Pills For The Soul?

DIETER K. MULITZE, PH.D.

PILLS FOR THE SOUL?

How Medication Falls Short of Christ's Healing of the Emotions

Sovereign World

Sovereign World Ltd
PO Box 784
Ellel
Lancaster LA1 9DA
England

www.sovereignworld.com

ISBN: 978 1 85240 487 1

Cover design by David Lund Design
Printed in the United Kingdom

Dedication

To my wife, Ellen, and my daughter, Karissa.

Caution to the Reader

If you are taking psychiatric drugs, do not make any changes in your medication without seeing your physician or psychiatrist. Withdrawal from taking psychiatric drugs without competent medical supervision can be hazardous to your health. The information in this book is not intended to replace your seeking a competent medical opinion.

Table of Contents

Acknowledgements

Foremost, I wish to acknowledge Ellen, my faithful wife over the years. Without Ellen's support and encouragement, especially during the many hours when I essentially "disappeared" into my study, this book could not have been written.

Special thanks to all the brothers and sisters in Christ who have shared their lives and their pain with me in experiencing the healing presence of Jesus.

The stories of people as recounted in this book have been written to safeguard the identity of the individuals involved. Names have been changed, along with some of the details. Any similarity with anyone else is purely unintentional.

To God be the Glory!

Forewords

D ieter Mulitze's third book is clearly his most challenging. Building on the case for a biblical healing ministry in his first two books, Dieter now moves to a critique of prevalent models of psychiatry and the Church's all too facile acceptance of "worldly wisdom" in this field.

In a volume that confronts the widespread prescription of a variety of drugs, in response to psychiatry's burgeoning list of "mental disorders" (represented by the fourth edition of the American Psychiatric Association's *Diagnostic and Statistical Manual of Mental Disorders*), Mulitze invokes the literature of both psychiatry and theology, together with the experience of generations of patients, to utter an urgent wake-up call.

Claiming that our modern Western society has gone after a false messiah and become addicted (literally as well as physically) to wares being peddled by a cartel combining the pharmaceutical and psychiatric industries, Dieter Mulitze says, in the most plain language of his writing to date, "Stop. Look. Listen."

Why are Christians, with others in society, willing to trade time-honoured and biblical concepts like the "soul" and "healing" for purely materialistic notions that reduce emotional sickness to brain chemistry?

Pointing out that, from biblical times onward, the "healing of the soul" and the "renewing of the spirit" have provided relief from despair, sorrow of heart, alienation, effects of abuse, unreconciled conflict, addictive behaviour, etc., Dieter calls for the Church to get back to its roots and make use of the abundant resources of the gospel.

In his first book, Mulitze showed that a gospel stripped of healing is a truncated gospel. In his second volume, he examined the nature of biblical healing and the centrality of Jesus as the Healer and Deliverer of the whole person. In this third volume, while affirming Jesus as the Healer of Souls, Dieter first builds a devastating critique of much of contemporary psychiatric "business," claiming that in place of real healing, we have become a society controlled by substances that cannot and will not mend anything.

In such a hard-hitting and critical approach, the reader is entitled to ask, "What does a scientist trained in quantitative genetics and computer science really know about psychiatry? Or, for that matter, theology?" The answers are to be found in the book itself, which evidences wide reading of secondary sources in both fields, together with reports of the work of those fully qualified to speak to the issues. But make no mistake, Dieter Mulitze is not some armchair novice quoting a few experts to make a superficial case; he has lived out the results of his studies in years as a practitioner of the care of souls. As in his earlier works, it is this combination of rigorous scholarship with years of observation and extensive practical application that makes the case so compelling.

Finally, I must confess that, in taking up the challenge of writing a foreword for this book, I realize afresh the limitations of my own experience, both in the field of psychiatry and in the kind of caring for souls that forms the focus of the volume. As such, I am in no position to pontificate on Dieter's formal critique of modern psychiatric trends. But I have spent a lifetime watching people and observing what makes for health and deliverance. And even from this vantage point, it is patently obvious that much in our modern approach has gone seriously wrong.

Dieter tells us what has gone wrong and builds a compelling case for where we have strayed, together with offering the Church a simple but profound means of recovery. If all were well with our collective soul, we might feel free to set aside this challenge. But, given widespread bondage to the pharmaceutical drug culture, in which Christians are fully complicit, together with the cries of the afflicted for help not being given by the "industry," we ignore this discussion at our peril. Dieter's call for a return to biblical categories ("Why are you downcast, O my soul?" Psalm 42:5) together with biblical solutions ("Come to me, all you who are weary and burdened, and I will give you rest. Take my yoke upon you and learn from me, for I am gentle and humble in heart, and you will find rest for your souls" Matthew 11:28-29) is surely one that we who claim to follow Jesus must heed. With the early disciples, should we not confess afresh, "Lord, to whom [else] shall we go? You [alone] have the words of eternal life" (John 6:68). If Dieter Mulitze is right, we have gone after other gods, with devastating results. Only by returning to the Living God and making use of the resources He has given will the Church again become a resource for God's salvation and healing.

CARL E. AMERDING, PH.D.
Emeritus Professor, Schloss Mittersill Study Centre
Senior Fellow, Oxford Centre for Mission Studies

Our Western world, as it moves from complacency with rationalistic modernism, to disenchantment as expressed by "postmodernism," is facing deep and radical changes. This then is a time for fresh challenges, not for further conformity to past assumptions, especially those which have strong vested interests.

In this courageous book, Dieter Mulitze takes on the challenge of how the science of psychiatry has treated the personal mystery of the nature of human suffering. As the author has indicated, it is a great reduction indeed, to move "from healing souls to fixing brains." It is a profound reductionism to view the nature of the human being as merely anthropologically, if in fact there is omitted all reference to the human mystery of being created "in the image and likeness of God."

As a Christian, the author accepts wholeheartedly that theology has a central place in any discussion about the human condition. Whereas our secular culture would omit all discourse about the relation of God and humankind. The field of psychiatry is peculiarly vulnerable to reductionism, in order to give it the respectability of being a "science," rather than of being caught in the tension between religious mystery and scientific materialism. It reminds us of the choice made by Sigmund Freud, that by his focus upon the sexual dimension, he could maintain at least the appearance of being "scientific," rather than caught up in the subjectivity of the relational self.

The scorn with which hard scientists today view psychotherapy as "science" may extend tomorrow to much of what psychiatry still claims to be a science also. Dieter's extensive reading on such issues as biochemical imbalances of the brain, psychiatric labels, the nature of drug testing by pharmaceutical companies, all indicate a growing professional crisis of credibility. His many references to the history of psychiatry likewise reflect adversely upon the pedigree of this "science."

Trained in the discipline of genetics, Dieter speaks from outside the profession, and yet with the scientific rigor and logic of "hard" science, to question many assumptions of the psychiatric profession.

So he does not write as peeved insider, frustrated with his own career. Rather he writes objectively, as he questions conflicts of interest, patient and profitability, or indeed the patient's human dignity versus the inbuilt professional self-interests. It is the kind of disclosure that will open the way for the self-interests of other professions to be scrutinized, as societal assumptions become more questioned in a postmodernist environment. For psycho-analysis is no longer the tool monopolized by therapy, but the instrument of increasing skepticism within our society.

However, Dieter does not write as a skeptic, but as a Christian believer. He practices what he preaches in the compassionate care and cure of souls. His ministry is dedicated to "healing prayer," to demonstrate the power of God's Spirit in Jesus' name, to give release of the emotional captive, and to give relational healing to profoundly wounded persons. So the individual stories of people he loves with the compassion of Christ are a moving testimony to the power of prayer on their behalf. This perhaps is the unique character of this book.

Other scholars have, and are critiquing, the crisis of credibility of the "science" of psychiatry. For there has been a growing chorus of dissent since the 1970's, from both Christian and secular sources. But Dieter has the moral courage to affirm against the compromise of many Christians, that the presence of Jesus Christ in the lives of many sufferers is more efficacious than the impersonal drug treatment many have endured. This is a bold challenge, like that of David's encounter against Goliath, which many will dismiss out of hand without opening this book. But I urge you to read with an open mind, as I have done, to read and decide for yourself, whether there is the ring of truth about the testimonies of these sufferers.

G.K. Chesterton observed that if the world is crazily upside down, then the only way of seeing it properly is to stand permanently upside down. Dieter does something of this, to help us be freed of professional brain-washing. The stakes played are high indeed, no less than the future of the human race. Shall human dignity remain protected by the mystery of God's love for us, or shall we sell our religious birthright for so-called "secular scientific progress?"

JAMES M. HOUSTON, D.PHIL.
Founding Principal of Regent College and
Professor Emeritus of Spiritual Theology
Regent College, Vancouver, BC

 Introduction

Tanya's Story:
Pain, Depression, and Psychiatric Drugs

My first encounter with depression was when I was in high school. I had recently broken up with my boyfriend. I was feeling alone, sad, and in need of attention. That was when I first considered that suicide might be an option. So, I double-dosed on cough syrup. It seems funny now, but I just wanted a little attention, not to actually die. I did not exactly receive the attention I was looking for. I eventually got over being sad and was perfectly happy and content with life for about three years.

In my first semester of Bible college I met a boy who swept me off my feet. Within months we were planning a wedding—or at least I was. He reluctantly went along with the plans until Christmas vacation. When we got back to school, he quickly informed me that we were through. His family had advised him to break off our relationship. Well, once more I got depressed. This sadness lasted only about two months, and I recovered with the help of two close friends. We spent many long hours talking, and I was not alone. Once more I was perfectly happy and content with life for about one year.

In my second year of college, I had the best year of my life. I was involved in many different ministry opportunities, and I was also dating one of the most popular guys in the school. We got along great.

We prayed together and had a lot of fun just doing silly stuff. I traveled extensively for ministry, and we communicated by letters over the summer. We were discussing getting married about a year or two after we were done school. I had it all planned out and was on top of the world. Then came the fall—he broke it off. But he didn't do it well—he said we could still be friends and that we would probably get back together.

This was the worst time of my life so far. I was incredibly hopeful and yet desperate. I thought I would have a mental breakdown. I saw my school counsellor, and with his help and the help of a couple of friends, I made it through. It took some structure in my life and focusing on other things rather than curling up in bed and hiding. During this time, I experienced excruciating headaches, so much so that I had one of my friends take me to emergency, thinking that maybe I had a brain tumour. I felt constantly nauseated, and I can't believe I actually completed my studies for that year. It took nine months to a year to feel well again, but I did. Once more I was fairly happy and content with life.

I graduated from college with my degree, and in a few months I found a ministry position. I became a licensed minister with an evangelical denomination and was the assistant pastor in a small town. I met my husband at this church. He was a member of the congregation I was ministering in. He had just returned home and was getting over a broken engagement. Not the best candidate for me, considering my previous breakups. But, we hit it off. We had many long and serious talks concerning our past relationships and their problems. Finally, I had found someone who loved me back. Within eight months we were married. Hindsight tells me that this was way too fast, but I was afraid he would change his mind and leave me.

The first years of our marriage were awful. I gained about twenty pounds in four months and knew I was no longer attractive to my husband. He made this clear by suggesting numerous diets and exercise routines as well as plainly saying I was not as thin as he would like. If it were not for the fact that both my husband and I were in ministry and

I had no place to run, we would have both left on several occasions and called it quits. It was nothing like I had imagined married life to be. I thought it meant I would never be alone again. Instead, I felt always alone even when I was with my husband or other people.

I was overweight and had low self-esteem, so I thought we should have a child. This would certainly make our marriage better. At least it would give me some companionship and acceptance. So we had a baby boy—he was perfect and wonderful. His delivery was a terrible process. I was induced for two days before they finally decided to do a Caesarean. I was so tired that I never really bonded with him. Motherhood was not what I had imagined it to be. I couldn't breast-feed, because it was extremely painful. So I failed in that respect and resorted to bottle-feeding. He demanded my attention at all hours of the day and night. I resigned my position at the church because I thought that was my duty as a good Christian mother. So I began to resent my son because he cost me my identity. I tried to stay home full-time but for financial reasons I had to go back to work—but at a job that demanded a lot of physical labor. Being at work was a relief for me, because then I only had myself to think about. My family cared for my son, and I think he saw more of them than me for the first three years of his life.

Shortly after his birth, I began to tell my doctor that I just didn't feel right. She asked if it was affecting my relationship with my son, and I said no, just my relationship with my husband. Apparently this did not warrant any help. So for six months I told her that something was wrong. I was sad all the time. I shirked responsibility in any way I could. I just wanted to sleep and eat all day.

I managed to make an appointment with a Christian counselling centre. I went to two sessions, each time seeing a different counsellor. They both told me the same thing, "Your husband is just too hard on you, and if he doesn't change, you'll never get better." This was exactly what I wanted to hear. I would like nothing better than to blame all of my problems on someone else.

Eventually it got to the point where I couldn't sleep or eat, and I went for three days without eating or sleeping. The good thing is that

I lost all my baby weight and more. I was finally at the point where I should have been attractive. But, I was beside myself. I thought I was going crazy. My husband thought I was going crazy. I went to emergency; they made an appointment with another doctor in a nearby city, and I got in to see him immediately.

The doctor asked how I was, and I told him. He immediately diagnosed me with postpartum depression, even though my son was ten months old. He said that the neurotransmitters in my brain were not transmitting properly and that he could prescribe some medication that would correct the imbalance. This sounded wonderful to me. I was hospitalized for one week while they stabilized the dosage of antidepressant and sleeping pills. This was another separation from my son, which I shamefully admit I thoroughly enjoyed because of my desire to get away from such responsibilities.

The medication made me feel numb to everything. There was nothing that was really joyful or really sad. Everything was simply uneventful—including our marital closeness. I felt nothing, emotionally or physically. Feeling no pain is supposed to be a wonderful thing, but I also had no joy or pleasure in anything.

Once more, we decided that what our family needed was another child. This would surely help cure all that ailed. So I became pregnant again. We asked the doctor if the antidepressant medication I was on would have any affect on the pregnancy, and he assured us that it was as safe as taking the occasional Tylenol during pregnancy. Still, I felt unsure about it. So at nine weeks conception I stopped my medication. I began having some slight cramping but thought nothing of it. At my twelve-week ultrasound it became apparent that something was wrong. The technician said nothing and didn't call in my husband to see the screen. They put a rush on the results, and I called my doctor the next day, only to discover that my baby had died at nine weeks. I would most likely pass the child over the weekend or require a dilation and curettage on the following Monday.

On Monday, I went for my first dilation and curettage. What an awful experience. The nurses all tried to be comforting, but I was still in shock. All seemed to go well, and I was home by the afternoon. I have never felt so alone. I was very thankful for my son, and I treasured him like never before. On the following Friday, my husband and I went to a marriage encounter weekend. I don't know if this was the best timing, but we went anyway because we had pre-registered. I was still off my medication and I could feel. I cried a lot. I also had some physical symptoms, such as continual vaginal spotting.

I had of course gained a lot of weight, again, because I had been three months pregnant. So, I felt huge and ugly beyond belief. But there was a supernatural peace that sustained me. A group of ladies from my church had been praying for me since the day of my ultrasound, and God upheld me by His grace. This was better than any medication prescribed by a doctor.

A month after my miscarriage, I went for my second dilation and curettage because of the continued spotting. They figured the surgeon had missed something in the first operation. This time I knew what I was in for. A month later, I was rushed to emergency—I was hemorrhaging. The doctor knew I didn't want to have more surgery, so he prescribed a high dose of birth control pills to stop the bleeding as well as intravenous drugs immediately. This worked, and I only had to spend one day in the hospital.

Two years later, I was still healthy and became pregnant again. I was happy and content during this pregnancy. Physically, I ached all over and was tired a lot. I didn't go out or do much. Our daughter was born by another Caesarean. This time it was planned, so I wasn't nearly as exhausted. I didn't even try to nurse, and the bottle-feeding was easy.

For financial reasons again, I went right back to work. So at three months old, she was left with family members so I could work full-time to supplement our family income. I must stress that this was not our choice but was necessary. My husband soon finished his job and was unemployed. He stayed home with our six-month-old girl and five-year-old boy for six months while I worked full-time. This was a growing and learning experience for all of us. My husband was offered a position, which he gladly accepted, and he became employed full-time. So, there we were both working with two kids and having to pay for daycare. That is a crazy way to live, and I am saddened that so many families actually *choose* to do this. I saw my family very little and missed them immensely.

Even through all of this stuff—a miscarriage, the birth of another child, the financial stress, and so on—I did not go back on antidepressants. I recognized that they cause more harm than good, and I knew that true healing would only come from God. He is the sustainer of all life, and in Him is the source of life.

My healing began when, out of desperation, I went for healing prayer. I was getting depressed again, and we didn't know if our marriage could survive with me having yet another bout of depression. I had heard that this pastor had a prayer ministry and incredible healings were taking place, so I thought I should give it a try. My husband and I went to see him; the whole way there I kept thinking that I was crazy to even try getting help from a pastor. I thought for sure that I was just overreacting and that I didn't even need help in the first place. I thought everyone had the deep-seated pain that I did and that it was normal.

The prayer time went well. God spoke to the pastor regarding a lot of hurts in my life. I received prayer for healing of the hurts caused by the demanding perfectionism of my mother and for the lack of the feminine in my life. When we left his office, I felt better. But I knew there was a lot more "stuff" that needed to be dealt with.

Later, I finally worked up the courage to deal with some other issues in my life. I made an appointment to see another minister of healing prayer. My husband also accompanied me to this session. I had been having a recurring memory of some past painful trauma. In the prayer session, God took me to the memory of the sexual trauma and walked through it with me. Jesus told me that it was not my fault and that I was not alone. In this memory, while I was being assaulted, I looked up and saw Jesus standing just off to the side and crying over the incident. This brought an incredible peace. This memory no longer made me fearful. I had found some comfort and strength in knowing that God was with me and that there was nothing to fear. I also prayed a prayer of forgiveness for the person who had violated me. During this same session, Jesus reminded me of another incident earlier in my life and healed and cleansed me from that trauma as well.

Once these memories were dealt with, I experienced a few weeks of peace and calm. Then it seemed that all hell broke loose. I began having anxiety attacks, depression, and strange thoughts. I was not looking after myself, and my husband told me that he had noticed. I thought I was losing it. Once more my world was collapsing. The difference was that now I knew there was a cure. So I prayed and asked God to reveal what the problem was. I also called to make another appointment for healing prayer, but I couldn't get one until the following month. I just couldn't wait that long. Thankfully, God is gracious and meets us right where we are. Through His very real healing presence, the Lord healed me from the hurt and pain of an early experience of sexual abuse.

What God has done has been truly exceptional. He is healing our marriage and restoring the connectedness that should have been there all along. He is healing my relationship with my son. He is truly a treasure to me that I could never imagine being without. He is no longer any inconvenience. I think I am actually becoming a mother, something that we all think is instinctual but isn't necessarily so. My relationship with my daughter has always been good, but it is getting even better. I am discovering whom it is that God has created me to be.

I experienced more healing, but it is hard to explain what happened to me at this point. I have heard it described like this: before I was walking alongside myself, and now I am walking as a whole person. I never realized how hard I had to work at living. I would try so hard to act like everyone else in a given situation, but I had no sense of my true self and the ability to just "be" in that situation. I saw my life as a set of roles that I needed to play out. For example, the role of the minister's wife was one that I filled by looking to other minister's wives to see how they carried themselves, what they said, and how they acted. That is what I would try hard to copy. It was a lot of work. This was all done at a subconscious level and became "normal" for me; I knew no other way of being. Since this incredible healing and the miracle that Christ has done, I can just be, with no pretense of what others think of me or how they will react. I used to measure every word as if in a script in order to elicit the desired response. Now, I can just express my ideas, thoughts, and feelings without fear of recourse or rejection.

As if this wasn't enough healing, God had even more in store, and He still has more and more. I felt God calling me to discover what it means to truly be feminine. For years I had placed my identity in my role of minister, and then wife, and then mother. When these weren't enough, I began to develop all kinds of other roles. I tried other jobs, vocations, crafts, gardening, music, anything that would give me a name and an identity. None of these worked.

It didn't take much to make me feel like I was worthless. Simply a comment about the state of our house and my lack of the tools required to make it a home would send me into despair. This comment was the trigger, the impetus needed to get me looking at my need for healing in this area. The trigger produced a train of thought in my head that I referred to as 'the lie'—what I believed about myself as a result of the trigger. This led to a strong feeling of despair and self-hatred. For most of us, this whole process happens unconsciously, and we get angry or sad and don't know why. It is when we stop to analyze the process and call it what it is that we can find the healing needed to make us whole again.

My next healing was not without demonic interference. At every step of the way in my healing, the enemy tried to prevent it by putting the thought in my head that I am going crazy or the thought that I don't actually need any of this "healing prayer" stuff.

The truth came soon after to combat this barrage of lies. To quote my journal: "*Memory:* No one connected with me at birth. Not mother, father, or grandparents. Generational stuff filled the gap with despair. *Lie:* I am alone in this world with no one to tell me who I am. *Truth:* Jesus told me that His hands were on me even inside the womb when He was creating me."

A short time later I went for more healing prayer. The issues were despair, lack of mother love, and no bonding with mother. The image of Mom scolding me for a messy room was symbolic of a conditional-love relationship, and I consistently failed those conditions. We also prayed a generational prayer regarding some relatives on my maternal grandfather's side. There were some incidents of people in my family line who were obviously dabbling with evil. When we prayed to break the bonds with these people using the sword of the Spirit and placing the cross of Christ between them and myself, a huge weight floated off my shoulders and I was filled with a profound sense of relief.

As we prayed, the Lord clearly spoke to me. During the prayer time for separation from my mom in infancy, Jesus said, "I am here." During prayer for despair and conditional love when I looked at that monumentally messy room, Jesus said, "It doesn't matter; it's not a big deal." I truly thank the Lord for changing me and helping me to just "be." The prayer team leader assured me that when healing is complete I will be able to mother without effort and without having to read books to figure it out. Thank you, Jesus, for the work that you are doing in me.

I had been reading some books by Leanne Payne and they speak of practicing the presence of Jesus, inviting Jesus to speak to you. I decided to give this a try and came face to face with the sin of self-hatred. I knew I never liked myself, but I would not have considered it a sin. I had to pray and renounce the sin of self-hatred, and right away Jesus came and filled me with His peace and with self-acceptance. I don't speak of self-confidence but of the confidence that Christ has restored within me.

I have also struggled with a sense of God's calling to ministry. I could not understand how that could possibly fit into my roles of wife and mother. So while practising the presence of Christ recently, I received this word from the Lord: "Don't be afraid to step out into the calling I place on you. Perfect love casts out fear." This was exactly what I needed to hear.

Our marriage is the best I could ever imagine or hope for. We have truly grown in love and friendship. Our rotten years were a result of two very hurt people triggering each other. We were both equally responsible for how bad it was. Thankfully, we have both received healing prayer and are enjoying life with each other. My depression would lead most people (including my husband) to blame our problems on me. In reality, we both were in need of help. This has been a great relief for me, to begin to see myself as no longer "the problem" or "the victim"; instead I helped move us to "the solution"—Jesus.

Emotional Pain Is for Real

Christians are not immune from emotional suffering and pain. There are many like Tanya in the body of Christ, including some in full-time ministry. The "walking wounded" are in our midst. Christians experience emotional problems as frequently as people in general—about 15 percent—and almost 32 percent of Christians "will suffer with a significant mental disease during their lifetime."[1] At a healing conference I attended, believers suffering from depression were invited to come forward for prayer. About 20 percent of the Christians present came forward, mostly women, and including those that some would not expect to suffer from depression. The prayer team was empathetic, full of grace and understanding, so everyone felt it was a safe place.

I have prayed with Christians suffering from deep depression, some with suicidal tendencies. Others have come with almost crippling fear, others with obsessions and compulsions, and still others with deep addictions. After hearing the painful stories of some Christians, I am amazed that they are still alive. Some believers live with deep shame, in an emotional prison. Some pastors and missionaries silently suffer from deep emotional pain, not wanting others to know about the true condition of their souls.

Anne did not feel worthy of God's love and was basically ruled by shame. As a very young girl, her father, uncle, and brother raped her. The "simple remedies" offered her did not remove the shame from her inner being. Her pastor and church told her that if she would only have faith, believe hard enough, and forgive hard enough, then she would "get over it." Martha has had a sleep disorder for decades and can hardly remember the last time she had a good night's rest—something that many people take completely for granted. Fred has intense feelings of loneliness and abandonment and at times "hears voices." Rebecca has uncontrollable and completely irrational anxiety with occasional panic attacks. And they all love Jesus.

These are real people with real pain. Each person is unique, with very real emotional and functional problems. In one sense it is easier to have physical pain, since there is rarely any stigma associated with it. Hopefully you just need medication or surgery or some other medical intervention and you will be healed. But what about depression or panic attacks, for example, and if there is no apparent cause? How could this ever be if you are filled by the Holy Spirit and have been born again, as some might ask?

I have met many Christians at healing prayer conferences and healing prayer services, including pastors and their wives, who have lived with deep emotional pain and inner woundedness for many unbearably long years. Typically, they love Jesus like other Christians and have been looking for healing and hope for years. I have absolutely no reason to doubt their commitment to Jesus.

Some Responses Are Unreal

The response of Christians to those with emotional problems has not always been very helpful. At times, it can be unreal, even adding to the pain. Comments like "just snap out of it," "try harder," "read your Bible more," "memorize Bible verses," "attend church more regularly," "you need more faith," "claim your victory," "pray harder," "speak out your healing," or "stop pitying yourself" are often insensitive and border on condemnation.

Most churches are embarrassed to have Christians with deep emotional pain in their midst. Not many churches openly welcome schizophrenics or the clinically depressed. Does yours? In some churches, Christians with emotional pain and deep spiritual wounds have a sense of shame "just by being there." Sometimes a church will completely deny or subtly suppress the problem. But are we not called to mourn with those who mourn, to exhibit the compassion of Christ to one another, and to love one another as Christ has loved us?

Some Christians simply minimize the emotional pain of others, as if it was some sort of phantom pain. I suspect that such people have not experienced much emotional pain themselves. I recall an old aboriginal proverb—"Don't judge another person until you have walked in his moccasins."

An all too common belief among Christians is that emotional problems are often due to personal sin or wrong choices.[2] After all, some say, if you are "walking right with God," you would not be suffering from depression. Another common belief in the Church is that emotional illness is due to personal or spiritual weakness.[3] To see a psychiatrist or a doctor is then interpreted as a lack of faith. The final verdict often results in some degree of shame or condemnation.

While praying with Charles, a Christian diagnosed with depression, I learned that his church had declared that his condition was caused by sin and if he would just walk righteously with the Lord, the symptoms would disappear. Charles had spent many hours searching his soul, confessing almost any sin he could think of, yet there was no relief. The result? He felt even more pain, since he now viewed himself as a failure in the body of Christ. Heaped onto his shoulders was condemnation from his church. Ironically for Charles, being a Christian was an added liability. Whatever happened to living by grace?

I know of others like Charles, both men and women, who attend churches where "success" and "victorious Christian living" are paramount. Depression is almost unbearable when you are surrounded by "victorious and Spirit-filled" Christians. For them, worship and fellowship are difficult because of the contrast between where they are and where everyone else is—at least on the outside. It is not unlike Christmas time when the suicide rate goes up since depressed people become even more depressed when surrounded by continual jolliness and happiness that poignantly reminds them, by contrast, of their inner state.

Let us not think for a moment that pastors and their wives are immune from emotional pain. One survey showed that 80 percent

12

of pastors and 84 percent of their spouses experience discouragement or suffer from depression.[4] I have ministered healing prayer to some very deeply wounded clergy and spouses, sometimes for almost unbelievable pain from the very people they were called to shepherd and exhibit the love of Christ to. I have personally seen Jesus bring deep, lasting healing to clergy couples who have even lived with suicide attempts and depression for years. Those who would argue that Christians with emotional problems are weak and should simply "snap out of it" must ironically agree that this applies to a larger percentage of pastors and wives than believers in general.

Job was a blameless and upright man who feared God (Job 1:1,5,8) and showed signs of depression, yet in the end he was still found faithful (Job 42:7-8). His "comforters" expected him to confess his sin and thus "get right with God" (Job 4:7;5:8). Jeremiah (Jer. 4:19-20), Elijah (1 Kings 19:3-5), and Jonah (Jonah 4:1-3)—among others in the Scriptures—also went through times of deep emotional turmoil. Thus, having a deep emotional problem is not necessarily a sin. But what, then?

From Sin to Neurotransmitters

Other Christian writers would argue that focusing on a person's sin in the midst of their emotional problems could be harsh, if not cruel. People need compassion and understanding—not condemnation. Not many would disagree here!

Another major and increasingly predominant view in the Church is that there are often genetic or biochemical reasons for a Christian's emotional suffering. It is more than theology or spiritual problems—it may well be a malfunction in one's body or brain. Maybe in some cases it is *only* a physical problem, an illness. A number of prominent Christian writers, referring to modern scientific research, claim that our neurological pathways or neurotransmitters, for example, are either imbalanced or malfunctioning. Therefore, we *need and must have medication*—typically psychiatric drugs. The Church has largely accepted modern biological psychiatry with its apparently scientific diagnoses and the widespread use of psychiatric drugs. Some Christian authors repeatedly advocate this view to the Church.

The acceptance of this view in the Church is typically founded on two major reasons. First, it has been repeatedly observed that the "usual approaches" in the Church to helping Christians with serious emotional and behavioural problems—like clinical depression, bipolar spectrum disorders, debilitating panic attacks, mood swings, attention deficit disorders, and more—are often not that effective. It is often written that prayer, counselling, therapy sessions, looking to the Scriptures, or seeing a pastor or priest, for example, are rather ineffective. The implication: it may not be only, or even fundamentally, a spiritual or relational problem in the first place.

Secondly, and most importantly, it is frequently argued that since *all truth is God's truth*, and that since psychiatry is a modern science, then as Christians we should just embrace the best that modern psychiatry has to offer. We must avail ourselves of the most recent scientific medical advances. We should then be thankful that Prozac or Zoloft or Luvox, for example, can help restore a neurotransmitters imbalance in our brains. After all, God has made our brains with great complexity, and He could also use psychiatric drugs to heal us, just like insulin helps with diabetes. Since there are some genes that apparently will cause or at least predispose a person to certain emotional problems, then medication is most definitely required. Clearly, it is argued, *a chemical problem requires a chemical solution.* This does not necessarily rule out pain and trauma from the past or childhood issues, but it is argued that brain chemistry will at times be a significant factor. Accordingly, Christians are encouraged to take psychiatric medications for their emotional problems, even upon the recommendation of some Christian doctors or psychiatrists. Not a few books authored by some Christian writers give almost glowing testimonies of how the psychiatric drugs have helped those with emotional problems, transforming their very lives, when prayer and counsel did next to nothing. In fact, some people even wonder how those drugs can accomplish things that the Holy Spirit apparently cannot.

Some Christians are being pressured by their doctors and psychiatrists to take psychiatric medication, while others are taking medication and long for the day when it will be needed no more. Some Christians have been helped by psychiatric drugs and are thankful. Then there are those who suffer from the side effects of psychiatric drugs, rightly wondering if the "treatment" is more costly than the relief from pain. There are many Christians under psychiatric care who are still in great need of healing. Many Christians ponder the significance and meaning of professional, scientific-sounding psychiatric labels that now define part of their life or even who they are.

But is this acceptance of psychiatry by the Church really wise or warranted? When Christians experience deep emotional pain, should the Church refer them so readily to psychiatrists? When some Christians are reluctant to taking psychiatric medication, could it ever be that the Holy Spirit is trying to tell them something? Are psychiatric diagnoses truly scientific? How valid are they? Where did they come from? Must Christians accept these diagnoses at face value, as well as the inevitably prescribed psychiatric medication? Should Christians surrender to these diagnoses that hold such power over people's lives? Should Christians readily agree that they have a chemical imbalance in their brains and therefore they must take psychiatric drugs to fix their brains?

Flawed Brains or Flawed Science?

For many years as a Christian I had never questioned the Church's general acceptance of psychiatry. Like most Christians, I had simply believed the widely held view concerning the imbalance of neurotransmitters, which many regard as fact or almost a "scientific mantra." I simply trusted the books written by prominent Christian authors on the topic. I was shocked to find out that there is another opinion on the matter and that the prevailing view in the Church rests on cracked and faulty foundations. This is most evident when we examine the assumptions behind the two main reasons for generally accepting psychiatric drugs in the Church. This has huge implications for many Christians, as well as for the ministry of healing prayer.

Firstly, the apparent inadequacy of the "standard spiritual remedies" assumes that everything that the Church could offer has already been tried. But as I read the books that advocate psychiatric drugs within the Church, I notice reference to almost *everything except* the healing presence of the living Christ. A glaring omission is a well-developed practical theology of the presence of Christ. The "usual" approaches rarely even mention any divine intervention of Jesus through His healing presence today. This is all quite predictable, since the authentic healing presence of Christ has been substituted in much of the Church by numerous therapeutic techniques and methods to heal the human soul.[5] Charles Kraft, professor of anthropology and intercultural communication at Fuller Theological Seminary and president of Deep Healing Ministries, wrote:

> When a person is struggling with emotional problems, we send him or her to a psychologist who, though he or she may be a Christian, depends on secular techniques built on secular assumptions, without including Jesus the Healer in the process…We practice a secular Christianity.[6]

Among evangelical churches, Kraft further characterized secular Christianity as:

> largely powerless—powerless to heal, powerless to free people from emotional wounds and largely powerless to bring about real-life change. Our churches are filled with hurting people, therefore, who have no understanding of how to gain the freedom Jesus promised us.[7]

The "usual approaches" are inadequate for the mysteries of the soul and the deep emotional pain of many Christians. This is another symptom of secularization within the Church. When the "usual approaches" do not work, we look elsewhere.

Secondly, those who state the view that "all truth is God's truth" are making an implicit, critical assumption that few believers ever stop to ask. Simply: *is it truth?* What if the logic and reasoning behind much of modern psychiatry is flawed and needs fixing? After all, science is not perfect, and neither are scientists. I was surprised to find out that there is a growing number of highly respected and even world-renowned scientists and psychiatrists who support this view. Some of them are committed Christians. Entire books have been written to document the flawed reasoning behind a lot of psychiatric research. This is explored in some detail in this book.

For the skeptics, I point out that some psychiatrists, including Christian ones, are able to bring healing to people with some of the most severe and bizarre emotional problems *without any psychiatric drugs*. No mention of neurotransmitters! This directly challenges the prevailing view in the Church. And don't forget the fact that not so long ago psychiatry was practised without psychiatric drugs of any kind, and to suggest that you would ever use such drugs was met with disbelief, scorn, and maybe even the accusation of being "out of touch with reality." How times have changed!

So what does this all mean? It turns out that many Christians' brains are just fine; it is modern psychiatry that needs fixing due to its inherent logic disorder. As explained later in this book, that logic disorder is due in part to modern psychiatry's separation anxiety and identity disorder over its place in the modern world.

When you stop believing in a miracle Jesus, you more readily believe in "magic bullets" and miracle drugs. The Great Substitution—Jesus replaced with method and technique to heal the soul—has resulted in the Great Reduction—the healing of souls shrivelled down to fixing brains. Consciousness now appears to result from brain chemistry, emotions from neurotransmitter irregularities. The latest advances in brain research have eclipsed the soul. Do we not need more love instead of more Luvox or lithium? Or more of the peace of Christ instead of more Paxil? The apostle Paul was beaten three times, ship-wrecked three times, stoned once, often in much danger, often sleep deprived, often almost starving, cold and naked, and burdened daily for the churches (2 Cor. 11:25-28). How on earth did he ever do that without Prozac?

So are we just back to sin being the cause of emotional problems? Not exactly. Sometimes one's personal sin is a factor, in which case the Lord is willing to forgive abundantly and show his mercy, compassion, and healing grace. More often one has been sinned against, and there are very real and deep wounds from the past (Ps. 34:8;147:3; Is. 61:1). The emotional problems are not so much sin but *signals*, indicators of the soul. We need to listen to the Spirit and understand how Jesus would want to help us deal with the toxic waste in our souls. The wisdom of Jesus and the Gospels is far more potent and profound than anything that psychiatry has to offer, as we shall see.

This is not an anti-psychiatry book, and I am not on a scientific witch hunt. I am for solid and well-researched psychiatry that would count as part of God's truth. As a trained research scientist, I am concerned when science is misused or devalued. I am also not against psychiatrists *per se*, since there are many who truly care for their patients and there are Christian psychiatrists who are offering their very best for their patients. I do not wish to trivialize the ethical and moral issues that many psychiatrists face. I am more concerned about what psychiatry as a whole has become and all the pressures that a larger mental health system imposes on everyone, especially patients.

Tattoo Needles, Lice, Alzheimer's and More

This book is not about the well-documented and well-researched organic or truly biological causes of emotional disorders. Medical conditions that can mimic or masquerade as depression or mania include hormonal or metabolic disorders like thyroid problems, Cushing's disease, Addison's disease, Wilson's disease, and diabetes.[8] Hypoglycemia (blood glucose too low) can result in depression, crying spells, insomnia, dizziness, and more.[9] Some infections that can mimic in similar ways include influenzas, mononucleosis, viral pneumonia, and AIDS.[10] Then there are also brain diseases, autoimmune diseases, and neurological disorders such as Parkinson's disease, Huntington's chorea, temporal lobe epilepsy, Alzheimer's disease, and similar dementia.[11]

Other medical problems that result in various emotional and behavioural problems include iron deficiency, anemia, mercury intoxication, pernicious anemia, Lyme's disease, carbon monoxide poisoning, Brill-Zinsser disease transmitted by lice, low calcium intake, parasites, seronegative syphilis—often from contaminated tattoo needles, and various brain tumours.[12] Lack of exercise and nutritional deficiencies, especially the B-vitamins that are so important for brain functioning and the nervous system, or too much refined sugar or starch should not be overlooked.[13] Toxins and various food additives that can affect some people's brains, essentially brain allergies, have been known to cause schizophrenia, depression, dyslexia, hyperactivity, and other mental illnesses.[14] In those cases, simply fasting can bring healing and relief from such mental illnesses.[15] The brain is restored to normal functioning while fasting promotes detoxification.

Emotional problems are typically secondary or related effects in the above medical conditions that can be determined by laboratory tests. After all, most people feel sad or discouraged if they have low energy or an illness. If any of the above is suspect, a thorough medical checkup and lab tests are in order.

Some of the above "organic" problems could have a relational or spiritual root. Psychosomatic medicine, the study of how emotions affect our health, has shown that hyperthyroidism, for example, can be caused by an emotional problem.[16] Fear, guilt, shame, self-hatred, anxiety, unforgiveness, bitterness, and other prolonged emotions can cause many physical diseases or chronic illnesses.[17]

Unfortunately, not all psychiatrists perform thorough medical tests on their patients. In some psychiatric institutions, as many as half of the patients with a true medical condition are misdiagnosed.[18] Misdiagnosing someone with a supposed psychiatric disorder and prescribing a psychiatric drug can have serious health consequences when there is a true medical condition. The medical condition is masked by the drug and gets worse. "Physicians using powerful drugs to mask symptoms of disease are, in effect, disconnecting the body's alarm systems and allowing disease processes to continue disrupting the brain."[19]

A psychiatrist diagnosed Martha, a wife and mother, with clinical depression. She was soon put on a normal dose of Prozac. Her depression steadily got worse over a few years, for which she was given a higher dose of Prozac. A week before she suddenly died it was determined that she had a brain tumour. How tragic—she might be alive today if she had been correctly diagnosed, but unfortunately Prozac masked the true condition.

This book is *not* about the above, but rather it is about situations where any suspected medical condition has been ruled out by appropriate lab tests. This book concerns the presumed biological cause—typically some biochemical imbalance in the brain—as the cause of emotional or behavioural problems.

The Most Important People in the Church

We must not get lost in doctrine, research, therapies, drugs, and ideology so that we lose sight of very real and hurting people. Ever wonder who are the most important people in the Church? Could it be the leaders or those with great ministries? Maybe those who are living victoriously or those who "have it all together"? Or those who tithe and give generously in order to finance all the programs and pay the pastor's salary? No. The most important people in the Church are those who suffer.[20] This would include the most deeply wounded, those with emotional pain. This resonates from 1 Corinthians 12:22-26—if one part of the Body suffers, then all suffer. How a church treats the suffering in its midst is a very real "litmus test" of a church's true spirituality and maturity.

I remember praying with a Christian lady suffering from depression who declared to me that she was a failure as a Christian, as a wife, and as a mother.[21] Her heart was broken as she shared about her years of pain and deep disappointments and years of medication on psychiatric drugs. I looked straight into her eyes and said that was simply not true—she was *not* a failure. Instead, I told her that she is a precious daughter of the living God who *has yet to experience more of the healing presence of Jesus.* Grace, not performance or labels, was the basis of her identity. As the truth sank in, she said that no one had ever put it that way. Then she suddenly released a torrent of tears, and her healing began as the Holy Spirit revealed the sources of her deep pain and Jesus gently brought healing to her broken heart. The only failure was her church's inability to bring her into the presence of Jesus for her healing. And that, I told her, was truly depressing.

The true stories of people in this book include those who have had negative and unhelpful, if not damaging, experiences with psychiatric drugs. This is intentional; I merely wish to communicate the "other side" of the story in contrast to books that repeatedly emphasize how amazing and how helpful the drugs have been. Of course, psychiatric drugs have helped some people, and one can be thankful. But that still does not rule out the possibility that the ministry of healing prayer could have helped them even more and the drugs could have been entirely unnecessary.

Endnotes ⎯⎯⎯⎯⎯⎯

[1] Dwight L. Carlson, *Why Do Christians Shoot Their Wounded?* (Downers Grove: InterVarsity Press, 1994) pp. 56-57.

[2] Carlson, pp. 11-19.

[3] Grant Mullen, *Emotionally Free: A Prescription for Healing Body, Soul and Spirit* (Kent: Sovereign Word International, 2003) p. 24.

[4] Mullen, p. 51.

[5] Dieter Mulitze, *The Great Substitution: Human Effort or Jesus to Heal and Restore the Soul?* (Belleville: Essence Publishers, 2003) pp. 33-58.

[6] Charles H. Kraft, *Confronting Powerless Christianity: Evangelicals and the Missing Dimension* (Grand Rapids: Chosen Books, 2002) p. 10.

[7] Ibid.

[8] Demitri Papolos and Janice Papolos, *Overcoming Depression* (New York: HarperPerennial, 3rd ed., 1997) p. 39.

[9] Udo Erasmus, *Fats that Heal; Fats that Kill* (Burnaby: Alive Books, 1986) p. 35.

[10] Papolos, p. 39.

11 Ibid., p. 40.

12 S. Walker, *A Dose of Sanity: Mind, Medicine, and Misdiagnosis* (New York: John Wiley and Sons, 1996) pp. 1-17.

13 Richard F. Berg and Christine McCartney, *Depression And The Integrated Life* (New York: Society of St. Paul, 1981) pp. 115-132.

14 Elmer L. Towns, *Fasting For Spiritual Breakthrough* (Ventura: Regal Books, 1996) pp. 178-180.

15 Ibid.

16 Howard R. and Martha E. Lewis, *Psychosomatics: How Your Emotions Can Damage Your Health* (New York: The Viking Press, 1972) pp. 33-42.

17 Henry Wright, *A More Excellent Way: A Teaching On The Spiritual Roots of Disease* (Thomaston: Pleasant Valley Publications, 2002, 5th edition).

18 Walker, pp. 13-14.

19 Walker, p. 55.

20 *Mike Mason, The Gospel According to Job* (Wheaton: Crossway Books, 1994) p. 211.

21 Mulitze, pp. 226-227.

Chapter One

The Church and Psychiatry: A Cozy Alliance

Do not conform any longer to the pattern of this world, but be transformed by the renewing of your mind. Then you will be able to test and approve what God's will is—his good, pleasing and perfect will (Rom. 12:2).

Woe to you when all men speak well of you, for that is how their fathers treated the false prophets (Luke 6:26).

Gerlinde's Obsessive Compulsive Disorder

Gerlinde was a mental health professional, having worked most of her life in a psychiatric institution. She came to me for healing prayer, out of great desperation. She told me that for over ten years she was battling a strange, irrational, and emotionally oppressive compulsion. It consumed about an hour a day of her time and was always quite intense. She had talked to a number of pastors and sought counselling numerous times, but with no help. The compulsion was deceptively simple: to reach for the phone and phone a certain individual that she hardly remembered. She did not want to do that at all and could not think of why, but it was a strong and growing compulsion over those ten years. It had become a spiritual battle all its own, and took all her effort to avoid phoning. This might seem as a small

23

thing to many, but to her, it was a compulsion that was attempting to take over her life.

I anointed her with oil and asked the Holy Spirit and Jesus to come. In about two minutes, the Lord brought back suddenly and very clearly an early memory of a brief and embarrassing encounter that she had experienced with that very individual she did not want to phone. Quite surprised, she remarked how she had totally forgotten about the incident, being such a long time ago. After reassuring her of Christ's forgiveness for her part, I asked the Lord to completely sever the soul and spirit connection between her and that individual as well as to release her from some defilement concerning the circumstances of that event. This might seem all very simple, but that short time of healing prayer with the Spirit's revelation broke the compulsion and brought her great emotional freedom.

From Injecting Horse Blood, Removing Ovaries, to Zapping The Brain

How would people like Gerlinde have been helped centuries earlier by the mental health profession? It all depends on the era and the ideology at the time. Before we look at the current theory of biochemical imbalances in the brain, it is instructive to look at some of the past approaches to helping the "mentally ill."

The history of psychiatry is littered with many discarded theories and treatments of the mentally ill. Until about 1650, it was believed that conditions such as epilepsy, madness, and insanity had supernatural or demonic causes and thus one should see a priest or undergo an exorcism.[1] But after the 1650s and the influence of Descartes and the Enlightenment, it was increasingly believed that madness had rational, natural, knowable causes.[2]

Eventually, the clergy were replaced by doctors in handling the insane, while psychiatry developed as a discipline to manage the mentally ill who were increasingly committed to insane asylums.[3] Formerly people were categorized as saints, sinners, believers, non-believers, and heretics, but with the rise of scientific secularism people were classified as rational and normal or mad or insane.[4] The "keys of St. Peter were replaced by the keys of psychiatry."[5] So what was the result of a rational approach to the many forms of madness and insanity? Relax and take a deep breath before reading any further. Rest in a "comfy couch" if you have one.

Therapy with water, or "hydrotherapy," was attempted in various ways. A popular method was to wrap people up in tightly tied wet sheets. As the sheets dried they would tighten, causing pain and near suffocation. Or, the mentally ill would be sprayed with water while they stood naked in a metal cage.[6] Or they might be kept in a continuous bath for weeks or even months.[7] The more extreme form of water therapy was to bring a person to near death by temporary drowning.[8] Apparently such a near-death experience shocked a person's nervous system and brought their thinking right out of their mental illness.

Mechanical devices were used. The swinging chair (and later spinning beds, if you can imagine) that revolved, even up to 100 times a minute, caused weakness, pain, and terror to induce "new associations and trains of thoughts."[9] Similarly, there was the gyrator, wherein people were strapped horizontally to a board that rotated at high speeds.[10] The tranquilizer chair was a chair designed to stop all body movement, strap a person rigidly in place, and even block a person's sight by a wooden contraption, after many hours causing a sedative or tranquilizing effect to "assist in curing madness."[11]

Temperature variations were employed. Harvard Medical School physicians experimented with dropping the body temperature of schizophrenics 10° to 20° Fahrenheit between specially cooled blankets for up to three days.[12] The theory was that upon warming up and regaining consciousness, the cold shock would cure the schizophrenics of their mental illness.

Injections or removal of body parts were tried. Schizophrenics were once injected with horse blood into their cerebrospinal fluid in order to cause aseptic meningitis with some fever and then relief from their mental illness.[13] The removal of endocrine glands, or the cervix, or ovaries, or even Fallopian tubes were said to alleviate mental illness. Gynecologists from the 1890s to about 1910 apparently looked at the "hospitalized mentally ill as a rich source of patients" and often claimed that about 50 percent of their insane female patients were healed by hysterectomies and ovariectomies.[14] Endocrine therapy was popular in the early 1900s, wherein the mentally ill were injected with extracts from animal ovaries, testicles, thyroids, pituitary glands—and especially sheep thyroid extract.[15] To abort or minimize a mental crisis, English psychiatrists even up until 1921 used cotton oil, which irritates the bowels and causes diarrhea.[16]

Sheer terror was advocated as "therapy." Another way to stop a mentally ill person's "fixed ideas" was through "therapeutic terror," which involved being immersed in a tub of eels or having sealing wax dropped onto the palms.[17]

Shock was induced by various chemical means. In the 1930s and 1940s, insulin injections were used to induce comas and Metrazol was used to induce convulsions.[18,19] Apparently the comas or convulsions would cure the insane. The growing consensus in those days was that induced insulin comas were more effective for schizophrenics whereas induced Metrazol convulsions were better for manic-depressives.[20] By 1939, 70 percent of American hospitals used Metrazol shock therapy, even though there was no evidence of long-term benefits.[21] Almost 37,000 American mentally ill patients received this treatment from 1936 to 1941, often against their will.[22] Some people never came out of a coma and died.

Purposely cutting up and damaging part of the brain was proposed as a cure for mental illness. From the 1930s to the 1950s it was believed that mental illness could be cured by actually cutting up or chopping parts of people's brains—hence prefrontal lobotomies.[23] The procedure was simplified to using an ice pick, driven right through a person's eye sockets in order to destroy the brain's frontal-lobe nerve fibres, and was actually even used to "cure" troubled children.[24] This was not a new idea—in the twelfth century it was believed that demons would leave a lunatic's brain when holes were cut into the scalp.[25]

Electroshock therapy, where the brain is subjected to an electrical current, was originally conceived from observing pigs being electrocuted in a slaughterhouse prior to slaughter.[26,27] The key was to stun the brain directly instead of running a current through the whole body, which might induce a cardiac arrest.[28] Electroshock therapy (ECT) soon replaced Metrazol and insulin shock therapy as a cheaper and apparently safer method to restore normal brain function.[29]

If the above past "therapies" for mental illness seem almost incredible to you, it's because they should. All those therapies were once hailed as effective cures, often with little or inconclusive proof. They were used by some or many and then over time discredited and no longer used today—although ECT is still in vogue. Such different, varied, and contradictory approaches demonstrate one thing for sure: hardly anyone really knew what the problem was and how to solve it. Everyone was "grasping for straws" over the centuries.

Would not those supposed therapies in themselves drive some people insane or at least cause deep emotional pain from the trauma or shock? What would being forced to lie in a tub full of eels for several hours do to you, followed by experiencing a near drowning? (On second thought, please don't imagine too hard!) Did not anyone wonder at the obvious contradiction of using more trauma to heal people who have been wounded by trauma in the first place?

Fad, more than science, was behind many of these therapies. Money was a factor at times. In the 1930s, American neurosurgeons made about $5,000 a year while just *one* lobotomy could fetch from several hundred to $1,500.[30] Few professionals resisted the temptation.

The latest in the series of treatments for those suffering with mental or emotional pain involves the more "scientific" approach with psychiatric drugs. The relatively crude attempts of the past now give way to the apparently precise, modern, and intricate world of neuroscience.

Moods, Emotions and Juggling Neurotransmitters

Modern psychiatry has adopted a strongly medical, biological view of mental illnesses and disorders. Stephen King, a Christian psychiatrist, summarized the prevailing central theory of psychiatry as follows:

> The dominant theory in modern psychiatry is that human behaviors and adaptive functioning or malfunctioning are biochemically based, with neurochemical imbalance in certain brain areas causing symptoms and resulting illness. Thus, symptoms of anxiety, depression, insomnia, irrational thinking, mood swings, and the like can be traced to a deficiency in brain cells of important chemicals such as serotonin, dopamine, and norepinephrine. Modern medications are prescribed to remedy these deficiencies or imbalances as specifically as possible in order to relieve the symptoms of the illness.[31]

A number of prominent Christian authors support at least some of the basic theories and premises of modern psychiatry. Minirth, Meier, and Arterburn, for example—among many others—support the view that flawed brain chemistry is often involved in emotional suffering and that psychiatric drugs are therefore necessary to correct that problem. The "brain essentially functions chemically"[32] and "normal behaviour and feelings depend on the right chemicals being in the right places in the right quantities."[33] The brain is so much of who we are—it originates our feelings, thoughts, emotions, and bodily functions—and when there is an "imperfection in our brains," it can result in emotional problems.[34] The brain effects emotions to the extent that even a small malfunction in brain chemistry can greatly effect one's emotions.[35] This would be consistent with the notion that we are "largely chemical creatures."[36]

What is the link between brain chemistry and emotions? It can be a chemical imbalance leading to depleted chemicals in the brain that can control emotions[37] or affect our moods and feelings.[38] Apparently the "key to balanced brain function...lies with the neurotransmitters and synapses."[39] A decrease in certain neurotransmitters is the physiological cause of depression.[40,41] Matthews, a Christian doctor who wrote about the healing power of prayer, concurred that an imbalance of neurotransmitters can cause depression.[42] Carlson, a Christian physician and psychiatrist, wrote that many emotional problems involve an imbalance of neurotransmitters.[43] Mullen, a Christian mental health physician who affirms healing prayer and deliverance ministry,[44] concurs that chemical deficiencies or imbalances in the brain cause mood disorders and also psychotic disorders.[45] Schizophrenia is caused by a chemical imbalance that is different from those causing mood disorders.[46] ADD and ADHD, as well as anorexia, are apparently caused by chemical imbalances in the brain.[47] Lockley, a Christian physician, wrote that when certain neurotransmitters are depleted, which might be caused by stress or continually thinking certain thoughts, neuron transmission across synapses is impaired such that thinking and feeling processes slow down, thereby leading to depression.[48] With improperly functioning synapses, depression can then be a "physical disease."[49] Even anxiety can become a medical problem with an altered body chemistry.[50] Emotions, then, become a function of processing neurotransmitters in one's brain. Stressful, painful, or traumatic life situations, if prolonged, can alter brain chemistry and cause a significant imbalance in the brain's neurotransmitters. Meier, Arterburn, and Minirth concur with the generally accepted belief that this is a sound theory.[51] John and Mark Sandford, of Elijah House ministries, while fully affirming inner healing and deliverance, concur that many people with a mental illness have a chemical imbalance in their brain.[52]

Biebel and Koening, in their book *New Light On Depression*, endorsed by the Christian Medical Association, understand depression as a whole-person disorder.[53] The four basic types of depression are spiritual, biological, developmental or often from one's childhood, or those from life situations—often overlapping and unique to each person.[54] Most people diagnosed with clinical depression experience biochemical depletion (imbalance of certain neurotransmitters) regardless of the type of depression.[55] Therefore, regardless of the cause of major depression, the "common denominator" for treatment should be medical, with antidepressants.[56] A survey of Christian psychiatrists revealed

29

that most considered psychiatric medicine the most effective means to treat schizophrenia and mania, while affirming a role for prayer.[57]

How does one correct the chemical imbalance? If that imbalance remains in one's brain long enough, as might happen in prolonged depression, drugs are required and necessary to correct the imbalance and enable the person to begin to work out the problem[58,59] and hopefully discover a root cause, such as anger, grief, woundedness, and more.[60] For depressed people, antidepressants restore "normal brain function,"[61,62] correct one's brain chemistry,[63] and "correct a biochemical flaw in the regulation of neurotransmitters."[64] Antidepressants straighten out a person's mind by increasing the level of neurotransmitters in the brain.[65] Psychiatric drugs will restore the normal chemical balance in one's brain and thus normal thought control[66] and mood.[67] There are approximately thirty antidepressants that correct a chemical imbalance in the brain by restoring normal serotonin levels, which restores concentration, mood, and control of one's thoughts.[68]

Sometimes it is not so much a chemical imbalance as rapidly firing neurons that are behind an emotional disorder. Obsessive and Compulsive Disorder (OCD) also appears to have a biochemical basis. Just as sparks can kindle or ignite into an ever-growing fire, nerves in a person's brains with altered brain chemistry can repeatedly misfire and cause racing, repetitive, and cyclic thoughts.[69] This brain phenomenon, known as "kindling" in psychiatry, is then the supposed basis for obsessions and compulsions and even intense emotions like rage or convulsions.[70] OCD is "normal thoughts constantly recycling and magnified to something weird."[71] The result can be a "biochemical trap" that requires a psychiatric drug to control the OCD.[72] When OCD has set in over years, psychotherapy will not help, and the only effective way to break the cycle of obsessions and compulsions is with drug therapy.[73] With the cycles broken chemically, the patient can then begin to work out the problem with counsel and therapy.[74] Drugs are necessary to enable healing and spiritual understanding for people with OCD.[75]

Mood Disorders and Genetics

Many mood disorders are apparently caused by genetics.[76,77] Many bipolar (from highs to lows) spectrum disorders, such as dysthymia (low-grade chronic depression),[78] Bipolar,[79] and Bipolar II,[80] can have a genetic cause. ADHD is apparently a lifelong genetic disorder.[81] Living victoriously with genetically caused mood disorders requires good therapy, loving relationships, and lifelong psychiatric medication.[82] A body of scientific evidence apparently supports the genetic and biological basis of many emotional disorders—such as schizophrenia, ADD, ADHD, and many more—that are understood as mental illnesses.[83] The gene DEP1 can apparently cause biological depression.[84] Genetics research, such as twin studies, adoption studies, and the study of families and communities such as the Amish, apparently provide evidence for the genetic predisposition of depression and other mood disorders.[85] John White, a late Christian physician and former associate professor of psychiatry at the University of Manitoba, concurred, pointing to adoption studies.[86] Mullen, like some other Christian authors, holds that the biological view is partially correct and that the spiritual (personal woundedness) and demonic views must be addressed as well for true healing.[87]

Biochemical and Neurological Gridlock?

So is there much hope without psychiatric drugs? Apparently, not much. In such a situation, seeing a pastor, thinking positive thoughts, obtaining counselling, having more faith, or depending on Jesus, for example, do not help.[88,89] Typically, "even the finest counsel does nothing to alter a person's mood."[90] Such people are in a "chemical gridlock," and no amount of counsel or prayer or self-effort will release them from the deep emotional pain, since it is deemed *a chemical problem that requires a chemical solution.* Apart from psychiatric drugs, then, there appears to be little hope. Concerning the physical causes of emotional bondage, Mullen concluded:

> It is important for the public to realize that people with depression, mania, anxiety and attention deficit disorder are

helplessly in the grip of a condition they can't control…These conditions are legitimate physical problems with medical treatments just like diabetes or any other chronic illness.[91]

Some addictions apparently result from altered neurological pathways. Sexual addiction is understood by Weiss, for example, as a disease with a very definite biological component.[92] Apparently certain chemicals in the brain, like endorphins and enkephalins, are progressively craved by the brain, and eventually neurological pathways are established behind legitimate sexual intimacy or sexual addictions.[93] The brain is neutral, not moral or immoral, with a neurological pathway that must be reprogrammed or reconditioned by various behavioural and other techniques along with other means of healing.[94] Since the biological and neurological aspect is so key to sexual addiction, any solutions without addressing the biological will not work. Recovery involves necessarily overcoming the imbalance of certain neurological pathways.[95] Spiritual solutions, such as prayer,[96] seeing a pastor, reading the Bible, or fasting,[97] are in themselves ineffective. Concerning his own sexual addiction, Weiss wrote that just coming to Christ and repeatedly receiving forgiveness was in itself ineffective—he was not healed.[98]

Some Christians have been quite enthusiastic and overly accepting of psychiatric drugs. In an article entitled "The Gospel According to Prozac: Can A Pill Do What the Holy Spirit Could Not?" the authors discuss the issues around the apparent ability of Prozac to do for Christians what the Holy Spirit, prayer, counselling, and self-help could not.[99] The authors wonder why a drug that changes neurotransmitter levels can appear so effective for people, while "prayer and good intentions" seem, in comparison, so inadequate.[100]

The article gives testimonies of Christians who had suffered with depression and were significantly helped by Prozac. The authors raise questions of the relationship between sin, personal responsibility, discipleship, and biology. A key question is the reliance on a "miracle drug for emotional and psychological well-being rather than on the God of miracles."[101]

Conclusion

The Church, in general, has clearly accepted modern biological psychiatry. Outright denial of emotional suffering, anti-intellectualism, suspicion or rejection of science, or blaming everything on sin are not attractive options. A strong case for modern psychiatry by Christians is often made by acknowledging its scientific basis. Since genetics, neurology, pharmacology, and so forth are the results of scientific research, and all truth is God's truth, then we should accept the findings of modern science. Carlson, among many other Christian writers, makes this point, affirming that regardless of the source, all truth is ultimately God's truth.[102] The insufficiency of spiritual approaches commonly offered within the Church, the apparent positive results from psychiatric drugs, and the strong belief in the biochemical theories behind the drugs all serve to bolster the acceptance.

Most pastors are encouraged to refer their parishioners to psychiatrists or mental health professionals when there are serious mental, emotional, or behavioural problems. Gary Collins, professor of psychology at Trinity Evangelical Divinity School and author, for one, recommends that Christian counsellors refer those who are "severely depressed or suicidal" or "appear to be severely disturbed emotionally," among others, to mental health professionals—including psychiatrists.[103]

Dan Blazer is a Christian, former medical missionary, author, and dean of medical education and professor of psychiatry at Duke University School of Medicine.[104] Reflecting on the long debate between psychiatry and Christianity in *Freud vs. God: How Psychiatry Lost Its Soul and Christianity Lost Its Mind*, he concludes that evangelical Christians and psychiatrists have developed a superficial friendship, "easily accommodating and frequently relying on one another."[105] Pastors, counsellors, and theologians have uncritically accepted neuropsychiatry.[106] Christian patients tend to willingly accept almost every drug prescribed.

A central theory in biological psychiatry is the supposed biochemical imbalance of neurotransmitters as a cause of depression and other emotional or behavioural problems. A huge edifice of drug therapy, professional reputations, scientific research, and profits for drug companies has been erected upon it. Prominent Christian writers and psychiatrists encourage many Christians to basically accept this belief and take the drugs as needed. But just how scientific and solid is this belief? After learning from Kathryn's true story in the next chapter, we will examine that belief closely in the following chapters.

Endnotes _____

[1] Robert Whitaker, *Mad In America: Bad Science, Bad Medicine, And The Enduring Mistreatment Of The Mentally Ill* (Cambridge: Perseus Publishing, 2002) pp. 28-33.

[2] Whitaker, pp. 34-61.

[3] Whitaker, pp. 33,100.

[4] Whitaker, p. 122.

[5] Roy Porter, *Madness. A Brief History* (Oxford: Oxford University Press, 2002) p. 122.

[6] Ty Colbert, *Rape of the Soul: How the Medical Imbalance Model of Modern Psychiatry Has Failed its Patients* (Tustin: Krevco Publishing, 2000) pp. 44-45.

[7] Whitaker, pp. 75-76.

[8] Whitaker, p. 12.

[9] Whitaker, pp. 12-13.

[10] Whitaker, p. 15.

[11] Whitaker, pp. 15-16.

[12] Whitaker, p. 83.

[13] Elliot S. Valenstein, *Great and Desperate Cures: The Rise and Decline of Psychosurgery and Other Radical Treatments for Mental Illness* (New York: Basic Books, 1986) pp. 36-37.

[14] Whitaker, p. 78.

[15] Whitaker, p. 79.

[16] Edward Shorter, *A History of Psychiatry. From The Era of The Asylum to The Age of Prozac* (New York: John Wiley and Sons, Inc., 1997) p. 196.

[17] Porter, p. 140.

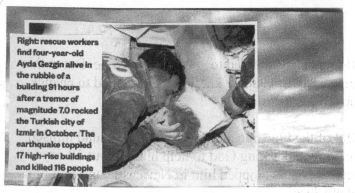

Right: rescue workers find four-year-old Ayda Gezgin alive in the rubble of a building 91 hours after a tremor of magnitude 7.0 rocked the Turkish city of Izmir in October. The earthquake toppled 17 high-rise buildings and killed 116 people

LIGHT THE DARKNESS

Today, many people's lives have collapsed around them and they are trapped under the rubble of fear, rejection, abuse, addiction, loneliness, guilt and many other problems.

Like the little girl in the photo, Jesus wants to come and rescue you and save you.

Jesus died on the cross and paid the price for all the sin in the world.

Ask Him to help you right now.

Say sorry in your own words and ask Him to forgive you.

Believe the gospel and read the Bible for yourself.

Be baptised in water and thank God for eternal life.

FROM THE FOG ON THE TYNE
TO THE LIGHT OF THE WORLD

The Policeman on horseback swung his baton and hit one of the fighting fans on the head. The Newcastle fans had spilled out of the pub in Sunderland city centre and Dougie wiped away the blood in the midst of the mayhem.

Just another day at the office for the Newcastle United Bigg Market Bender Squad.

Millwall on the Old Kent Road, the biggest soccer riot Sheffield had ever seen. Dougie was always there (if he was not serving time in prison). But there's gangs in prison, so the action does not really stop.

Unless you've had enough of violence and you're looking for a different way to live.

He was also addicted to speed and cocaine. But at this time early in 1986 he knew something had to change now ....(Psalm 121)

Out of the blue one day in February he found himself praying and asking God to help him. About 10 days later two girls stopped him in Newcastle and told him about Jesus.

He went to a church near the football ground, and on 18th Feb 1986 he was born again by the power of the Holy Spirit, and his life changed forever.

The drugs, drink, women. violence, anger, were now history.

He began preaching the Gospel in Newcastle city centre, and to this day God has sent him to 47 countries worldwide with the Good News of Jesus Christ.

Today Dougie lives in Gateshead over the river from Newcastle.

0793 1044832

[18] Valenstein, pp. 48-49.

[19] Whitaker, p. 94.

[20] Whitaker, p. 96.

[21] Ibid.

[22] Ibid.

[23] Valenstein, pp. 51-62.

[24] Whitaker, pp. 132-135.

[25] Whitaker, p. 111.

[26] Shorter, p. 219.

[27] Whitaker, p. 97.

[28] Ibid.

[29] Whitaker, pp. 98-106.

[30] Whitaker, p. 130.

[31] Neil T. Anderson, Terry E. Zuehlke, and Julianne S. Zuehlke, *Christ Centered Therapy: The Practical Integration of Theology and Psychology* (Grand Rapids: Zondervan Publishing House, 2000) p. 349.

[32] Frank Minirth, Paul Meier, Stephen Arterburn, *Miracle Drugs* (Nashville: Thompson Nelson Publishers, 1995) p. 3.

[33] Minirth et al., p. 4.

[34] Paul Meier, S. Arterburn, and F. Minirth, *Mastering Your Moods. Understanding Your Emotional Highs and Lows* (Nashville: Thomas Nelson Publishers, 1999) pp. 74-76.

[35] Minirth et al., p. 23.

[36] Minirth et al., p. 29.

[37] Ibid.

[38] Minirth et al., p. 29.

[39] Minirth et al., p. 25.

[40] Frank B. Minirth and Paul D. Meier, *Happiness Is A Choice: A Manual on the Symptoms, Causes, and Cures of Depression* (Grand Rapids: Baker Book House, 1978) pp. 215-217.

[41] Meier et al., pp. 82-83.

[42] Dale A. Matthews, with C. Clark, *The Faith Factor: Proof of the Healing Power of Prayer* (New York: Viking, 1998) p. 89.

[43] Dwight L. Carlson, *Why Do Christians Shoot Their Wounded?* (Downers Grove: InterVarsity Press, 1994) p. 74.

[44] Grant Mullen, *Emotionally Free: A Prescription for Healing Body, Soul and Spirit* (Kent: Sovereign Word International, 2003) pp. 87-187.

[45] Mullen, pp. 18,35.

[46] Grant Mullen, *Moods: What Christians Should Know About Depression, Anxiety and Mood Disorders* (Orchardview Medical Media, 2004) p. 64.

[47] Mullen, 2003, pp. 73,47.

[48] John Lockley, *A Practical Workbook For The Depressed Christian* (Milton Keynes: Authentic Publishing, 1991) pp. 43-47.

[49] Lockley, p. 45.

[50] Minirth et al., 1995, p. 71.

[51] Ibid., p. 82.

[52] John Loren Sandford and Mark Sandford, *A Comprehensive Guide to Deliverance and Inner Healing* (Grand Rapids: Chosen Books, 1992) p. 180, cf. p. 170.

[53] David B. Biebel and Harold G. Koening, *New Light on Depression* (Grand Rapids: Zondervan, 2004) pp. 31-53.

[54] Biebel et al., p. 21.

[55] Biebel et al., pp. 23,26.

[56] Biebel et al., pp. 36,173.

[57] Mark A. Pearson, *Christian Healing: A Practical And Comprehensive Guide* (Grand Rapids: Chosen Books, 1995) pp. 156-157.

[58] Minirth et al., 1995, pp. 3-4.

[59] Meier et al., p. 93.

[60] Meier et al., pp. 111-137.

[61] Minirth et al., 1995, p. 10.

[62] John White, *The Masks of Melancholy. A Christian Physician Looks at Depression & Suicide* (Downers Grove: InterVarsity Press, 1982) p. 133.

[63] Minirth et al., 1995, p. 27.

[64] Ibid.

[65] Biebel et al., pp. 173-176.

[66] Mullen, 2003, pp. 36,60,61,62,74,164.

[67] Biebel et al., p. 173.

[68] Mullen, 2003, p. 47.

[69] Minirth et al., 1995, p. 74.

[70] Minirth et al., 1995, pp. 74,84.

[71] Minirth et al., 1995, p. 83.

[72] Minirth et al., 1995, p. 82.

[73] Minirth et al., 1995, p. 98-99.

[74] Ibid.

[75] Minirth et al., 1995, p. 104.

[76] Meier et al., pp. 11,32,65,97,233.

[77] Mullen, 2003, pp. 28,35,43,50,73,164.

[78] Meier et al., p. 19.

[79] Meier et al., p. 46.

[80] Meier et al., p. 42.

[81] Meier et al., p. 30.

[82] Meier et al., pp. 217-218,220.

[83] Carlson, pp. 19,69-86.

[84] Biebel et al., p. 38.

[85] Stephen Arterburn, *Hand-Me-Down Genes And Second-Hand Emotions* (Nashville: Thomas Nelson Publishers, 1992) pp. 70-78,141-148.

[86] White, p. 136.

[87] Mullen, 2003, pp. 164-165.

[88] Minirth et al., 1995, pp. 3-4,28.

[89] Arterburn, pp. 93-94.

[90] Minirth et al., 1995, p. 3.

[91] Mullen, 2003, p. 84.

[92] Douglas Weiss, *The Final Freedom: Pioneering Sexual Addiction Recovery* (Fort Worth: Discovery Press, 1998) pp. 13-17,81.

[93] Weiss, pp. 18-23.

[94] Weiss, pp. 24-63.

[95] Weiss, pp. 20.

[96] Weiss, pp. 17.

[97] Weiss, p. 158.

[98] Ibid.

[99] A.T. Tapia, C.E. Barshinger, and L.E. LaRowe, "The Gospel According to Prozac. Can a Pill Do What the Holy Spirit Could Not?" *Christianity Today*, August 14, 1995. pp. 1-8.

100 Tapia et al., p. 1.

101 Tapia et al., p. 3.

102 Carlson, p. 85.

103 Gary R. Collins, *Christian Counseling: A Comprehensive Guide* (Waco: Word Books Publisher, 1980) p. 54.

104 Dan Blazer, *Freud vs. God: How Psychiatry Lost Its Soul & Christianity Lost Its Mind* (Downers Grove: InterVarsity Press, 1998) pp. 17-23.

105 Blazer, p. 21.

106 Blazer, p. 112.

Chapter Two

Kathryn: Shame, Depression, and Psychiatric Drugs

Though my father and mother forsake me, the Lord will receive me (Ps. 27:10).

I have come that they may have life, and have it to the full (John 10:10).

Mental health professionals diagnosed Kathryn as clinically depressed and prescribed psychiatric medication for her. She was informed that she had a biochemical imbalance in her brain. While she experienced some relief from the drugs, which almost ended her life, the cause of all her emotional pain had nothing to do with brain chemistry. Kathryn shares her life in detail, to show that relational imbalances, not chemical imbalances, were at the root of her suffering over many years. In later chapters, we will resume her story, with even more first-hand details on the effects of antidepressants on one's soul and spirit. I expect that more than a few readers can identify with various parts of her journey.

Roots of Pain in the Early Years

This is my story, my journey over the past twenty-eight years of being a believer and yet struggling with depression, low self-esteem, and all that goes along with that. I know that I am not alone in these struggles.

Mental and emotional illnesses are increasing in epidemic proportions these days—and Christians are not exempt. Yet Jesus said that He came to give us abundant life. Where have we gone wrong? Where has the Church gone wrong?

I was the second of six children. I arrived only eleven months after my older sister, and from what I've heard over the years, mine was one of those "unwanted" pregnancies.

As the story goes, told to me by my dad many times over the years, I was supposed to be a boy. My name was to be Michael Patrick. Even though my parents weren't ready for a second child, a redeeming factor would have been that I was a son instead of a daughter. One of the comments that my dad made often over the years, usually at the dinner table, was "Damn, why couldn't you have been a boy?" I was tall, and by the time I was in grade school, he was coaching basketball. I think he had dreams of a son who could be his star centre.

My brother was born two years after I was. From Day One, he was my father's pride and joy. Memories of my childhood and adolescence are overshadowed by the life of my brother. In retrospect, and knowing what I do now, I believe that for the most part my dad pretty much lived his life through my brother. David was the best—in sports and later in business—and my assigned role in the family was to enhance my brother's existence. There were many examples of my dad's preference for my brother over me and the sacrifices I was forced to make on his behalf. The problem was, I grew up believing this was normal—that David was more important than me and that my life did not hold the value that his did.

At a very early age, and I'm not sure why, my dad gave me a new name. It was "Dummy"—and it stayed with me until the day he died. No, I take that back. He died almost twenty years ago, and the name stayed with me long after his death. Even well into my twenties, I recall hearing, "Hey, Dummy, make me another martini," or, "Hey, Dummy, where's my coffee?" I laughed when he called me that—but I later realized that the wound went deep, so deep that for many years later I would hear "Dummy" when I make a mistake, and I had to stand against that lie.

My brothers and sisters agree that, for some reason, I was my dad's "punching bag." Perhaps it was my place in the family; perhaps it was the work of the enemy—more than likely it was a combination of both. All I know is that my dad's verbal and emotional abuse escalated over the years—and proportionately to his growing abuse of alcohol. In my story I will later share how, after years of verbal and emotional abuse from my family (my father set the pace), I accepted Christ and sought healing from the Church, only to discover that the abuse continued—this time in the guise of spirituality and truth.

The overall theme of my childhood would be one of *learned co-dependency*. From what I've been told, my mother had two nervous breakdowns before I was five years old. I don't have any memories of ever being held or nurtured by her. In fact, to this day it's always more about what I can do for her than her role towards me as my mother. I know my sister, brother, and I spent the better part of our early childhood years living with relatives—as my mom was hospitalized and/or emotionally incapacitated most of the time. The overall picture that I have of my mom is one of her in the distance—either very sad or crying.

I don't know when my dad's drinking started, but I do recall being afraid of his anger at a young age. I learned early on that my job was to keep Mom from being sad and Dad from being angry. That mindset, along with the forced acquiescence to my brother's needs for the remainder of my growing up years, pretty much created a Kathryn who existed only for the benefit of others. Needless to say, that carried over into all of my other relationships. To this day I realize that if I am not consciously aware, I can still default to feeling responsible for others' feelings and making the necessary adjustments personally to avoid making any waves.

By the time I was in grade school, I had two more sisters. So now there were five children—four girls and one boy. My mom was doing better emotionally by that time, and I believe she had actually bonded with one of her babies. She and my sister Jennifer have always been close, and even to this day, Jennifer shares a relationship with my mom that the rest of us did not have with her. We've always referred to

Jennifer as "the princess"—as she is the favoured daughter who can do no wrong. Doesn't every family have one of those?

During our grade school years, my dad coached every team that my brother played on—baseball in the summer, basketball in the winter. Our entire life as a family revolved around my brother's activities. Most evenings in the summer there was a baseball game—and my job was to sell candy at the refreshment stand. For basketball during the winter months, my job was to keep track of rebounds and give "stats" at the end of the game. There was never even a discussion of activities for "the girls."

My brother also had an interest in playing drums at a very early age. He used to take my mom's Tupperware and turn it upside down for a drum. I developed an interest in art and wanted to take art lessons. During my freshman year in high school, we moved into a new home, and my parents could not afford any living room furniture right away—so we were told that the living room would stay empty for a time. That year I asked if could take art lessons at school, which would cost an extra $10 per year. I was told they could not afford that. They did, however, purchase a $500 set of drums for my brother (I recall my parents discussing the cost), and the drums were our "living room furniture" for a long time. It didn't even cross my mind that there might be something wrong with this picture—this was a normal life.

During my senior year in high school, my dad was not coaching my brother's teams any more. However, he attended every game that my brother played in on Friday and Saturday evenings. One Saturday evening in February of my senior year, my school was having a father-daughter dance. My dad reluctantly agreed to attend with me, but only after my brother's basketball game. I went to the dance earlier with a friend and her dad—and sat alone for most of the evening as my friends danced with their dads. My dad arrived at the dance at 11:00 pm—and we had one dance together, during which he complained for having to be there.

Becoming A Single Mother

When I was twenty-two years old and attending college, my dad was transferred to North Dakota. Since I was not financially able to make it on my own, I decided to move with the family. I took a job as a waitress when we arrived in North Dakota and purchased my first car—a brand new Toyota. I remember the payments were $72 per month, and I was so thrilled to have my very own new car.

At that time, my brother was attending college in Iowa. He called home one weekend and told my dad that he needed a car. I recall walking into the family room as my dad was hanging up the phone—and he said to me, "David needs your car." I vividly remember the sense of shock and hurt that I felt at the time—but in my mind there was no option other than to give my car to my brother, as the word "no" was not in my vocabulary. So, my sister and I drove with two cars to Iowa, where we met my brother and I turned over my new car to him. I, of course, had to continue to make the payments while I drove the family station wagon when it was available. I got my car back six months later, only to then be told that Jennifer and her new husband needed a car—so they could have mine. Again, "no" was not an option.

When I was twenty-three years old I started dating Tony. He was a professional singer and worked in the same hotel where I was a waitress. Tony and my dad were friends before I started dating him, as my dad had stayed in that hotel during the months prior to our move to North Dakota. Tony was seven years older than me. To make a long story short, we dated for two years and became sexually involved very early on in the relationship. Even though I was not a believer at the time, I knew this was wrong, and I would usually spend all day Sunday alternating between crying and sleeping—after having been with him for most of the weekend. We were planning to be married, and I wanted to wait until marriage but he didn't—so guess who won? I became pregnant the next summer.

Tony wanted me to have an abortion—saying that he just wasn't ready to be a father. When I refused, he said, "Then it's your baby," and we broke up.

I was living with my parents at that time and was able to hide my pregnancy from them until I was five months along. All they knew until that time was that Tony and I had broken up. My dad and Tony continued to remain friends, however, and my parents went to see him every Friday night at the place where he was singing—as they loved to dance. Even after I told them that I was pregnant and that Tony had broken up with me, they continued to socialize with him on weekends. It was as if Kathryn did not even exist—other than to be the "bad girl" who got pregnant.

Coming To Christ and a New Life

During my pregnancy I met a wonderful friend who invited me to church with her. I accepted Christ early in the pregnancy, and it was as if God carried me through those months on a pillow. I sensed His forgiveness and looked forward to being a mom. I was not able to love myself, even then, but I loved the baby inside of me with all of my heart. He became my reason for living. In fact, I recall—even before attending church or hearing about Christ—asking God to please change me because I knew that the life I had been living would not make me a fit mother. He heard and answered that prayer. Over the years I have wondered what would have become of me had I not had a child. Not having any personal sense of identity and/or purpose left a huge void in my heart—but being a mom gave me a reason to live. I was not worthy, but my son was!

The church we attended was non-denominational. There were several "founders" of our church, who had joined together some forty years earlier to start the church. These four or five families purchased a large building to live in and formed a commune for the purpose of saving money and ultimately being able to send out missionaries. They also started what became a Bible school and missionary college. By the time I started attending the church, it was quite large, and the fellowship probably consisted of fifty families who had sold all they owned and joined this fellowship or community. This was my only exposure to Christianity, and as I look back, I realize that the fellowship was rather "cult like" and very legalistic. But to me, at that time, it was my new life.

I grew in my relationship with the Lord. Even my friend who led me to Christ said that she had never seen someone change so much, and she knew it could only be the work of the Holy Spirit. I was truly a new creation in Christ—I felt it, and others noticed it. Prior to getting saved, I was also quite the party person. I loved to drink, smoke, and party until the early morning hours. To this day my mom tells my son, "Your mom was a lot of fun before she got religion." Needless to say, my new faith was not well received by my family at that time—especially by my parents.

Cynthia was the name of my friend who led me to Christ. She had been raised in a conservative Christian home and had never "strayed" as I had. She was a petite blonde, soft-spoken and quiet—pretty much opposite of me in every way. We laugh about this now, but I recall, in my new life as a Christian, trying to act like Cynthia. She was the only Christian with whom I had a friendship at the time—so I thought all Christian women must be like Cynthia. So I tried to walk like Cynthia, talk like Cynthia, and even eat (more slowly) like Cynthia. Surely this was what it meant to be a Christian—right? I loved my new life and the peace and sense of belonging to my new "family" that I had.

When my son Tyler was three years old, I went to work for a man in our church who was starting a new business. I'm not sure why, but he approached me one Sunday after church, saying that he was starting this business and that he felt God wanted him to hire me to be his secretary. He offered me more money than I was making at the time—so I readily accepted. I was very flattered at his offer and grateful for the opportunity that he was providing for me to make more money. By this time, I was on my own as a single mom and struggling to make ends meet. This was my first daily encounter with a "Christian" man—and I don't think I need to tell you that, in my mind, anything he said was "the gospel truth." So when he told me that I needed to work sixty hours a week, that to me equaled obedience to Christ.

After several months of working long hours and having very little time with Tyler, I said to my boss one day, "I'm a single mother, and I don't feel right about working such long hours and not being with my son."

His comment was, "You do what I say, and God will take care of your son." So I did what he said.

Coping With Shame And an Emotional Breakdown

One night—very late, when I was sleeping—the phone rang, and it was Tyler's dad. He had just gotten off work and asked if he could come and see me. I hadn't seen him for about three years. I had been praying for his salvation for all these years and was excited that he called and saw this as an answer to my prayers. My pastor had also encouraged me to pray for his salvation and for us to be together "as a family." So, I said he could come over. Long story short, we ended up in bed—instead of in church together.

Needless to say, I was devastated. How could I do this again? I was a Christian. It wasn't long before the combination of the long hours of work and the guilt for having fallen into sin led to an emotional breakdown.

It started with an inability to sleep and anxiety attacks during the day. Pretty soon, I was unable to eat and cried all the time. I was literally coming undone—day by day. I went to see one of the pastors from our church and confessed my recent fall into sin with Tony. I was sure that God was punishing me for my sin.

The sleeplessness, anxiety, and other problems became worse, and I finally sought the help of a medical doctor, who diagnosed me with "psychogenic" fatigue. He told me to take three months off for rest. The pastor from my church invited Tyler and I to come and live at the fellowship for that time—so that I could get the rest I needed and also have help from the other women in the fellowship in taking care of my son. Now God was providing for me, and I experienced what I would describe as a strange sense of gratitude for His mercy and yet a strong sense of shame and guilt for having let myself get into this mess.

My "Christian" boss was not happy with my doctor's diagnosis and prescribed treatment. When I told him that the doctor wanted me to take three months off work, he said, "Forget what your doctor says and come back to work for me." I probably would have complied with his wishes if I had even an ounce of physical or emotional strength—I desperately wanted his approval—but I was a mess. There were days when I was so emotionally spent that I was not even able to look at Tyler. I think just being a mom equates with "giving," and I had *nothing* left to give. I was physically, mentally, and emotionally spent, and, even with rest from my normal responsibilities, I continued to struggle with depression, fatigue, and an overwhelming sense of being lost—wondering what it meant to be a Christian relative to all that I was going through. I went to every healing service and even to one woman who supposedly had an inner healing ministry. I received some temporary relief but nothing really lasting or noteworthy.

There was an older couple in our church who committed to pray for me daily, and I even spent some nights in the recliner in their living room. When they prayed for me, I again received some temporary relief—but it didn't seem to last.

At one counselling session I asked my pastor if there might be some medication that I could take to help me sleep or to feel better, and he said that I did not need medication—that he and God would bring me out of this. By this time, I had what another counsellor later described as a "thought disorder." The same tormenting thoughts would go through my head like a tape recorder—over and over again. Other than the fear that I might be pregnant again, I don't recall what the thoughts were specifically. I think that it was whatever would get hold of me at the time and instill fear—then the tapes would start.

I was under terrible oppression. I could feel it physically "in my head," and my mind was tormented. I also recall having a sense of paranoia. When I returned to work at a new job, if there was a meeting "behind closed doors" I was certain that it was about me and that I was going to be fired. Even though I now had a boss who continued to demonstrate Christlike love to me, I had never been able to trust a man, so why should I start now? I was certain that he would abandon me too.

In an effort to "be good enough" and find healing from this hellish existence, I tried a healthy diet, vitamins, exercise—everything I could think of or that people would suggest—and of course prayer, but nothing seemed to work. I also recall one day when our pastor came to visit me, and he seemed frustrated that I wasn't getting better, as I was in bed a lot. He said I just needed to get out and take a long walk, get some exercise. So, that began a daily routine of even more walking—sometimes miles—believing that the pastor must be right and that God would heal me if I obeyed him.

Some Unconditional Love

After three months off work, I was starting to have some good days and felt that I could go back to work at least part-time. God, in His mercy, brought a truly wonderful Christian man into my life at that time. His name was Mark. He had heard from someone else in our church about this single mom who was struggling—and he called me into his office one day. He said, "I want to help you by giving you a job. How much [money] do you need to live on?" I suggested a monthly amount—and he increased it by $200. To this day, I know that Mark was a living, breathing Jesus in my life at that time.

I went to work for Mark's company as a receptionist. I was still having some pretty rough days, and on more than one occasion, I would get to work, last until about 9:00 a.m., and have to go home. The anxiety and fatigue were unbearable at times. I never heard a cross word or reprimand from Mark about this. Usually when I got back to work the next day there would be flowers or a kind note of encouragement. I had *never* in my life experienced the kind of unconditional love and acceptance that he showed to me—not just for a short time but for the six years that I worked for him. We are still friends to this day. I would also add that I missed a lot of work during the first two years on that job, and I was always paid for my time off—God's incredible provision for Tyler and me!

I continued to struggle with good days and bad for the next two years, believing that this was my lot in life and that, short of a miracle, I would probably end up in a mental hospital someday. My days and nights consisted of fearful, anxious thoughts, insomnia, loss of appetite, and *severe* depression. It was God's grace that kept me even as functional as I was—and that wasn't much.

Drawn Into A Codependent Relationship

Another significant dynamic in my life during this time was my friendship with a woman named Margo. From the first day we met, there was a "chemistry" that I thought was God giving me a single friend. To me, Margo represented the kind of Christian that I wanted to be. I never had a sense of my own identity; I always wanted to be like someone else. She seemed strong, confident, and godly and had never fallen into the kind of sinful lifestyle that I had. We soon became "best friends" and were inseparable. She would often help me with Tyler by taking him to the park or to a movie. She sort of became his second mom, which to me at the time seemed a wonderful blessing. In mentioning that I wanted to be like the women I admired, I should add here that I thought I was the only woman who had ever had premarital sex—and that God was still punishing me for my former lifestyle. The church that I was attending did not talk about these things. As I look back now, I realize I was not alone in my struggles, but at the time it seemed that I was the only "sinner" among saints.

Margo had never had a relationship with a man. She was very strong and had been a "tomboy" when she was young. She quickly took control of my life and soon became angry or jealous if I wanted to socialize with other friends or my family. When I was at the worst point in my "breakdown" she took complete control—even to the point of answering all of my phone calls. I later found out from friends and family that they did not come to see me when I was sick because she told them I was not able to have visitors.

That relationship later developed into inappropriate touching on Margo's part, under the guise of wanting to comfort me. When I was having trouble falling asleep, she would lie next to me on the bed and stroke my hair or rub my back. Looking back now, I know that this relationship, along with the other contributing factors that I've mentioned, led up to my having a complete breakdown, but at the time I misinterpreted this as the one thing in my life that was good. I recall feeling very

49

uncomfortable (I know now it was repressed anger) with the way she touched me and her control of my life, but I was so sick and weak at the time that I thought I could not live without this friendship. It's hard to believe, but I was so "boundary-less and clueless" that it never occurred to me that Margo might have inordinate affection for me or that I should (or could) say no when her touches made me feel uncomfortable. I know now that was all part of my lack of a sense of being. I had always felt that I had no doors to close at will, that if someone wanted something from me it was theirs for the taking. Sad, I know, but true as can be.

Depression, Psychiatric Drugs, and Near Death

I had lived with this chronic depression for about two years when the pressures of life started to overpower me again. I felt that I was coming close to another "breakdown" and decided I had to find a counsellor other than the pastor I had been seeing intermittently. I found a wonderful counsellor through a mutual friend who, when I first called his office, had said that he could not see me for two weeks. I told his assistant about my history of depression and that I knew I was close to a breakdown, and they got me in the next day. I took the standard tests (MMPI), saw a medical doctor in the same clinic for a complete physical, and was diagnosed as clinically depressed. The doctor told me that it was no different than having diabetes or another disease and that I needed to be put on an antidepressant right away.

The first drug they put me on—I don't recall the name—did nothing. I was on it for about two weeks. However, when I noticed a rash developing on my arms, I called the doctor. He instructed me to stop taking the medication right away and to go to the pharmacy and purchase some Benadryl to counteract my allergic reaction.

The way I felt at the time and the lack of concern that I expressed to the doctor over the phone are clear indications to me, in retrospect, of the path of destruction I was (unknowingly) on by not even realizing how sick I was. I had called my sister who is a nurse to tell her about the reaction I was having, and she said that I should just follow the doctor's advice. The crazy thing was that I was also running a temperature of 104° Fahrenheit and having heart palpitations and trouble breathing—but I didn't even mention those things to my sister or the doctor. It seemed that the ability to sense danger or take care of myself just was not there. Later that night, my sister said she had a strong sense that she should stop by to see how I was doing. She took one look at me, instinctively checked my pulse, and said that we needed to get to a hospital right away.

When we arrived at the hospital, a doctor immediately saw me, because the nurses were shocked at my appearance. I looked as though I had been in a fire. My body was covered with a reddish-purple rash; my face and eyes were swollen; and I was barely recognizable. One of the nurses who took care of me said that she wished they had a camera because I was a "classic textbook case" of a severe allergic reaction. I was admitted to the hospital and put on an IV with steroids. I was too sick to ask questions that night.

The next morning my doctor came in to see me, and I asked him how serious my condition was. *He said that if I had not gotten to the hospital I would have been dead by morning.* He told me that when we arrived the night before my pulse was 130 and my blood pressure was 90/60 and dropping. He told me I would have gone into shock or cardiac arrest, either of which would have killed me. The really bad news was that they could not give me another antidepressant for at least two weeks and a side effect from the steroids I now needed to be on was depression. Argh!

So, deeper and deeper I sank into depression for the next two weeks. I was not even able to get out of bed. How did I feel? The saddest part about all of this is that I saw it as God's judgment on me for having sinned with Tony two years earlier. I had repented every day for those two years—but why else would this be happening to me? I was certain that I was the *only* woman in my church who sinned by having sex outside of marriage. I was the Scarlet woman, and there was no one in my life to tell me differently.

The church that I attended was all about appearance, and they weren't quite sure what to do with someone with my problems. Margo continued to take care of me and kept me isolated from other friends and family members, though I didn't know that at the time. As I look back now, I believe that the sicker I got, the better it was for her, as it gave her more control over my life. Also, the more she "took care of" me, the more dependent I became on the relationship. I can't call it a friendship. The inappropriate touching continued, and I recall feeling very angry about it—but the words *no* and *stop* were not in my vocabulary.

How did I feel? Like a person with a sick mind and body and no choices or hope for anything different. The only way I know to describe it is a feeling of intense shame, that I was someone who was intrinsically flawed and just not like other people. It's like I was living on one side of a river, watching everyone else live on the other side. Life was not for me—I did not exist as a person with feelings, rights, or purpose. I recall being in church on a Sunday, looking at women my age with their husbands and children, and *knowing* that would never be for me. I did not deserve it. I was bad! I think the only thing that kept me from considering suicide was my love for Tyler. He was my life, my reason for living, and I wanted desperately to be a good mother.

I continued to see the counsellor who had put me on the antidepressants. I was started on another drug, and within about two weeks I started to feel better. They also put me on a drug for the "thought disorder" I had—I believe that drug was called Navane (this was twenty years ago). Here's the description of this drug: "Thiothixene (Navane) is an anti-psychotic drug of high potency. Used in the treatment of disorganized and psychotic thinking. Also used to help treat false perceptions (e.g., hallucinations or delusions). *This drug may cause neuroleptic malignant syndrome.*"

My counsellor was a kind man, and I felt very comfortable with him. He had such a non-shaming way about him—so I'm not sure if I got better because I finally had someone I could talk to and who seemed to care about me or because I was on the medications. The doctor had explained to me that the *neurotransmitters in my brain were not functioning properly and that, without medication, there was no hope of my getting well.*

Rejection and Shame from a Bible College

During the early days of living at the fellowship and working on getting well, the pastor who was counselling me encouraged me to apply for Bible school. The fellowship had with it a four-year accredited Bible school, and he felt that I would benefit greatly from this. He said that, if accepted, Tyler and I could just move onto the campus permanently and that he would be enrolled in preschool while I attended Bible school. I was really excited about this and made arrangements to meet with the registrar right away.

I don't recall how long the application process took, as I had to provide references, have an interview, etc. But one day I received a letter in my mailbox saying that I had been accepted for the fall classes at the college. I was ecstatic and felt that this was a new start for me. Perhaps I really was worthy of a better life than what I had known so far. Others in the fellowship congratulated me and said that this was a "first" for the school—to have a single mom enrolled. Tyler and I had been in temporary housing on campus and now were preparing to move into student housing.

Shortly after my acceptance to Bible school, I received a phone call from the office of the head pastor and president of the school. I had met him on only two occasions for prayer, once when I was pregnant and the second time when I first experienced signs of depression. His secretary said that he wanted to see me in his office that afternoon.

The pastor shared with me that he had just recently found out about my acceptance to Bible school. His exact words to me were (I will never forget them): "We can't accept you here because your life still shows the consequences of sin. If you come back with a husband, we will accept you." He then said, "I need to ask you to leave the campus as soon as possible. I am the shepherd of this flock, and it is my responsibility to protect them from a woman like you."

I was numb. The only vivid memory I have around this incident is the intense sense of shame that I felt as word travelled around the campus—the "the single mom" needed to leave and would not be attending Bible school. I remember sitting in the fellowship dining room the next day, feeling like the adulterous woman at the well. The sense of shame was deep, and yet it only served to confirm what I already believed about myself—that I was set apart by God for punishment and as an example to others. Tyler and I moved off campus shortly thereafter, into a low-income housing unit, and I returned to work.

Deepening Depression and Band-Aid Solutions

I recall being so very sick and trying for so long to get well without medication (just have enough faith), but to no avail. One pastor who saw me on one of my worst days said, "You just need to claim the resurrection power."

I thought, "He doesn't have a clue..."

When I finally got on antidepressants, I started sleeping again, got my appetite back, and, best of all, the tormenting thoughts subsided. I believe I still had serious underlying depression—but at least I was having some relief from the horrible physical symptoms. I was remembering how very sick I had been, how I had tried to get well without medication, and that the only relief I eventually got was with medication. When anyone suggested that medication is not the answer, I thought, "Then what *is* the answer?" I tried the faith thing and it didn't work. The problem, as I see it, is that others, like me, are suffering from the same kind of problems that I had—and the Church doesn't have the answers. I believe now that if I had received the right kind of prayer and ministry, I would not have needed the drugs.

The shame that I felt throughout all of this, along with the feelings of worthlessness and guilt, affected every area of my life. Even saying that sounds like an understatement—as I *was* "shame." The only thing I was good at was being a mom, and yet, now I know that a lot of my problems deeply affected my son as he was growing up as well. How could they not? That is another story altogether.

The deep sense of shame and worthlessness that I lived with contributed greatly to my inability to choose healthy relationships and thus

54

to a codependent way of relating to others who often, like me, had a shame-based identity or some other deficit with regard to a sense of self. I felt so unworthy of being loved simply for who I was. I had never heard the words "I love you" from my parents. So, in order to get a sense of worthiness, I would "attach" myself to another person. In my mind, Margo was a godly woman, so if I, shameful as I was, could be known as "Margo's best friend," then that would give me some sense of identity and worthiness. It was as if I did not really exist anyway. The only problem was, I also had to give up control of my life in order to keep this new identity. Margo later shared with me that she eventually saw a counsellor about her issues and was told that her attraction to me was an effort to devour the feminine qualities that she saw in me and felt lacking in herself.

Help from Healing Prayer and Wise Counsel

Well, as I mentioned before, I was on the medications for about a year when I met a couple from our church who had an inner healing ministry. I don't recall how we really got together, but we scheduled a prayer session for one Sunday afternoon. I remember that before the session the husband was careful not to "promise" me anything. He said, "Kathryn, if God doesn't show up, nothing will change." Well, God showed up.

When we got together they spent a good deal of time asking me about my family history and, more specifically, if there was a history of depression in past generations. I told them that my maternal grandmother had suffered with depression for as long as I could remember, and my mother had suffered two nervous breakdowns, had gone through several series of shock treatments, and lived with depression during most of my early childhood years. Both were very fearful women, and my mom still is to this day. She suffers from panic attacks, intermittent dizzy spells that can last for days, and some forms of agoraphobia.

This couple went into prayer and took authority over generational bondage and the sins that had been passed down in my family. After that day *I knew I was different.* Something had lifted. I don't recall exactly how long it was before I knew I was better—perhaps a week or two—but I decided on my own to go off the antidepressants. I knew deep in my heart, with a knowing that only He can give, that God had touched me and that I was different.

Part of my ongoing healing was found in seeking godly counsel and obeying what God showed me about unhealthy emotional dependency and idolatry. While I was seeing my counsellor he somehow became "tuned in" to the unhealthy dynamics of my friendship with Margo, with whom I was sharing a duplex at the time, and he encouraged me to sever that relationship and to move back home with my family. When I told Margo that I was moving out, she became very angry and called the counsellor, telling him that I needed her and that my family would destroy me if I went back to them. He called me at work that same day, and said he wanted to see me as soon as possible. I think he knew that the news he was going to give me would be very shocking and he wanted someone else there to validate what he was going to tell me, because when I arrived he also had another female counsellor in the room. He said, "Kathryn, you need to get out now. Margo is in love with you." He told me to have nothing more to do with her.

As I look back now, I don't think I fully comprehended what he was saying. I thought Margo was a godly woman, so the two didn't go together. Long story short, I ended the friendship—because I really trusted my counsellor, felt safe with him, and trusted that my healing would be maintained as I followed the counsel of this wise and godly man.

A Faithful Father

It has been twenty-five years since my emotional breakdown. Tyler is twenty-eight years old now, having graduated from college, and is pursuing a career in music. He lives in another city, and I only see him once or twice a year. That is difficult for me, as I would like to be able to see him more often, but I believe that God, in His wisdom, knew that it would be better for Tyler to have some space of his own in which to grow and mature as a man apart from the mom who raised him alone. Tyler recently told me that he has come to realize that my faith was handed down to him and that now he needs to have his own. My mother's heart aches at times as I see him struggle to find the Father's love, having grown up without a dad, but I continue to hold on to God's promises for Tyler, believing that God will work *all things* for his good as we continue to look to Him for answers.

As I think of how to bring closure to this chapter, the consistent theme that runs through my mind is that God is faithful. Through it all I have found that His word can be trusted. I would love to be able to say at this point that my healing from the painful effects of childhood abandonment and neglect, along with spiritual abuse from the Church, is total and complete. But I would be less than honest to say that. There are times when I still struggle with bouts of depression or the pain of rejection that causes me to wonder if I have received any healing at all. At other times it seems that growing up in a home where I was given a shame-based identity in place of the one that God intended for me created sort of an "Achilles heel" that is vulnerable to rewounding and for which I need to maintain an awareness and sensitivity to God that others may not need. What I do know now that I didn't know twenty-eight years ago, however, is that He alone "restores my soul" and that my healing is truly found in His presence. Yes, there are medications that can numb the pain or provide some sense of stability during times of crisis or intense pain, but there is so much more to healing that God has for us, and that is what I experienced and continue to experience as I seek Him "at every turn."

The Abiding Presence

We live in a fallen world, and none of us is exempt from the pain of betrayal, rejection, or the wounding that comes to us, often undeserved, and many times seemingly enough to "take us out." In recent years, I have gone to God with new pain, sometimes resembling the old pain and sometimes from a wound that is altogether new and unfamiliar. Through it all, I have learned time and time again that He is faithful and that deep and abiding healing is found, not in medication or religious methodologies, but in His presence as I spend time with and get to know more intimately the lover of my soul. Psalm 27 assures me that if my father and/or mother abandons me, the Lord will take me and adopt me as His child. Yes, it would be easier in some ways if the healing would come "once and for all" or if I could wake up one day knowing that I will live "happily ever after," but that would constitute a one-time encounter, rather than a relationship. It is that relationship with Jesus, walking with Him in good times and bad, that brings a growing assurance of His presence—like the intimacy between a husband and wife that grows stronger as they experience one another in new and different ways. It is in going through the "ups and downs" of everyday life with Him that we discover His faithfulness and His ever-abiding presence. It is not in the freedom from trials or in living with "perfect" circumstances that joy is experienced, but rather in His presence, no matter what the circumstances.

Chapter Three

Biochemical Imbalances: Flawed Brains or Flawed Research?

The Lord is close to the brokenhearted and saves those who are crushed in spirit (Ps. 34:18).

You have been weighed on the scales and found wanting (Dan. 5:27).

James: A Fight With Antidepressants

My journey with depression and the medical field's push to prescribe antidepressants began in the mid 1990s when the local female medical doctor of our small community prescribed an antidepressant for my wife. Instead of getting better, my wife seemed to withdraw from me more over the following five years. She seemed to be getting more unhappy and despondent despite her prolonged relationship with antidepressants. She did make an attempt to wean herself from the drugs, but every attempt seemed to be followed by an even greater dependency on the antidepressants. To make things worse, one winter my wife was involved in a vehicle accident that left her bedridden for several months.

During this whole time I was struggling with my wife's growing emotional and physical distance from me. Situations in my workplace also precipitated a series of consequences that involved my administrators and higher authorities. I was at risk of losing my job, possibly my career. In short, my entire world came tumbling down one winter.

Having trained in the field of Christian family counselling, I had a very skeptical view towards the competency of most counsellors. As a result, I only reluctantly sought out the help of a trained stress counsellor recommended by my union. Though she did proffer a few helpful suggestions in stress management, she strongly suggested I see a psychiatrist and seriously consider taking antidepressants for a period of time.

As I was being emotionally and physically stretched to the breaking point, I had a complete physical exam. During the follow-up, my doctor proceeded to tell me that I was very fit and there was no physical reason for my distress. He recommended and booked an appointment for me to see a psychiatrist.

My visit with the psychiatrist was quickly brought to a halt when I made it clear to him that I was not interested in drug therapy. After seeing the effects of antidepressants on my wife—dependency on the drug, etc.—I asked him if I had any alternatives. His simple response was, "If you refuse to take medication, I cannot help you."

My situations seemed to just escalate. On top of it all, I was beginning to slip into that black void of sensory deprivation (no feelings), a sense of profound loss for my wife and job, and an overwhelming sense of aloneness—there was no one who could help me. In January of that year, with the permission of my wife, I booked myself into a crisis management safe house in a nearby city in an attempt to have some completely uninterrupted time to evaluate my life situation. They quickly admitted me, taking every precaution to prevent me from committing suicide. Though I have had two uncles commit suicide, I had already unequivocally determined that suicide was not an option for me.

Where was God in all of this? He was carrying me. As I reflected on who I was as God's beloved child and on the promises He has given us in His Word, a deep conviction began to settle in me that He would never leave me or forsake me. He was, and has been, with me all the time. I had a good rational-spiritual handle on which to keep pushing on in my circumstances.

The crisis management team recommended that I see a Christian psychiatrist. Though I thought this might be an oxymoron, I pursued the appointments in the hope that God might use the wisdom of this man to guide me in this time of hopelessness. I was not disappointed. Though he did highly recommend taking a short course of antidepressants, he did not abandon me when I pursued a drug-free solution to my problem. His godly counsel came at a divinely appointed time. We carefully looked at alternatives such as spiritual solitude, diet, trigger foods, physical exercise, and mind breaks (minute vacations). I did compromise by agreeing to take a short course of St. John's Wort, the "herbal" equivalent of an antidepressant, for about a month.

Today, I continue to pursue a drug-free life. I have a very profound assurance that Jesus not only lives in me, He walks with me. I still occasionally face those despondent times, those ugly situations that rear their ugly heads. My wife has divorced me. However, in spite of being occasionally enveloped by a cloak of darkness and having no feelings, I have learned to thank God and praise Him for His faithfulness in spite of circumstances and the absence of feelings. The frequency and length of those despondent spells are shortening. I am so thankful to God for giving me a deep, profound, settling sense of joy that is becoming more of the norm for me. I have every reason to live!

Leah, Rachel, and Neurotransmitters

For years, Rachel was barren and unable to bear Jacob a child (Gen. 29:31). Meanwhile, God blessed Leah with children (Gen. 29:32-35), then Bilhah (Gen. 30:1-8), and then Zilpah (Gen. 30:9-13). There was envy and strife between Rachel, Leah, and the sisters (Gen. 30:1). During harvest, Rueben found some mandrakes in the field and brought them to Leah (Gen. 30:14). Rachel insisted that Leah give her some of the mandrakes, but Leah agreed only if she could have conjugal rights with Jacob for the night, to which Rachel agreed (Gen. 30:14). This resulted in another son for Jacob (Gen. 30:16-18).

Why did Rachel so desperately want the mandrakes? Because they were thought to have aphrodisiac powers—which is why they are called "love apples"—and thus would help her fertility, and perhaps she would become pregnant.[1] Mandrakes are common in Israel, appearing as large leaves at ground level with violet flowers and yellow fruit resembling a tomato, with a very distinct, pleasant fragrance (Song. Sol. 7:13).[2]

Is there anything scientific to these "love apples?" Genesis 30 is actually an early example of neurotransmitters "behind the scenes." Hyoscine and mandragora, found in the mandrake root, can actually calm the nerves because they block the action of acetylcholine, a neurotransmitter.[3] These drugs, known as "anticholinergics," cause euphoria in low doses or even hallucination or delirium in higher doses.[4] Rachel was on to something more than simple folklore. Nevertheless, brain chemistry and neurotransmitters were not the solution for Rachel's situation—it was entirely God's favour and mercy when God opened her womb (Gen. 30:22-23).

Coal Tar, V2 Rockets, and Psychiatric Drugs

Whatever could coal tar, German V2 rockets, and psychiatry have in common? Did you ever wonder about the origin of the first psychiatric drugs? If you are even just a bit curious, please read on!

In the late 1800s, coal-tar chemistry was a very active industry. Organic chemists began to make synthetic dyes in response to an increasing demand.[5] In 1883, a phenothiazine was synthesized from methylene blue, which was derived from coal tar. Through a search for an antimalarial drug and then for an antihistamine, RP4560 was synthesized by Rhône-Poulenc in 1950.

Animals were first used in 1950 for screening drugs. The absolutely amazing discovery was that when rats were given RP4560, they lost interest in climbing up a rope to a platform for their food.[6] The drug was eventually given to psychiatric patients, many of whom emerged from psychoses. The first psychiatric drug, an antipsychotic, was released as chlorpromazine (Thorazine) and spread quickly through asylums and began a new era in psychiatry.[7] The drug was used without any idea at all as to how it worked on the brain and mind.[8]

During World War II, when the Germans ran out of liquid oxygen and ethanol as fuel for their V2 rockets, they used hydrazine. After the war, chemical companies claimed the stockpiles of hydrazine. But what to do with tons of this stuff? Many of those companies were developing pharmaceutical divisions.[9] In 1951 in New Jersey, iproniazid was synthesized from hydrazine in the quest for a drug for tuberculosis. Patients treated for tuberculosis also exhibited seemingly positive mental effects, and interest for psychiatry soon caught on. News spread—it was even reported that mental patients taking iproniazid "were dancing in the wards even though they had holes in their lungs."[10]

The first psychiatric drugs, then, were discovered completely by accident, with no real idea of how they worked.

How Much Serotonin Is in Your Brain?

The Church basically agrees that an imbalance of neurotransmitters is closely involved with, if not mostly causative of, severe emotional pain and disorders. Neurotransmitters are chemicals that float in the gap or synapse between the nerve cells of the brain. A decrease in those neurotransmitters is considered to be the major factor in depression.[11] To help alleviate clinical depression, for example, people like Kathryn in the previous chapter are prescribed antidepressants to increase the neurotransmitter level and restore normal brain function.

But how reliably can anyone measure the amount of serotonin in people's brains? Can serotonin levels—or any other neurotransmitter level, for that matter—in the human brain be measured as reliably as a lab test can measure levels of uric acid, creatinine, folic acid, sodium, LDL cholesterol, or triglycerides? Since a low level of serotonin is supposed to cause depression, this is a critical question.

I was quite surprised to learn that there is *no* test to accurately measure the level of these neurotransmitters in the brains of patients, and therefore there is no way of knowing if this is truly the problem for any given patient.[11,12,13,14,15,16,17] Psychiatrists, therefore, "cannot pin down the neurochemical status with specific accuracy."[18] There isn't a "shred of evidence" like from other clinical lab tests.[19] There are no reliable, objective tests to determine if anyone has a mental health condition.[20] Mental health professionals rely on *checklists of symptoms* to determine the probability (not certainty) of a possible chemical imbalance in one's brain.[21]

Neurotransmitter levels in the brain can only be determined *indirectly* from their metabolites with tests using urine or cerebrospinal fluid. Those tests are weakened by the fact that *less than one-half of these metabolites come from the brain; more come from other organs of the body.* When attempts have been made to measure the neurotransmitter levels, given the serious limitations and problems with such measurements, the results are either inconclusive or actually *contradict* the chemical imbalance theory. Elliot Valenstein, author and Emeritus Professor of Psychology and Neuroscience at the University of Michigan, estimated that of the metabolites involved, about one quarter of patients with depression test for low levels and some of them even have high levels, while most patients with depression have normal levels and paradoxically some patients who have never experienced depression actually have low levels.[22]

Glenmullen is an author, clinical instructor in psychiatry at Harvard Medical School, on staff at Harvard University Medical Services, and in private practice. He concluded in a comprehensive and critical review of the research that *any* measured deficiencies of such metabolites are not specific or diagnostic for *any psychiatric condition.*[23]

To restore a supposed low level or imbalance of serotonin, or any other neurotransmitter, one must be able to test *when the level is restored.* Since restoring the balance is so important, it is profoundly unfortunate that there is no way to measure when the balance is "corrected." If you can't measure the level like you can measure blood sugar level for insulin, for example, then psychiatric drugs can obviously cause elevated levels in the brain. Remember: those who advocate the biochemical imbalance theory claim that the brain requires the *correct neurotransmitter balance for proper functioning* with normal moods and feelings. Logically, "if the brain requires such a fine balance, too much should pose a problem as much as too little."[24] But such authors and researchers have painted themselves into a corner, arguing that something should be fixed while not being able to prove if fixing is required; and if they try to fix the problem, they can't prove when it's fixed either. Is this the "Achilles Heel" of psychiatry? A disturbing dilemma when you really think about it, especially when it involves *your* brain!

Terry Lynch is a medical doctor and author of *Beyond Prozac: Healing and Mental Distress*, a well-researched and highly acclaimed book. He wrote that it has never been established what a "normal" level of serotonin is for people.[25] But if we do not know what the normal level or range is, then what is an "abnormal" range? When someone stops taking an antidepressant that has been supposedly maintaining the "normal" neurotransmitter level, how does the level stay that way—by some miracle?[26] From diagnosis to every stage of "treatment," doctors and psychiatrists do not know the patient's neurotransmitter level at all. These simple facts seriously undermine the biochemical imbalance theory.

Now here's a more disturbing thought: what if someone diagnosed with depression has in fact a *normal, correct* neurotransmitter level (entirely possible according to what scientific evidence we have) and is now given a psychiatric drug? The obvious result will be artificially elevated—or maybe even toxic—neurotransmitter levels with all the side effects. No gain and all pain? Remember: if someone tells you that your serotonin is low or imbalanced, it is *not because of fact, but because the theory requires it. Your serotonin is "low" simply because it's supposed to be.*

There are more complications still. Even if these neurotransmitter levels could be reliably measured, what about differences due to gender, age, diet, and other factors? How variable are neurotransmitter levels for any given person? Would it approach daily fluctuations and variation as observed in blood pressure readings? How many tests would one have to take to assess the level for a given person? Don't forget that diet can affect serotonin (metabolite) levels in the body. For example, carbohydrates have tryptophan, an amino acid that is a precursor of serotonin and thus raises serotonin levels. Nutrasweet, found in many diet sodas, blocks the entry of tryptophan into the brain and thus reduces serotonin levels.[27]

Reserpine, believed for many years to reduce brain amines, has been offered as proof for the biochemical imbalance theory.[28] However, recent critical reviews of the literature and the early research refute that, with actually as much evidence for the *opposite* view.[29] An authoritative historical review of psychiatry concurs totally.[30]

There is even more evidence to challenge the chemical imbalance theory. There are drugs that increase serotonin and norepinephrine activity, like amphetamine or cocaine, and yet do not cure depression.[31] There are even some drugs that equally alleviate depression yet have minimal or no effect on serotonin or norepinephrine, directly contradicting the theory.[32] Furthermore, most antidepressants cause other effects in the brain in addition to increasing the activity of serotonin or norepinehprine, which challenges the simplicity of the theory.[33]

Even if some depressed people were found with a measurable biochemical imbalance, that would still not prove that the imbalance caused the depression, since other causes could account for it equally well.[34]

Magic Bullets or Shotgun Blasts?

The selective serotonin reuptake inhibitors (SSRI) are touted as being selective only for serotonin, like a "magic bullet" zeroing in on one neurotransmitter in your brain that needs tweaking in order to fix your emotional problems. Thus some authors contend that the only action of an SSRI is to increase the level of one neurotransmitter—serotonin.[35] But is this even remotely the case?

The whole idea is implausible, because *only* 5 percent of a person's serotonin is in the brain while the other 95 percent is in the rest of the body.[36] The serotonin nerves are a "vast, complex network."[37] Most of the serotonin is in the gastrointestinal tract, with some in the cardiovascular system and also the reproductive system and the genitals, where it affects one's hormones.[38] This is the obvious reason behind the numerous sexual dysfunctional side effects—because it is *not truly selective for serotonin in the brain* in the first place. About 60 percent of women on Prozac have inhibited sexual arousal, increased difficulty with orgasm, and reduced libido, while men on Prozac experience increased impotence and inability to ejaculate.[39] No wonder Viagra sales have skyrocketed some years after Prozac appeared. The U.S. has apparently graduated from a Prozac nation to a Viagra nation. A new definition of progress?

Since the brain is so complex, the supposed selectivity of SSRIs lacks plausibility. Each neuron (nerve cell) branches out tens of thousands of times as it connects with other neurons.[40] The brain has about one hundred billion neurons.[41,42] The claim that a SSRI could be "selective" is simply incredulous.[43] It is a "leap of faith" to ever believe that artificially altering one of the brain's biochemical functions could improve the brain and mind.[44]

SSRIs cannot be selective because neurotransmitters do not function independently of one another—they interact continuously and often in complex ways.[45] For example, raising serotonin lowers dopamine, which has been long known to cause serious side effects.[46]

Some writers refer to serotonin and norepinephrine as the brain's "main" amines.[47] This idea is a historical artifact, since the early psychiatric drugs were discovered when little was known about brain chemistry, and subsequent theories were based on the first-discovered neurotransmitters (dopamine, serotonin, norepinephrine). But now these theories are in question, since over *one hundred neurotransmitters* to date are known to affect the brain. Just because those three neurotransmitters were discovered first, it does not logically follow that they are the "main" ones. One can definitely challenge the idea that serotonin, among over one hundred neurotransmitters, could really be the "major regulator" of so much human behavior—holding to such a belief testifies to simplistic thinking and reductionism.[48]

If SSRIs are really that selective, you would expect those drugs to be specific for certain emotional and behavioural conditions. But the facts are otherwise. Results from clinical trials show that SSRIs can help alleviate depression, OCD, social phobia, generalized anxiety disorder, post-traumatic stress disorder, and panic disorder.[49] SSRIs are even more effective in treating premature ejaculation than depression.[50] Wellbutrin, an atypical antidepressant, was simply renamed as Zyban in 1997 and marketed as a drug for smoking cessation.[51,52] Serafem, prescribed for severe menstrual problems, is in fact Prozac under a different name.[53] Some SSRIs are used to treat bulimia, while imipramine, which was first developed as an antidepressant, also works for panic disorder.[54] Some psychiatrists prescribe Prozac for migraine headaches, arthritis, autism, and even alcohol addiction.[55] Even major tranquilizers are prescribed for many psychiatric disorders, which questions their supposed specificity.[56]

How do you explain this paradox wherein psychiatric drugs are used for unrelated disorders? The best explanation for the apparent effectiveness of SSRIs across such a wide range of unrelated emotional problems and conditions is that they are definitely *not* specific to or selective for serotonin.[57] Then it is also true that different psychiatric disorders have *no* biological specificity.[58]

There are still more problems with the theory. Antidepressant drugs typically increase serotonin or norepinephrine activity to the maximum level in a day or so, yet the corresponding mood improvement often requires several weeks or more. How can this be, if the theory is so specific for those neurotransmitters? During those weeks, many other brain chemistry and related changes and complex interactions will have occurred, making it very difficult to understand what actually caused the positive therapeutic effect—if there was one. Many of those changes do not involve neurotransmitters (like serotonin and norepinephrine), further challenging a theory of depression based on biochemical imbalance.[59]

Another indictment of the supposed specificity of psychiatric drugs is the simple fact that people are often given a "cocktail" of drugs to alleviate symptoms.[60] Instead of a "magic bullet," it is more like a "shotgun blast."

The supposed selectivity of SSRIs is simply untrue. The facts scream against any such notion. Perhaps the only "selectivity" of SSRIs is that *people are selected* by psychiatrists and others, based on certain diagnostic criteria, to take these drugs.

Excuse Me, Mrs. Rat, But How Do You Feel?

The serotonin imbalance model relies heavily on results from test-tube studies using rat brains.[61] The behaviour of rats that were given antidepressants or none was noted; then the rats were killed and their brains analyzed for the amount of serotonin. Then researchers extrapolated from rat brains to human feeling and behaviour. As Glenmullen points out, there is just one little tiny problem with this—rats cannot talk.[62] Since researchers cannot (at least not yet!) discuss a rat's experience with depression, researchers presumed that some measurable and observable behavior of a rats actually relate to depression in people.[63] So if a rat does not climb a rope in a cage or run around after her tail as often as before, there is some presumed degree of depression. If a rat lies in a corner of the cage and hardly moves, how sure can you be that it is severely depressed? Might there be other explanations? Unfortunately, you can't ask the rat. Studies with rats have been invaluable in assessing toxicity or drug levels for people, early warnings on dangerous side effects, and so forth. However, the extrapolation from rat behaviour to human feelings and emotions is problematic.

Aspirin Deficiency

In psychiatry, any positive effect from a drug treatment is often used to argue back to a biological basis for the emotional problem. If you take an antidepressant and feel better, many psychiatrists and researchers conclude that your brain needed the chemicals. Therefore, your depression really is a biological problem.

But such reasoning is erroneous and an example of biological reductionism, confusing causation with correlation and also causes with mechanisms.[64] It is fallacious reasoning dubbed as "pill before change is proof that change is due to pill," or "*post hoc, propter hoc.*"[65] Drawing conclusions about the nature of an illness and even making a diagnosis based on the effectiveness of a treatment has been called *ex juvantibus* reasoning (Latin: "from that which produces health").[66] For example, lithium helping manic-depressive patients does not imply a lithium deficiency in those patients any more than aspirin bringing relief from headaches implies an aspirin deficiency in the brain.[67]

Modern psychiatry is littered with the fallacies of *ex juvantibus* reasoning. For example, if your child is diagnosed with ADHD, takes Ritalin, and there is an improvement, many mental health workers would conclude that there was a biochemical problem. But in a study by the National Institute of Mental Health, *normal children* of professionals in the biomedical and mental health community were given Ritalin. The results? Those children *also* showed decreased activity and increased attention span—that is, the *same* response as children diagnosed with ADHD.[68] So do we conclude that these normal children also suffered from the same biochemical problem? Is it even remotely possible that *all* children then suffer from ADHD?

The history of psychiatry is full of such examples of false cause and effect. For example, in the late 1800s in England, women wanting a divorce were assumed to have a biological mental disease because after the "treatment" of having their clitoris surgically removed—which would have been incredibly painful in the days before anaesthesia—they typically returned to their husbands without any desire for divorce.[69] Shocking and illogical! Maybe the true cause was a new law in Britain that permitted women to file for divorce? But then you have to believe that members of Parliament created a mental disease by passing a new law.

An example from modern medicine illustrates the problem for psychiatry. Drinking fluids reduces a fever, but this does not mean that dehydration causes fever. In fact, dehydration is often a *result* of fever. Similarly then, changing serotonin levels that might help depression does not mean that a serotonin imbalance causes depression.[70] It is also logically possible that a serotonin imbalance is the *result* of depression.[71] The explanatory power of the chemical imbalance theory for a patient is equivalent to saying to the patient "you're alive."[72] "Biological psychiatry has trapped itself in a logic box that will self-destruct."[73]

Almost anyone who takes enough LSD or cocaine or some other hallucinogenic drug will experience hallucinations or delusions. Too much alcohol or caffeine, as we all know, will interrupt thought processes, feelings, and behaviour. Chemical substances certainly do affect the brain, and hence our thoughts and emotions, and can often alter one's neurotransmitters, and might even cause a biochemical imbalance or chemical dependency in the brain. However, one cannot *simply reason in reverse* and claim that if a person has altered feelings, thoughts, moods, or behaviour then the cause is biological. That is an *error in logic,* since there are other causes besides biological or neurochemical ones that can explain the condition.

The DST Debacle

During the 1980s, the Dexamethasone Suppression Test for depression was very common in psychiatry.[74,75] Psychiatrists believed that by injecting a person with dexamethasone, a synthetic hormone, and then taking blood tests for cortisol levels, they had a reliable test for biological depression not caused by life situations or relationships. Apparently depressed people would suppress cortisol levels in their blood for a significantly shorter time than non-depressed people.[76] The test became popular, widely used, and looked upon as a clinical test to help identify or confirm depression in patients.

Finally, psychiatry appeared more scientific, with a lab test like much of modern medicine! That was short-lived, however. It turned out that simply a decrease in food consumption, as often caused by a lack of appetite by depressed people, usually resulted in the DST results associated with supposedly depressed people.[77] Upon more research with conflicting results, psychiatrists eventually abandoned the DST.[78] By 1997, the DST virtually disappeared from psychiatry,[79] while the underlying erroneous thinking has not. The pseudoscientific enthusiasm is now shifting to PET

(Positron Emission Tomography) scans.[80] It is only a matter of time before the same thing happens to PET scans in psychiatry. The logical errors in the research behind the DST have been clearly published and documented.[81] Remember, this is but one of many such examples in psychiatry.

Does Carrying an Umbrella Cause Rain?

Imagine being in an office building in some city and looking out the window onto the street while it is raining. You notice many people with umbrellas and those without umbrellas running rather quickly. A few people are really getting soaked. You are quite happy that you are dry and not getting drenched. Would you ever conclude that people deciding to walk outside with their umbrellas open caused the rainfall? Perhaps such an idea never crossed your mind. Or would you ever argue that drought is caused by a lack of people carrying umbrellas? That idea probably never crossed your mind either—and for good reasons.

Yet this type of thinking confuses causation with correlation, a common error in scientific reasoning but almost epidemic in psychiatry. You simply cannot argue that carrying umbrellas causes rainfall just because umbrella carrying is highly associated with rainfall.[82] Likewise, you cannot conclude that if low serotonin levels are observed in many people diagnosed as depressed, that depression is necessarily caused by low serotonin levels. Yet such simplistic reasoning helps determine drug therapy for our loved ones. You can, however, just as readily argue—and there is scientific evidence to support this—that any observed biochemical changes in the brain are a *result* of one's emotions and feelings and thus are a function of the soul.[83]

So just because brain chemistry is involved in our behaviours and moods, does it necessarily follow that brain chemistry is the real problem? Certainly not! It is an error in logic as well as reductionism. Thomas Szasz, Emeritus Professor of Psychiatry, State University of New York, argued in his book, *Myth of Mental Illness*, that the brain's involvement in human behavior doesn't make moral or personal issues treatable by medicine any more than the use of nuclear energy in warfare renders international behavior treatable by nuclear physics.[84] Unless a clear causal mechanism or process is demonstrated, it is mere correlation. It would appear that psychiatry is not immune from logic disorder.

Healing or Disabling the Brain?

Many authors, including many Christian authors, believe that psychiatric drugs restore correct brain chemistry by fixing a biochemical flaw in the brain's neurotransmitter regulation. Thus, such drugs are believed to restore and heal the brain. But do they really?

Ironically and unfortunately, the *reverse* is true. Psychiatric drugs *cause, rather than correct*, chemical imbalances in the brain.[85,86] They actually impair normal brain function. SSRI antidepressants, in particular, damage the brain.[87] This view is supported by a considerable amount of scientific research.[88] Psychiatric drugs cause a general dysfunction of the brain and demonstrate their apparent healing by actually "impairing higher human functions" (on both "normal" people and psychiatric patients) as well as creating a "medical spellbinding" effect wherein patients deny the loss of emotional and other functions. [89]

Antidepressants raise neurotransmitters to toxic or pathological levels, which begins an assault on the brain's normal functioning.[90] When the brain's biochemical balance is artificially upset, it begins to compensate and adjust itself to the toxic substance in order to restore the normal balance.[91] The brain "fights back" to restore the balance by producing less serotonin and shutting down receptors—a phenomenon known as "downregulation."[92,93] Rather than "correcting" anything, the drugs actually cause a new pattern of brain dysfunction.[94] Some call it "Prozac backlash," the brain's attempt to counteract or neutralize the drug's neurological effects.[95] That's why suddenly stopping taking the medication can be so dangerous—the new artificial balance built over weeks and months is suddenly disrupted when the antidepressant is no longer taken. The brain cells don't have enough time to adapt to the sudden change.

About 30 to 40 percent of people on SSRI drugs eventually notice that the "effectiveness" wears off, most likely due to the brain's success in finally compensating and restoring the balance.[96] Psychiatrists call it "Prozac Poop-out."[97] Most psychiatrists will simply increase the dosage, often reasoning that the depression is worsening, which just makes matters worse in the long-term.

Neuroleptics, typically prescribed for schizophrenics, bind the dopamine receptors and induce brain pathology and impaired brain function.[98] Since there is no conclusive scientific evidence to show that abnormal dopamine levels (or any other neurotransmitter level) cause schizophrenia, taking neuroleptics does not correct any imbalance at all.[99] At best, they change brain function such that certain symptoms (sometimes) are diminished.[100] Thorazine, the first neuroleptic, was initially characterized as causing a prefrontal lobotomy by chemical means, making patients feel "immobile," "waxlike," and "emotionally indifferent."[101] But Thorazine was later marketed as "safe and effective."[102]

The above is no surprise since psychiatric drugs are synthetic, toxic substances, an example of *toximolecular* medicine. Toximolecular medicines do not cure any disease; they "disrupt the delicate, precise architectural design of our body" and its functions and always cause side effects.[103] Unlike natural substances for the human body (vitamins, hormones, etc.), these synthetic toximolecular substances can be patented by drug companies to ensure huge profits.[104] The desired approach is *orthomolecular* medicine where natural substances are taken to promote health and help prevent diseases.[105]

The Side Effects Are the Effects

Imagine opening up the case for your computer and looking at the circuit board for the central processing unit, the computer's "brain." You see a wire, unplug it, and notice some strange behaviour by your computer. But just because you can undo what you just did—and restore normal computer functioning—does that mean that you know how the computer functions? Does that make you a computer engineer?

Just because we know something about brain dysfunction does not mean we know a lot about *correct* brain function. It is incredibly easier to learn how something gets broken than to understand how it really functions.[106]

Given the complexity of the brain and our limited understanding, the "side effects" of psychiatric drugs, which are many, are *the* effects.

The brain dysfunctions are *the* effects.[107] The human brain has about 100 billion neurons, or about as many stars in the galaxy.[108] Each neuron is connected to about 10,000 other neurons, comprising an intricate and incredibly complex network of 100 quadrillion connections.[109] Since the brain is so complex, with billions of neurons and pathways that we know next to nothing about, why not leave it alone rather than pretend we can tweak or fine-tune the brain with psychiatric drugs?

Most people's serotonin and other neurotransmitter levels—even when they are suffering from depression, for example—are within a *normal* range. The brain is happily working with its current level of serotonin. Taking antidepressants disrupts the level of serotonin and other neurotransmitters. That's why many people have side effects. The brain now struggles to adapt and to compensate for the artificially changed serotonin level, as research has demonstrated. When a person stops taking the drug or reduces the dosage, the brain again encounters a wrong level of serotonin and works to normalize the level. The side effects *and* withdrawal effects are best explained by antidepressants messing up a normal serotonin level in one's brain, rather than restoring a correct balance.

Antidepressants or "Psychic Energizers?"

But what if an antidepressant "worked" for you or for someone you know? There are stories of people who "got their life back" with the help of psychiatric drugs. One can't deny an apparently positive effect, and one can be thankful for whatever benefits were realized. But what really happened?

Many people on SSRIs experience more energy, especially for those in depression, and of course this is a welcome effect. This is largely due to the fact that SSRIs are similar to amphetamines or cocaine, with similar stimulation and side effects.[110,111] At low prescription-level doses, stimulants have these common effects: increased energy, more focused attention, and brightened mood.[112] *These exact same effects have been observed in many research studies with normal, healthy people.*[113] Amphetamines and cocaine initially interfere with serotonin,

75

dopamine, and norepinehprine, whereas SSRIs initially interfere only with serotonin.[114] It's like taking a low dose of cocaine for a much lower "high" and energy boost. In fact, in the early history of antidepressant drugs, they were called *psychic energizers,* but that term never caught on since it would not be as "useful" in marketing to the public as *antidepressant.*[115] The term *antidepressant,* therefore, is misleading since it implies that depression has been treated when in reality people have been stimulated and energized.[116] Is it any surprise that aerobic exercise—with its endorphins and stimulation of the cardiovascular system—has been associated with lessening of depression?[117]

The picture is even more complex when a person experiences prolonged stress. Stress affects hormones, steroids, and more. Over time, the body gets used to elevated levels of adrenaline, which can lead to mania with its heightened energy and alertness.[118] Eventually, the body needs to "crash" to hopefully rest and heal. This is the "depressive" stage where the body (and soul!) long to be replenished.[119] Therefore, increasing serotonin levels via antidepressants, which increases blood corticosteroid to give more energy and thus an "amphetamine"-like effect, leads to more depression and inevitably a more serious "crash."[120] In this context, taking a drug with a stimulant effect "could be compared to forcing a breaker on your electric box to go back and stay on when it has already, as a safety measure, cut itself off."[121] The better approach is to find out what is causing stress and robbing one's peace so that one cannot fully enter His rest (Heb. 4:9-10; John 14:27).

Reign of Error

The theory of biochemical imbalance in the brain as a cause of emotional and behavioural problems, such as depression, is full of holes and more myth than fact. It is but the latest in a series of theories of the cause and cure of mental illness.

This chapter considered only a *few* of the many logic errors behind much of the flawed research used to prop up this theory. A recent critical review of the scientific literature outlined the problems with research studies involving brain serotonin levels and behaviour, clearly showing the inconsistencies and at least nine methodological problems that "plague the research findings."[122] The research data clearly does not support the theory.[123] In the larger picture, "a complex network of interlocking cognitive errors is active in biological psychiatry."[124] Indeed, it has now become apparent that research in psychiatry "has been woefully unscientific and seriously flawed", with major statistical errors in about 40 percent of papers in even reputable psychiatric journals—in addition to other types of errors.[125]

David Healy is a world-renowned researcher, author, historian of psychiatry, Reader in Psychological Medicine at the University of Wales College of Medicine, and former secretary of the British Association for Psychopharmacology. In *Let Them Eat Prozac*, published in 2004, concerning the theory of chemical imbalances as a cause for depression, he wrote:

> Talk of sexual complexes yielded to a new patter: "You have a chemical imbalance; these pills will restore your brain to normal."…This myth still flourishes in popular consciousness almost forty years later…Indeed, no abnormality of serotonin in depression has ever been demonstrated.[126]
>
> It is important to note what is not being said here. There are variations in serotonin levels and serotonergic receptors from person to person, and these may make us more or less sensitive to the effects of SSRIs and even to stress. SSRIs do act on serotonin, but there is no evidence of a serotonergic abnormality in depression.[127]

Psychotherapeutic terminology is no longer required to understand depression. The new language of chemical imbalances is scientific and easily understood. It is simple—your serotonin is just out of whack—that's all.

Psychiatrists very rarely do any critical reading or thinking, and medical students tend to accept the information and theories as dogma and truth uncritically.[128] Hardly anyone takes the time to really stop and think. *The scientific research, not your brain, is flawed and needs fixing.* Chances are, your neurotransmitters are doing just fine—I hope mine are also!

So what keeps this theory alive instead of dead and buried? Psychiatrists and especially drug companies must have a way to explain the action of these drugs to their patients so that they will more readily take them. What would you think if a psychiatrist or doctor told you that no one really knows how the drug will work, but you should take it anyway? How could drug companies market their product if they would also confess they really didn't know how they work? The discussion about biochemical imbalances serves to promote psychiatric drugs.[129] The chemical imbalance theory is not supported by science but by the marketing of psychiatric drugs by the pharmaceutical companies.[130,131]

Scientists prefer to hold on to a wrong theory when there is none to take its place. In the meantime, error and confusion reigns. Rather than admit ignorance, which requires humility, some researchers would rather support a flawed theory.[132] It is like turning one's ears away from the truth and turning aside to myth (2 Tim. 4:4). When theories of drug action and mental illness first appeared, the knowledge of brain chemistry was insufficient to explain or substantiate them, but nevertheless they have become widely accepted in spite of subsequent research and "defended, propped up, and heavily promoted." [133]

This supposedly modern theory of brain chemistry virtually determining our emotions was actually proposed thousands of years ago by Hippocrates (c. 460-c.377 BC), who taught that the brain caused joy, sorrow, pleasure, grief, tears, and so forth.[134] There is nothing new under the sun (Eccl. 1:9-10).

Conclusion

The biochemical imbalance theory behind mental illness, most notably depression, is unproven and flawed. Philosophy and the ideology of scientific materialism, not real science, are behind this theory.[135] When psychiatric drugs help people, it is not for the reasons commonly understood. For the diehard skeptics who still wish to hold on to the chemical imbalance theory, my final point is that more and more psychiatrists no longer believe it themselves either after years of research with even better technology. That led a prominent researcher and professor of psychiatry to state, jokingly, in 1999 to a room full of about 300 psychiatrists "We have been lying to everyone for years concerning the chemical imbalance model."[136] Significantly, not one researcher in the audience challenged that statement.[137]

The Church has been taken captive to the basic principles of the world (Col. 2:8). It is not the chemicals in anyone's brain that are imbalanced; rather, it's the weighing of "scientific" data to support this theory that is imbalanced. Like Belshazzar, it has been *"weighed on the scales and found wanting"* (Dan. 5:27).

When I lived in Syria, one of my favourite historical sites was an amazing Crusader castle, *Krac De Chevalier*, not far from Aleppo and on the way to Lebanon. This castle was unique, having two walls and two moats. Richard the Lion Hearted was there centuries earlier; you can see his coat of arms on some of the archways to this day. I have my own photos to prove it! Think of the neurotransmitter imbalance theory as a cause of mental illness as the outer wall, now breached, since the theory has been shown as flawed, indefensible, and full of holes. The second wall and moat to cross would be genetics as a biological cause of mental illness. Will the castle fall? The next chapter will take a hard look at that supposed solid evidence for psychiatric and behavioural genetics, as also endorsed by many Christian authors.

Endnotes

[1] Victor P. Hamilton, *The Book of Genesis, Chapters 18-50* (Grand Rapids: Eerdmans Publishing Co., 1995) p. 275.

[2] Hamilton, p. 274.

[3] David Healy, *The Creation of Psychopharmacology* (Cambridge: Harvard University Press, 2002) p. 58.

[4] Healy, p. 59.

[5] David Healy, *The Antidepressant Era* (Cambridge: Harvard University Press, 1997) p. 43.

[6] Healy, 1997, p. 45.

[7] Healy, 1997, p. 46.

[8] Healy, 2002, p. 46.

[9] Healy, 1997, p. 61.

[10] Healy, 1997, pp. 61-62.

[11] P. Meier, S. Arterburn, and F. Minirth, *Mastering Your Moods: Understanding Your Emotional Highs and Lows* (Nashville: Thomas Nelson Publishers, 1999) p. 82.

[12] Elliot S. Valenstein, *Blaming The Brain: The Truth About Drugs And Mental Health* (New York: The Free Press, 1998) p. 100.

[13] Joseph Glenmullen, *Prozac Backlash: Overcoming the Dangers of Prozac, Zoloft, Paxil, and Other Antidepressants with Safe, Effective Alternatives* (New York: Simon & Schuster, 2000) p. 201.

[14] Peter R. Breggin, *The Antidepressant Fact Book: What Your Doctor Won't Tell You About Prozac, Zoloft, Paxil, and Luvox* (Cambridge: Perseus Publishing, 2001) pp. 21,135.

[15] Ty C. Colbert, *Rape of the Soul: How the Medical Imbalance Model of Modern Psychiatry Has Failed its Patients* (Tustin: Krevco Publishing, 2000) pp. 57-58.

[16] Peter R. Breggin and D. Cohen, *Your Drug May Be Your Problem: How and Why to Stop Taking Psychiatric Drugs* (Cambridge: Perseus Publishing, 1999) pp. 33-34.

[17] Terry Lynch, *Beyond Prozac: Healing and Mental Distress* (Douglas Village: Mercier Press, 2005 edition) pp. 27-28,42,57,113.

[18] Neil T. Anderson, Terry E. Zuehlke, and Julianne S. Zuehlke, *Christ Centred Therapy* (Grand Rapids: Zondervan, 2000) p. 349-350.

[19] William Glasser, *Warning: Psychiatry Can Be Hazardous To Your Mental Health* (New York: HarperCollins Publishers, 2003) p. 26.

[20] Grant Mullen, *Emotionally Free: A Prescription for Healing Body, Soul and Spirit* (Kent: Sovereign Word International, 2003) pp. 71,32.

[21] Mullen, p. 73.

[22] Valenstein, p. 101.

[23] Glenmullen, p. 197.

[24] Ann Blake Tracy, *Prozac: Panacea or Pandora? Our Serotonin Nightmare* (Salt Lake City: Cassia Publications, 2nd ed., 2001) p. 101.

[25] Lynch, p. 153.

[26] Ibid.

[27] Tracy, pp. 88-90.

[28] Meier et al., p. 82.

[29] Valenstein, p. 98.

[30] Healy, 1997, pp. 148-161.

[31] Valenstein, p. 98.

[32] Valenstein, p. 99.

[33] Ibid.

[34] Glenmullen, p. 197.

[35] Meier et al., p. 266.

[36] Glenmullen, pp. 20,16.

[37] Breggin, 2001, p. 31.

[38] Glenmullen, p. 16.

[39] Glenmullen, pp. 106-123.

[40] Glenmullen, p. 202.

[41] Meier et al., p. 77.

[42] John White, *The Masks of Melancholy: A Christian Physician Looks at Depression & Suicide* (Downers Grove: InterVarsity Press, 1982) pp. 82,128.

[43] Glenmullen, p. 202.

[44] Peter R. Breggin and Ginger Ross Breggin, *Talking Back to Prozac* (New York: St. Martin's Press, 1994) p. 35.

[45] Glenmullen, p. 17.

[46] Glenmullen, p. 20.

[47] Frank Minirth, Paul Meier, and Stephen Arterburn, *Miracle Drugs* (Nashville: Thompson Nelson Publishers, 1995) p. 82.

[48] Valenstein, pp. 102-103.

[49] Healy, 2002, p. 313.

[50] Healy, 2002, p. 63.

[51] Breggin and Cohen, p. 70.

[52] Charles L. Whitfield, *The Truth About Depression: Choices For Healing* (Deerfield Beach: Health Communications, Inc., 2003) p. 125.

[53] Ibid.

[54] Colin A. Ross and Alvin Pam, *Pseudoscience in Biological Psychiatry: Blaming The Body* (New York: John Wiley & Sons, Inc., 1995) pp. 92-93.

[55] Valenstein, p. 105.

56 Peter R. Breggin, *Psychiatric Drugs: Hazards to the Brain* (New York: Springer Publishing Co., 1983) p. 3.

57 Healy, 2002, p. 313.

58 Ross and Pam, p. 93.

59 Valenstein, p. 99.

60 Healy, 1997, pp. 257-259.

61 Glenmullen, p. 201.

62 Glenmullen, p. 204.

63 Ibid.

64 Ross and Pam, pp. 38-39.

65 John Warwick Montgomery, editor, *Demon Possession: A Medical, Historical, Anthropological and Theological Symposium* (Minneapolis: Bethany Fellowship, Inc., 1975) p. 260.

66 Valenstein, p. 132.

67 Valenstein, p. 133.

68 Ibid.

69 Ty C. Colbert, *Broken Brains or Wounded Hearts: What Causes Mental Illness* (Santa Ana: Kevco Publishing, 1996) p. 20-21.

70 Elio Frattaroli, *Healing the Soul in the Age of the Brain: Becoming Conscious in an Unconscious World* (New York: Viking, 2001) p. 92.

71 Ibid.

72Ross and Pam, pp. 95,39.

73Ross and Pam, pp. 94-95.

74 Valenstein, p. 131.

75 Whitfield, 2003, p. 31.

76 Valenstein, p. 131.

77 Valenstein, p. 132.

78 Glenmullen, p. 196.

79 Valenstein, p. 132.

80 Ross and Pam, pp. 95,101.

81 Ross and Pam, pp. 95,101-102.

82 Valenstein, p. 125.

83 Colbert, 2000, pp. 63-64.

[84] Thomas S. Szasz, *The Myth of Mental Illness: Foundations of a Theory of Personal Conduct* (New York: Harper and Row, 1974) p. 26.

[85] Breggin, 1994, pp. 33-34.

[86] Colbert, 2000, pp. 67-80.

[87] Breggin, 2001, pp. 27-42.

[88] Breggin and Cohen, pp. 34-35.

[89] Peter R. Breggin, *Brain-Disabling Treatments in Psychiatry. Drugs, Electroshock, and the Psychopharmaceutical Complex.* Second edition. (New York: Springer Publishing Company, 2008) pp. 1-21.

[90] Glenmullen, p. 17.

[91] Glenmullen, p. 48.

[92] Breggin, 2001, p. 34.

[93] Colbert, 2000, p. 72.

[94] Breggin, 2001, p. 35.

[95] Glenmullen, pp. 75,50.

[96] Glenmullen, p. 91.

[97] Glenmullen, p. 92.

[98] Robert Whitaker, *Mad In America: Bad Science, Bad Medicine, And The Enduring Mistreatment Of The Mentally Ill* (Cambridge: Perseus Publishing, 2002) pp. 162-164,190-192.

[99] Whitaker, pp. 196-199.

[100] Whitaker, p. 291.

[101] Whitaker, p. 154.

[102] Whitaker, pp. 154-155.

[103] Udo Erasmus, *Fats that Heal, Fats that Kill* (Burnaby: Alive Books, 1986) p. 183.

[104] Erasmus, p. 184.

[105] Erasmus, pp. 181-183.

[106] Breggin, 2001, p. 33.

[107] Breggin, 1983, p. 2.

[108] Scott Veggeberg, *Medication of the Mind* (New York: Henry Holt and Company, 1996) pp. 96,10,18.

[109] Veggeberg, pp. 96, 18.

[110] Breggin, 1994, pp. 65-71,104.

[111] William Glasser, *Warning: Psychiatry Can Be Hazardous To Your Mental Health* (New York: HarperCollins Publishers, 2003) pp. 33,59.

[112] Glenmullen, p. 214.

[113] Ibid.

[114] Breggin, 1994, p. 126.

[115] Healy, 1997, pp. 259,66-67.

[116] Glenmullen, p. 215.

[117] Glenmullen, pp. 259-261.

[118] Tracy, p. 76-78.

[119] Tracy, p. 78.

[120] Tracy, pp. 84-85.

[121] Tracy, p. 78.

[122] D.F. Calbreath, "Aggression, Suicide, and Serotonin: Is There a Biochemical Basis for Violent and Self-Destructive Behavior?" *Journal of the American Scientific Affiliation* 53(2), 84-95, 2001. p. 90-91.

[123] Calbreath, p. 94.

[124] Ross and Pam, p. 101.

[125] Terry Lynch in Glasser, 2003, p. xviii.

[126] David Healy, *Let Them Eat Prozac: The Unhealthy Relationship between the Pharmaceutical Industry and Depression* (New York: New York University Press, 2004) p. 12.

[127] Healy, 2004, p. 291.

[128] Ross and Pam, p. 95,87.

[129] Breggin, 2001, pp. 21,135.

[130] Healy, 2004, p. 12.

[131] Healy, 2004, pp. 1-469.

[132] Valenstein, p. 96.

[133] Valenstein, p. 57.

[134] Veggeberg, p. 101.

[135] Frattaroli, pp. 8,83.

[136] Colbert, 2000, p. 12.

[137] Ibid.

Chapter Four

The Genetics of Depression, Schizophrenia, Greed, and Spirituality

The hearts of men, moreover, are full of evil and there is madness in their hearts while they live (Eccl. 9:3).

Take my yoke upon you and learn from me, for I am gentle and humble in heart, and you will find rest for your souls (Matt. 11:29).

Sonia: Release from Schizophrenia

I first met Sonia at a healing prayer meeting. She is a very quiet, sensitive, and soft-spoken young lady. For the first two prayer sessions, she just wanted a blessing and seemed to appreciate the attention and a listening heart. In reality, she was also building up a "comfort level" with our prayer team. At the third prayer session, she shared, somewhat hesitantly, that she had been diagnosed as schizophrenic. That was the real reason why she was coming to our prayer team. She seemed a bit embarrassed by that, being a Christian. We reassured her that, nonetheless, she is a precious child of the living God and *that* was her identity. The psychiatric label was simply a label and in no way her true identity.

As we began in healing prayer, asking Jesus and the Holy Spirit to come and reveal the deeper issues in her life, she wept a number of times as the Lord revealed his love for her and a number of very deep lies that she had believed about herself and God the Father. There are times when a personal revelation of the living Christ is so overpowering that there are no adequate words for it, and it heals the deepest places. This happened to Sonia on several occasions, and we were immensely privileged to have a tiny part. There were moments of real tears in the presence of Jesus and His Spirit.

Sonia had also struggled with a deep sense of insecurity as to her salvation for a number of reasons, but after two more prayer sessions that was entirely resolved. At the last prayer session, we noticed how she had a sparkle in her eye, her hair was well kept, and she walked with much more confidence. She told me that for the first time in many years, she could truly experience joy. Soon after our prayer sessions, she was able to reduce her psychiatric medication under her psychiatrist's direction and come off her "meds" completely. She was able to resume a normal life without the former "symptoms." It turns out that, aside from some good friends who were praying for her, she just needed to come into the healing presence of Jesus in a safe, quiet place.

The Supposed Genetic Basis of Mental Illness

Modern psychiatry firmly claims that many mental illnesses are brain abnormalities with a genetic cause.[1] Depending upon the mental illness, one major gene or many genes or "linked loci" inherited together are involved. While realizing the importance of deliverance, inner healing, and healing prayer, Mullen, a Christian mental health physician, affirmed the general scientific consensus:

> It is now well established that mental illnesses are usually the result of an imbalance in the chemicals associated with mood control. This tendency to malfunction is usually inherited.[2]

Therefore, genetics is ultimately behind mental illnesses such as schizophrenia or depression. The associated biochemical imbalances have a genetic origin.[3] Adolescent depression is among mood disorders that are strongly inherited.[4] Some forms of depression may be inherited down generations, at least through genetic vulnerability.[5]

We often hear that a gene has supposedly been found for some mental illness. And if there isn't a gene as yet, then there is some sort of predisposition. Arterburn, for example, makes the case for genetic predisposition to suicide and depression by referring to family and adoption studies.[6] Many researchers would argue that this is much more solid evidence for a biological cause of mental illness than the theory of biochemical imbalances in the brain. Most people accept, without much investigation, results from twin and adoption studies, as if this is "slam dunk" proof. Carlson, among others, agrees that results from twin studies offer solid evidence for the genetics behind panic attacks.[7] Similarly, adoption studies support the belief that genetics is behind schizophrenia.[8] But as we shall see, this has little scientific basis and provides still more examples of flawed reasoning in psychiatry. This discussion is not just an academic one. Consider the story of Mark and Loretta, two young Christians.

Mark and Loretta

Mark is a handsome young Christian man in his early twenties. He has been diagnosed with clinical depression for a number of years, and with some antidepressants he copes reasonably well with life. He is quite athletic, has good grades in college, and attracts many young women. Through his church fellowship, he met Loretta, a beautiful, spiritual Christian woman his same age. They soon began a friendship and eventually started dating.

About six months later, he is seriously thinking of asking her to marry him. One day he discovered, quite by accident, that she is also taking antidepressants and will do so for life since it is apparently genetic, as it is for him. In fact, when he met her parents, he found out that depression runs in her family even more than in his.

Mark could hardly sleep that first night after he found out about her depression. He has read some popular books on depression written by Christian authors. Mark prayed for guidance, since should they marry there is apparently up to a 75 percent chance that any of their children will also suffer from depression.[9] If they had four children, three of them may well have to live with depression and thus antidepressants for life. Not a very comforting or reassuring thought—in fact, just thinking about it is depressing! But she's such a beautiful blonde, and he knows that he really loves her. They seem to "click" when they talk about spiritual things. What should Mark do? He is even beginning to lose more sleep over this issue. Let's consider this question of genetics in more detail and return to their story later.

Genetics and Mental Illness: A Fundamental, Basic Problem

Colin Ross, physician, psychiatrist, author, and past president of the International Society for the Study of Dissociation, argued that according to the theory of genetic causes for mental illness, one would expect separate genes or groups of genes for specific diseases in mental illness.[10] For example, there should be separate genes for bipolar disorder I or II, panic disorder, major depressive disorder, general anxiety disorder, schizophrenia, and so forth. But if the same genes inherit them all, then these disorders are not really different, even though psychiatrists would like to pretend otherwise—we might as well just go home and forget this whole exercise. If they really are separate diseases or illnesses, they should be inherited independently and thus have independent probabilities of occurrence. This is a basic, simple point before we go much further into the more complex world of genetics and psychiatry. But this poses a fundamental problem.

Most patients admitted to psychiatric hospitals are diagnosed for not one but several disorders or mental illnesses at the same time or in their lifetime—the technical term is *comorbidity*. How often should this occur if mental illnesses are genetically based and inherited more or less independently? Assuming the commonly agreed occurrence in the general population of 1 percent for schizophrenia, 10 percent for major depressive episode, 3 percent for panic disorder, 10 percent for alcoholism, and 2 percent for obsessive compulsive disorder, one would expect

0.01 x 0.10 x 0.03 x 0.10 x 0.02 = six in 100 million people, or about fifteen people in the entire U.S., to have those five diseases at once or in the same lifetime.[11] This is not unreasonable; how many people do you know who suffer from, say, Lyme's disease, Parkinson's disease, diabetes, colon cancer, and Wilson's disease? Even if those mental illnesses or "diseases" do not occur with completely independent probabilities, it still presents a major problem.

In stark contrast, the most reliable survey in the U.S. from 8,098 people showed over half of those with a serious disorder in the previous year had three or more psychiatric disorders—and that's 1,120 people right there and only one survey.[12] The best statistics and probabilities show that only one person on the face of the earth should have the degree of comorbidity for the number of disorders commonly found in dissociative identity disorder, but there are 6,000 such people admitted to hospitals in the U.S. each year. And that's just the U.S., and just one year! Simple mathematics using commonly accepted survey data refutes much of the genetic basis for mental illnesses and disorders.

The genetic basis of mental illness falls apart right here at the outset. It's like horses lined up at a race, tensed up in their starting gates, jockeys leaning forward with adrenalin already starting to pump, everyone silent with strained expectation. Then there is a pistol shot, the gates open suddenly, and everyone hears the thunderous pounding of many hooves. People start cheering and getting excited. But unexpectedly, within several gallops all the horses fall down and the race is over. I would imagine those who placed bets would be angry! Unless, of course you do not suffer from gambling disorder and thereby would not gamble in the first place.

"It Runs in Families": So Does Arrogance and Impoliteness

It is often argued that if depression, for example, runs in families, then there must be a genetic basis and one can inherit depression, or at least a predisposition for it. Where did this idea first come from?

Sir Francis Galton (1822-1911), while studying the British elite, came up with this idea in his attempt to purify the human race and identify the biologically unfit with mental disorders that exhibited "degeneracy."[13,14] This was the beginning of eugenics in the human population. Apparently madness was actually a family line's last step in progressive deterioration.[15]

Galton's ideas were exported and further developed in the U.S. In 1914 at an American eugenics conference, it was concluded that in the next forty years about 5.26 million Americans should be sterilized in order to reduce the percentage of "defectives" in the population to an "acceptable level."[16] In 1927, the U.S. Supreme court passed laws for the sterilization of people with mental deficiency since it was considered genetic.[17] The state of Oregon passed its sterilization law in 1917, and until it was repealed in 1983, 3000 people in Oregon had been forcibly sterilized.[18] In many states, Americans judged as mentally ill were prohibited from marrying.[19] It was also believed that criminality was genetic since it "ran in families."[20]

Many Christian authors agree with the "it runs in families" concept. Although family relationships and other factors play a role, since depression runs in families, it is argued, some family members may be "born with a genetic vulnerability to depression."[21] Medically speaking, tendencies for mood disorders are genetic "because the problem runs in families."[22]

But this is simplistic reasoning. Any family history or pattern could also be environmental, or a learned behaviour, or genetic, or a mixture. Just because members of the same family for generations are Anglicans, it does not mean that there is a gene for Anglicanism. The same may be said for membership in a political party. Who would ever suggest there is a gene for Conservatism or Liberalism that governs voting behaviour? After all, "it runs in families." Could there be a gene for atheism if for generations in a family no one had any faith or belief in God? Or more related to depression, which is an issue of behaviour, what about genes for impoliteness, arrogance, or snobbery, which has certainly been known to characterize whole families for possibly centuries? Why not consider these also as highly inherited traits? Since faith ran in Timothy's family line (2 Tim. 1:5), was it therefore genetic? Was Timothy saved by grace (2 Tim. 1:9) or was it wired into his genes? Researchers today concur that the "runs in the family" idea and such "family studies" provide no sure basis for the genetics of any behaviour.[23] Having abandoned family studies and the "it runs in families" thinking, researchers moved on to something else.

Twin and Adoption Studies

Many researchers now look to twin and adoption studies as more solid proof for the inheritance of mood disorders and mental illnesses. In fact, such studies have all but become the foundation or "linchpin" of behavioral genetics. Now, apparently, researchers can separate genetic effects from environmental effects.

For example, let's say that out of 100 sets of identical twins observed with schizophrenia there were 56 sets where both individuals were diagnosed with schizophrenia. That would give a "concordance" rate of 56 percent. If sets of fraternal twins were similarly observed and the concordance rate was, say, 14 percent, one might conclude that genetics caused the higher concordance rate, assuming an "equal environment" for identical and fraternal twins. Even better, if identical twins reared apart exhibit schizophrenia or depression, for example, one might infer that genetics is responsible for the similarity. The critical assumption is that of equal or same environments for the behaviour being studied. Results from such studies on the surface, at least, seem to support the genetics of certain behaviours. But is it really that simple? Here are just a few problems:

Attempts to increase the similarity of twins: Parents of twins sometimes attempt to make the twins as similar as possible, and there are even international twin conventions to identify the most similar twins.[24] This directly violates the equal environments assumption, because twins are then not raised the same as any other two siblings. Some adoption studies involved twins raised by different members of the same extended family, in the same village, and with the twins going to the same school and even playing together.[25] Such factors undermine the "equal environments" assumption.

Twin bonding or identity confusion: Sometimes a twin *wants* to be like the other twin since his or her identity is wrapped up in being one of the twins. It's like living up to a reputation or image. Or what about a twin *not wanting* to be like the other twin since he or she wants to establish their own identity apart from the other twin? That issue might cause anxiety or depression for both of them, since this is a deep-rooted issue of their individual being and identity. Any identity confusion and emotional bonding between the twins will confound the interpretation of any data.[26] But even genetically identical twins are different, because *their souls are unique and different.*

Some of the results directly disprove the genetics of behaviour: Going against genetic expectations, the concordance rate for fraternal twins is higher than for non-twin siblings even though they are *different* genetically.[27] So, Jack and Susie are much more likely to share a common mental illness because they were born at the same time instead of say three years apart, which has nothing to do with genetics. It has more to do with a common schooling, friends, same age, and other factors when born together. Similarly, female identical twins or female fraternal twins show higher concordance rates than male identical twins or male fraternal twins, again defying genetic expectations.[28] Same-sex fraternal twins have double the concordance rate than opposite-sex fraternal twins.[29] Children of the same gender can bond more closely, which involves relationships and not genetics. All such results undermine behavioural genetics. No wonder behavioural geneticists ignore those results and cannot offer any explanation consistent with their theory, concludes Jay Joseph, clinical psychologist and author on numerous papers on genetic research in psychiatry and psychology.[30] This is probably the most serious criticism of this type of research.

Researcher bias: Studies are not made blindly. If one twin is diagnosed as schizophrenic, the other is observed for any possible signs of schizophrenia, and so the diagnostician is already biased.[31] The best approach is to observe hundreds of people with no prior knowledge of whether anyone is schizophrenic and to have independent researchers ensure that no one observes both individuals from a set of twins.

Researchers don't even agree on what behaviour is schizophrenic, and there are no biological markers or tests for it, so researcher bias and preference is inevitable.[32] No one is sure what they are even looking for! This is most blatant when deceased or absent people are judged schizophrenic by a "pseudo-interview" from hospital records or interviewing relatives or friends—that is, the results are actually fabricated.[33]

Inflated results: The most accepted way of calculating the concordance rate, the "pairwise method," is to simply add up the number of sets of twins found wherein both of the twins have the mental illness or behaviour being observed. But the "pro-band" method has been advocated to count the individuals among the sets of twins instead.[34] This leads to higher results, like for one study where the rate went from 13.8 percent to 43 percent upon "correction."[35]

Pre-birth experiences can account for some twin similarities: Some researchers argue that when identical twins are reared apart and there are some striking similarities, then genetics is involved. But such similarities can often also be explained by their pre-birth experience and hence prenatal psychology, since twins shared the same womb. One study of 1300 children and families showed that a woman in a stormy relationship with her partner is 237 percent more likely to give birth to a psychologically or physically affected child.[36] Psychiatric disorders, especially schizophrenia, are much more likely should the father die while the child is in the womb.[37] A mother's neurohormonal secretion irregularities can cause a child's reading difficulties and behavioural problems.[38] A man's anxiety attacks and feeling of hot flushes (I was tempted to type "hot flashes"!) was traced to his mother's attempt to induce aborting him by sitting in a tub of very hot water.[39] Even a child's familiarity or preference for music can originate from the womb.[40] Depression, eating disorders, schizophrenia, and more can originate from birth events and even type of delivery.[41]

Those are just a few examples. Imagine twins sharing exactly the same womb experience and delivery—can you so quickly declare similarities even when raised thousands of miles apart as caused by genetics? Certainly not! To complicate things further, each child is unique with its own soul, so there can be a different reaction to the same womb experience.

A major glaring weakness of behavioural genetics is that the genetics is *inferred* from families and relatives *after the fact*. Genetic experiments with "planned matings," for obvious reasons, are not possible. The best approach would be to study twins. But the analysis of twins data, strictly speaking, will *not* provide valid estimates of heritability.[42] Aside from the critical assumption of equal environments (nurture, family life, and upbringing) for identical or fraternal twins, there is the absolutely critical assumption of similar total genetic variance.[43] Also, the environment for twins must be similar to that of all non-twins in general for a heritability estimate from twins to mean anything for non-twins—which is almost certainly not the case.[44] Using the term *heritability* in behavioural genetics is totally inappropriate and "inherently misleading."[45] So the next time someone tells you that depression is "highly heritable," be nice and just smile, but don't ever believe them for a second.

A major study using Danish health records supposedly offered solid evidence for the genetic basis of schizophrenia.[46] That research has been subsequently soundly discredited by a number of researchers.[47]

Another approach is to use genetic markers. For example, a researcher claimed to find a gene for manic-depressive illness in a population of Amish people.[48] Apparently the gene was located on the short arm of chromosome 11. A number of Christian authors have referred to this "landmark" study as more proof for the genetics of mood and behaviour. However, this study has been found misleading and incorrect and was later fully retracted by the researcher.[49]

Segregation analysis, another method of psychiatric genetics, is fundamentally flawed, since it rests on violated assumptions.[50] A complex segregation analysis of the families of British medical students has shown a major gene behind attending medical school.[51] Should we then really believe that attending medical school has a genetic basis? Then why not similarly question the supposed genetics of schizophrenia or mood disorders?

Ted, Eileen, and Their Schizophrenic Daughter

Ted and Eileen, a committed Christian couple, came to see me about their daughter Lucy, who had been diagnosed with schizophrenia several years previously. They were discouraged about the situation and under a lot of stress in their family because of Lucy's bizarre behaviour, which at times was terribly embarrassing. As they shared some examples where Lucy seemed to be psychotic or out of touch with reality, it was not hard to see why she was diagnosed as schizophrenic. They were concerned also about the drugs that their daughter was on as prescribed by her psychiatrist. Lucy didn't always take the medication, since she claimed that it made her feel "weird" and had some noticeable physical side effects.

After listening for some time, I told them that unless there was an undiscovered truly organic problem, their daughter's condition was certainly not genetic and not due to any chemical imbalance at all. I briefly explained why that is the case and cited some references they could study. They were quite surprised at my comments, since all the mental health professionals told them matter of factly that schizophrenia has a biological origin and Lucy would require lifelong medication. I reassured them that while the cause is most probably a relational or emotional one, Lucy's condition did not necessarily stem from bad parenting or a dysfunctional home. There could be numerous other causes even with the most loving, Christian upbringing. I certainly did not want to heap any shame or condemnation upon them—they had experienced enough already over the years.

As we talked, they said that something did happen to Lucy in grade nine that "changed" her, but she never, ever, told them what it was. The symptoms of schizophrenia started right after that time. I never did get to pray with Lucy, since she was unsure about the whole idea of healing prayer. However, Ted and Eileen did leave with some hope because now they knew that Lucy could be healed without drugs and her future was not genetically determined.

Schizophrenia: An Example of Impossible Genetics

Was I correct in telling Ted and Eileen that genetics was not the issue at all? I believe so, since schizophrenia is genetically impossible. Not convinced? Here's even more reasons.

Firstly, about 60 percent of schizophrenics have parents who both have no history or trace of schizophrenia for many generations back. Unless you believe in mutations operating here, this poses a serious problem for genetics.[52] This was true for Ted and Eileen; schizophrenia just "suddenly appeared" in Lucy.

Secondly, data from thousands of schizophrenics and their relatives show that the observed rates for children, parents, aunts, uncles, cousins, siblings, and so forth do not fit any Mendelian ratio or group of genes at all and actually show the importance of nurture.[53,54]

Thirdly, long-term studies of schizophrenics for twenty-two to thirty-seven years show that around half of all schizophrenics recover and improve significantly without drugs—and that includes many who cannot tolerate the drugs and even those who had severe schizophrenia.[55] How on earth is this ever possible if schizophrenia is genetic?

Fourthly, schizophrenic symptoms can actually "come and go" depending upon surroundings and people.[56] Does this mean that the genes suddenly turn off and on if Aunt Hazel is around or you are in Orlando, for example? (In case you are wondering, I have nothing against Florida or anyone's aunt.)

Fifthly, the two-year Soteria house research project showed that about 85 to 90 percent of newly diagnosed schizophrenics requiring acute hospitalization recovered without conventional hospital treatment or drugs, doing as well or better than those assigned randomly to a psychiatric hospital with the usual drug treatment.[57] If a peaceful, healing community can help people recover from schizophrenia, then why bother about genetics and drugs?

Sixthly, an emotional and relational model that understands people's inner pain, confusion, and even trauma explains many case histories of schizophrenia much better than a biological model.[58] People diagnosed with schizophrenia are actually normal people, often very sensitive, with normal genes, but who have experienced either abnormal family life or some other environment or some traumatic event. They typically experience a psycho-spiritual crisis with feelings of outrage and overwhelm and communicate in ways that usually reflect the core problem.[59] Diagnosing children as schizophrenic "is to fix them in psychiatric formaldehyde."[60]

Still not convinced? Simple population genetics pose even more problems. It is commonly agreed that the fertility rate of schizophrenics is about 20 percent of the general population. This means that within three generations, the frequency of schizophrenics should be less than 1 percent (0.20 x 0.20 x 0.20 = 0.008, again assuming no mathematics disorder) and virtually disappear within the fourth generation.[61] However, the schizophrenia rate is acknowledged as *stable* at 1 percent worldwide. Calculating in reverse from the current 1 percent worldwide, this means that the frequency of schizophrenia must be about 100 percent four generations backwards.[62] This is hardly possible. Again, the mathematics poses serious problems for the genetics of schizophrenia, as it would for other psychiatric disorders.

Biochemical theories of schizophrenia have appeared and disappeared. It was once believed that schizophrenics have a peculiar skunk-like odor in their sweat due to TMHA (trans-3-methyl-2-hexanoic acid).[63] This would, in theory, help to identify schizophrenics. Later, there was a massive scientific breakthrough when it was discovered that 43 percent of "normal" people also have TMHA. The theory was immediately discarded. I have often wondered if any clinical trials were conducted with and without Old Spice.

Since 1961, no less than 33,648 research studies have been undertaken to determine a genetic or biological cause of schizophrenia; not one has been found.[64] Could there be a message here? Meanwhile, at least 110 peer-reviewed research reports on studies involving 31,551 people have shown a strong relationship between psychoses or psychotic symptoms that include diagnosed schizophrenia in most cases and childhood trauma.[65] In one study, 322 children of schizophrenic mothers were adopted. Children that grew up in a "disturbed or traumatic" adoptive family were 8.5 times more likely to develop schizophrenia than those simply having a schizophrenic mother."[66] Such studies refute and contradict any genetic or biological theory of schizophrenia.

An exhaustive review of all the research into schizophrenia over sixty years, and especially the last twenty years until 1980, has revealed inconclusive and flawed research but not one reliable diagnostic test for schizophrenia, which would be required if schizophrenia really was a disease.[67] None have been found since, in spite of advances in medical research. Nevertheless, the majority of mental health workers and psychiatrists believe that schizophrenia is biologically caused, either genetic or biochemical. This is an example of psychiatry taking a "leap of faith."

But There Is Schizophrenia in Our Family!

The "trauma" from the past may not be always that obvious. This is certainly true for loving parents who cannot recall any instance of abuse, physical or emotional or otherwise. Sometimes, committed Christian parents have a child who becomes schizophrenic in the late teens or early twenties. What then? First, remember that it is not so much trauma but woundedness in the soul. One's child might have been traumatized when staying with a relative, or on a trip, or at summer camp, or some other time and place out of the immediate influence of parents. Not a comforting thought, but possible nevertheless. Or, the child—being deeply sensitive—may have made a deep internal choice or decision in response to something in the family that is "normal and functional" according to most people. This is no fault of the parents, who probably were oblivious to the child's inner thoughts. Or there might be an intergenerational factor or, at times, even a demonic influence. Or, the root cause could have been from the womb experience. This all requires discernment and the revelation of the Holy Spirit.

At first, one might want to reject relational causes, especially childhood trauma, since it appears to shift the blame to the parents.

Many people would rather shift the blame to genetics or faulty brain chemistry. But lifelong medication on antipsychotics is typically hazardous and damaging to the brain. Of the people I have ministered to in healing prayer who were on lithium, for example, all have found the side effects major and negative. Would we not rather believe, as a large body of scientific evidence supports, that relational issues is the cause? It's not a matter of illness but a need for discernment, love, empathy, and a healing presence. And even if there was trauma as abuse from parents, which implies sin, there is always forgiveness, healing, and the power of the cross. A malfunction in relationships is more forgiving in the end than a malfunction in the brain.

The Genetics of Greed, IQ, and Criminal Behavior

Why are predominantly negative, "different," or "unacceptable" emotions, behaviours, or moods the focus of human genetics and neuroscience? Why stop there? On what basis do we limit it to the negative or pathological side of life? If neurotransmitters and genetics can be invoked as the reason behind mood swings, depression, and OCD, for example, then why not do the same for joy, gentleness, or compassion?

Why not study the genetics of greed? One could construct a checklist to measure different scores for greed (twenty-five to thirty for really greedy, sixteen to twenty-four for moderate greed, nine to fifteen for sometimes greedy, and one to eight for possibly generous or at least averse to greed) and then compute the heritability for families and relatives with varying scores for greed.

Or the how about the genetics of generosity or the genetics of the ability to worship? Or what about joy? If compulsive hand-washing as an example of obsessive compulsive disorder is inherited, as some claim, then why not compulsive shopping or gossiping?

Some researchers claim that criminality has a genetic root, or at least a predisposition. In 1907, Indiana became the first state in the U.S. to pass a law permitting compulsory sterilization of "confirmed criminals" who were deemed by physicians as showing no hope for improvement.[68] Such people should not be allowed to procreate, it was argued, since their "bad genes" should be progressively removed from the population. What does this say for responsibility and one's will or any hope of repentance and change of heart? If criminal behaviour is genetic, how can anyone be punished for it? A scholarly and critical review of the supposed evidence that defective genes causes criminal behaviour reveals that the supporting evidence and methodology, including that of twin and adoption studies, is flawed and inconclusive.[69]

Other researchers argue that intelligence is genetic. Apparently, some races or ethnic groups are more intelligent than others. The accuracy and assumptions of IQ tests have been hotly debated. The supposed genetic basis for intelligence collapses completely because there is no agreement on what "intelligence" is, since it is an abstract and immaterial reality; the emphasis on abilities is only one approach; the IQ tests themselves have known racial and class bias; and all the twin and adoption studies have serious flaws.[70] The thinking behind the supposed genetics of intelligence is not very intelligent.

The Genetics of Spirituality

The latest scientific claim is that even spirituality has a genetic root. Apparently the VMAT2 gene (vesicular monoamine transporter) has been linked to spirituality, defined as the ability to experience self-transcendence.[71] People with cytosine in that spot on their VMAT2 gene ranked higher on the self-transcendence test than those with adenine. Of the 35,000 genes and 32 billion chemical bases in the human genome, the researcher confined himself to just 9 genes (0.025 per cent of all genes), those known to regulate brain chemicals known as monoamines.[72] Apparently spirituality can now be measured on a rating scale with fourteen and up for "highly spiritual," twelve to thirteen as spiritually aware, eight to eleven for those with average spirituality who could do better, six to seven for practicing empiricists who don't experience self-transcendence, and one to five for skeptics who resist developing any spiritual awareness.[73] Apparently being drawn to God in the first place is "hard-wired" into our genes.[74] Furthermore, it seems that spirituality is good for community survival and fits the evolutionary development of the human species.[75]

This entire line of research falls apart when you redefine spirituality as loving your neighbour or obeying Jesus or walking in the light as Jesus is in the light (1 John 1:5-10). The self-transcendence test for spirituality is biased, since it assumes a more eastern concept of spirituality based on meditation and "higher consciousness." People respond to God due to grace—not genetics—and resist Him due to hardness of heart and sin—not adenine in VMAT2.

Into the Quagmire

I went on a canoe trip in Saskatchewan with some friends some years ago. It was a nice, warm, relaxing summer day as we were quietly paddling along a rather peaceful river. We were having great fellowship and could also hear a few birds and the occasional beaver flapping his tail on the water. No one in our group had canoed this river before. There was a slight sound up ahead, and the water seemed to pick up just a bit in speed. But we were having such a great, relaxed time that nobody noticed. A few minutes later, we turned a bend, and suddenly we heard the sound of rushing water. The current quickly became very strong, and ahead of our canoes were rapids and what appeared to be a small (hopefully!) waterfall. No one was talking any more! Three of our canoes, including mine, managed to avoid getting capsized—probably more luck than skill! Two canoes capsized in trying to avoid a few large rocks, and four people ended up in the water. One person unfortunately lost his glasses.

Why mention this story? Because those who simply advocate "it runs in families" or the other common arguments or beliefs for the genetics of mood disorders or human behaviour probably don't realize where this thinking will lead.

The belief that mood disorders and other human behaviours are highly inherited ultimately leads into a huge quagmire. This belief is part of sociobiology, an ideology of naturalistic human nature from

17th century philosophers who rejected the idea that man was created in the image of God.[76] That step was necessary to later apply evolution to man, with a biological determinism wherein "human nature is encoded in our genes."[77] Man, who was made a little lower than the angels, now becomes just a little higher than his DNA.

If the genetics of behaviour is accepted in principal, then why not declare a master race? Don't forget that it was American academics who argued in the 1920s that whenever Negroes intermarried with another race, that race began to deteriorate and the average intelligence began to drop.[78] IQ tests were therefore used to monitor average American intelligence and any possible lowering as more Negroes arrived in the U.S. and eventually intermarried.[79] A truly appalling concept. Supporting the genetic and biochemical basis of depression, mood swings, and more is not as simple and innocent as it seems.

But What Is a Gene?

Those who argue for the genetics of mood swings and so forth are relying on the commonly held belief that "one gene leads to one effect." Remember your high-school genetics? Most scientists believe that a section of DNA has a specific effect on some part of the organism, like hair colour, width of one's big toe, size of one's belly button, eye colour, or the ability to experience "self-transcendence." If this is not always true, the arguments for the genetics of emotions and behaviours falls apart.

Ironically, molecular genetics is steadily undermining the "gene" concept. If you are "genetics-challenged," then the world of molecular markers, functional genomics, transposons, restricted fragment length polymorphisms (RFLP), single nucleotide polymorphisms, quantitative trait loci (QTL), linkage blocks, and so forth sounds daunting. But please read on anyway!

Contrary to popular opinion, simply knowing the sequence of one's amino acids doesn't give an understanding of biological function.[80] Amidst all the gene sequencing, geneticists are less sure of where a gene begins and ends on a chromosome.[81] Recently discovered regulator genes that control the rate of protein synthesis control the effects of other genes.[82] Many genes are actually split and "occur" in several places on a chromosome.[83] Alternative gene splicing causes the same sequence of "genes" to make proteins in different ways, while the one and same "gene" can actually make different proteins.[84]

To make matters more confusing, the same protein can have different functions depending upon the context.[85] Repeated genes, redundant genes, overlapping genes, cryptic DNA, nested genes, multiple promoters, and antisense transcription add even more complexity.[86]

Each of us has many defective genes "covered up" by normal ones.[87] Due to different DNA sequences between everyone's genome (all one's chromosomes), we differ by about three million nucleotides to the next person.[88] Then there are different DNA variations of the *same* gene.[89]

Even worse, only about 3 percent of the human genome actually codes for amino acid sequences.[90] Thus, if scientist are looking at the "wrong" 97 percent of the genes, their research is misleading. This does not even consider one's all-important interaction with the environment during one's development. R.C. Lewontin, renowned geneticist and Professor Emeritus of Zoology at Harvard University, concludes that for all these and other reasons, claims for the human genome project can be challenged as dubious dreams involving simplistic scientism and ideology.[91]

The idea of a gene as a "clear and distinct causal agent" is common and popular but not a very useful concept any more, concluded Evelyn Fox Keller, author and professor of history and philosophy of science at MIT.[92] The classical "gene" concept has worked well for single-gene disorders like Tay-Sachs, Huntington's disease, cystic fibrosis, and more—but these are rare examples.[93]

A "gene" or "genes" for depression or mood swings or spirituality, for example, is borderline illusion. This is a main reason why researchers often claim to have found "a gene" for some behaviour or emotion only to have it contradicted later or simply never repeated. *Authors who support such notions do not realize that they are out on a limb that in due course will be cut off.*

The search for genes behind mental illness is flawed and problematic from the outset. It is only a matter of time until molecular geneticists will experience their "Waterloo."[94] Mendel was an Augustinian monk. How ironic it would be if the Church unwittingly replaced the doctrine of grace with the laws of Mendel.

Mark and Loretta Revisited

So should Mark ask Loretta to marry him? Assuming that he has earnestly sought the Lord and truly believes this is God's will for his life, then *yes, of course!* In fact, Mark should find the most romantic time and place to ask Loretta and pray that it would be a moment they would always remember.

Should Mark and Loretta be concerned about the "genetics" of depression for their future children? *Absolutely not!* There is no basis to that concern. How freeing, like a weight has been lifted off! This also means that there is no genetics of depression in their life either. Neither Mark nor Loretta need to take their "meds" for the rest of their life. They would benefit from wise counsel and the ministry of healing prayer that intentionally expects the presence of Christ and His Spirit. With healing prayer, it is entirely possible that they will soon move towards more wholeness. As the Lord brings healing and restoration to their souls, they could reduce the doses of the antidepressants under the direction of their psychiatrists, until no more drugs are used. They can look forward to having four absolutely wonderful children who will probably stress them out a bit in their teen years.

Mental Illness and Green Laughter

Is "mental illness" for real, as supported even by Christian authors? The consensus of the best scientific research is that there are no biological or genetic causes, lab tests, or markers associated with any psychiatric "illnesses" or "disorders." They are unproven and unfounded hypotheses.[95,96,97] Breggin, in his *Toxic Psychiatry*, wrote

"There is no evidence that any of the common psychological or psychiatric disorders have a genetic or biological component."[98] Ty Colbert, author and licensed clinical psychologist, in private practice as a psychotherapist, concluded in his book *Broken Brains or Wounded Hearts: What Causes Mental Illness*:

> the truth is that researchers have never discovered a single defective gene or accurately identified any chemical imbalance that has caused an emotional disorder; nor have they ever proven that brain abnormalities are responsible for even one emotional disorder. In fact, the National Institute of Mental Health (NIMH), the United States agency in charge of funding research for the study of mental illnesses, openly admits that the causes of schizophrenia, depression, mania, anxiety, and hyperactivity are unknown.[99]

More and more mental health workers and some psychiatrists are raising serious doubts about the supposed biological causes of mental illness.[100] In 2003, a group of Ph.D. and MD clinicians and researchers challenged the American Psychiatric Association to identify *one* published research study that would prove the theory of a biological or genetic cause of mental illness.[101] They were unable to do so and in fact affirmed the absence of any conclusive proof or evidence for the theory of mental illness.[102]

The concept of mental illness is myth and fiction. The human mind, being an immaterial substance, cannot have a disease like the physical body does. Should we not wonder at turning unhappiness into a disease? Having a mental illness makes as much sense as green laughter or purple concepts or wise colour—the two realities just don't connect. Brains can have a disease, but not minds. This does not in any way deny or minimize deep emotional pain and suffering, which is real and can be profoundly debilitating. Mental illness or mental diseases is myth and illusion; wounded souls and broken hearts are for real. Recognizing the shaky ground for "mental illness" or "mental disease," mental health professionals now talk about "disorders" and "syndromes."

For people with emotional pain or "behavioral dysfunction," modern psychiatry offers almost nothing beyond psychiatric drugs.[103] But prescribing drugs requires an illness or disease. Therefore, psychiatry and the pharmaceutical industry must defend, promote, and support the notion of mental "illness" or at least mental "disorders." At all costs, the public in general must believe in "mental illness" since the profits, prestige, power, scientific credibility, and reputation of psychiatry and the pharmaceuticals are built upon it. A vast "house of cards" has been erected on this basic concept. Transforming unhappiness, stress, discontent, and emotional wounds into diseases has proven too profitable to discontinue.

Mental illness is often given as an "explanation" when confronted with emotional behaviours and symptoms that are beyond analysis and understanding. Rather than exercise humility and admit that they really don't know, mental health experts engage in mythology by pretending to understand. By contrast, the following stories demonstrate how healing prayer in the presence of Christ and His Spirit can bring direct revelation and deep healing.

Barbara, Laura, and Kara

Frank and Catherine Fabiano, ordained ministers and professionally educated in psychology and counseling/sociology respectively, wrote about Barbara, who was severely depressive with suicidal thoughts.[104] The cause of her condition was unknown. In prayer, the Lord took her back to the womb and revealed that her life had been cursed by her own father, who wished that she and her mother would die. As she called out to the Lord, His healing presence came so powerfully that the depressive, hopeless, and suicidal thinking completely disappeared.

Laura suffered from autism, fear of death, fear of abandonment, anxiety, and grief.[105] The healing presence of Christ—again in a womb experience—was so real. He appeared to her and held her lovingly so that the fear of "not connecting" was totally overcome. In the end, nothing would separate her from the love of Christ. Laura was completely healed of autism, fears, and anxiety.

Kara, a thirty-five year old woman, was totally exhausted, frequently ill, and began to appear half-dead.[106] Through healing prayer, the Lord revealed that the cause was the death of her brother, who had died in her mother's womb before Kara was conceived. From her mother's actions Kara believed that her brother's life was more important than her own, and then she felt guilty for being alive. Essentially, she was exhausted "living for two people" and was giving in to a spirit of death. The Lord's presence and the authority in His name to rebuke evil spirits and break demonic powers set her completely free.

The above three women could all have been declared mentally ill, although Kara's diagnosis might have been problematic. Drugs were not the solution—these women simply needed to experience the healing presence of the living Christ.

Conclusion

The theory of a genetic basis for mood swings and "mental illness" is flawed as much as the supposed biochemical theory. All the uncritical and simplistic thinking associated with it has unfortunately crept into the Church. With a Ph.D. in quantitative genetics involving the computer simulation of genetic models, I could write much more, but further discussion is beyond the scope of this book.

With reference to the two walls and moats of the Crusader castle as discussed at the end of the previous chapter, the second moat and wall have been thoroughly breached. Accordingly, "mental illness" as a concept has crumbled as well.

One might argue that even if there are no sound theories behind taking psychiatric drugs, at least they are effective and safe. But even this involves still more assumptions and is not terribly wise, as we shall see in the next chapter.

Endnotes ⎯⎯⎯⎯⎯⎯

[1] Charles L. Whitfield, *The Truth about Depression: Choices for Healing* (Deerfield Beach: Health Communications, Inc., 2003) pp. xix,24,29.

[2] Grant Mullen, *Emotionally Free: A Prescription for Healing Body, Soul and Spirit* (Kent: Sovereign Word International, 2003) p. 35.

[3] Mullen, p. 50.

[4] Mullen, p. 43.

[5] David B. Biebel, and Harold G. Koening. *New Light on Depression* (Grand Rapids: Zondervan, 2004) pp. 38-39.

[6] Stephen Arterburn, *Hand-Me-Down Genes and Second-Hand Emotions* (Nashville: Thomas Nelson Publishers, 1992) pp. 141-144.

[7] Dwight L. Carlson, *Why Do Christians Shoot Their Wounded?* (Downers Grove: InterVarsity Press, 1994) p. 62.

[8] Carlson, pp. 72-73.

[9] Mullen, p. 28.

[10] Colin A. Ross, *The Trauma Model: A Solution To The Problem of Comorbidity In Psychiatry* (Richardson: Gateway Communications, Inc., 2000) p. 28.

[11] Ibid.

[12] Ross, p. 29.

[13] Colin A. Ross and Alvin Pam, *Pseudoscience in Biological Psychiatry. Blaming The Body* (New York: John Wiley & Sons, Inc., 1995) p. 10.

[14] Robert Whitaker, *Mad In America. Bad Science, Bad Medicine, And The Enduring Mistreatment Of The Mentally Ill* (Cambridge: Perseus Publishing, 2002) p. 42.

[15] Whitaker, p. 44.

[16] Whitaker, p. 49.

[17] Ross and Pam, p. 12.

[18] Jay Joseph, *The Gene Illusion: Genetic research in psychiatry and psychology under the microscope* (Ross-on-Wye: PCCS Books, 2003) p. 177.

[19] Whitaker, p. 42.

[20] Ross and Pam, p. 14.

[21] Arterburn, pp. 82,70.

[22] Mullen, p. 50.

[23] Joseph, p. 5.

[24] R. C. Lewontin, *Biology as Ideology: The Doctrine of DNA* (Concord: House of Anansi Press Ltd., 1991) p. 33.

[25] Ibid.

[26] Joseph, pp. 13,10,156.

[27] Joseph, p. 41.

[28] Ibid.

[29] Joseph, pp. 41,149-151.

[30] Joseph, pp. 151-156.

[31] Joseph, p. 41.

[32] Joseph, pp. 41,135-136.

[33] Joseph, p. 201.

[34] Joseph, pp. 141-145.

[35] Joseph, p. 145.

[36] Thomas Verney, M.D., with John Kelly. *The Secret Life of the Unborn Child: How you can prepare your unborn baby for a happy, healthy life* (New York: Dell Publishing Co., 1981) p. 49.

[37] Verney, p. 57.

[38] Verney, p. 59.

[39] Verney, p. 67.

[40] Verney, pp. 20-23.

[41] Verney, pp. 104-125.

[42] D.S. Falconer, *Introduction to Quantitative Genetics* (New York, Longman, 1981, 2nd ed.) p. 159.

[43] Falconer, p. 43.

[44] Falconer, p. 159.

[45] Joseph, pp. 131,119-130.

[46] Ross and Pam, p. 30.

[47] Ross and Pam, pp. 28-35.

[48] Ross and Pam, p. 35.

[49] Ross and Pam, p. 37.

[50] Joseph, p. 282.

[51] Ibid.

[52] Ross and Pam, p. 14.

[53] Ross and Pam, p. 18.

[54] John Modrow, *How to Become a Schizophrenic: The Case Against Biological Psychiatry* (Everett: Apollyon Press, 2nd ed., 1992) pp. 199-202.

[55] Modrow, p. 209.

[56] Modrow, pp. 211-121.

[57] Loren R. Mosher, "Soteria and Other Alternatives to Acute Psychiatric Hospitalization," in *The Journal of Nervous And Mental Disease* 187:142-149, 1999. pp. 142-146.

[58] Modrow, pp. 9-21,221.

[59] Peter R. Breggin, *Toxic Psychiatry: Why Therapy, Empathy, and Love Must Replace the Drugs, Electroshock, And Biochemical Theories of the "New Psychiatry"* (New York: St. Martin's Press, 1991) p. 46.

[60] Breggin, p. 287.

[61] Ross, 2000, pg. 33.

[62] Ibid.

[63] Modrow, p. 178.

[64] Whitfield, p. 171.

[65] Whitfield, p. 187.

[66] Whitfield, p. 182.

[67] Seth Farber, *Madness, Heresy, and the Rumor of Angels* (Chicago: Open Court, 1993) p. 128-129.

[68] Joseph, p. 242.

[69] Joseph, pp. 240-263.

[70] Joseph, pp. 267-277.

[71] Jeffrey Kluger, "Is God in Our Genes?" *Time Magazine, Canadian Edition* (Oct. 25, 2004, Vol. 164:17), pages 44-52. p. 48.

[72] Kluger, p. 48.

[73] Kluger, p. 51.

[74] Kluger, p. 48.

[75] Kluger, pp. 50-51.

[76] Lewontin, p. 63.

[77] Lewontin, p. 61.

[78] Lewontin, p. 25.

[79] Ibid.

[80] Evelyn Fox Keller, *The Century of the Gene* (Cambridge: Harvard University Press, 2000) p. 6.

[81] Keller, p. 59.

[82] Keller, p. 56.

[83] Keller, p. 52.

[84] Keller, pp. 60-61,63.

[85] Keller, p. 64.

[86] Keller, pp. 67,111.

[87] R.C. Lewontin, *It Ain't Necessarily So: The Dream of the Human Genome and Other Illusions* (New York: Review Books, 2000) p. 50.

[88] Lewontin, 2000, p. 154.

[89] Lewontin, 2000, p. 155.

[90] Keller, pp. 58-59.

[91] Lewontin, 2000, pp. 133-186, xviv, 17.

[92] Keller, pp. 131,67.

[93] Keller, p. 68.

[94] Joseph, p. 292.

[95] William Glasser, *Warning: Psychiatry Can Be Hazardous To Your Mental Health* (New York: HarperCollins Publishers, 2003) pp. xii-xix.

[96] Whitfield, p. 39.

[97] Joseph, p. 97.

[98] Breggin, 1991, p. 291.

[99] Ty C. Colbert, *Broken Brains or Wounded Hearts: What Causes Mental Illness* (Santa Ana: Kevco Publishing, 1996) p. 2.

[100] Colbert, pp. 2-3.

[101] Whitfield, p. 256.

[102] Whitfield, pp. 256-259.

[103] Terry Lynch, *Beyond Prozac: Healing and Mental Distress* (Douglas Village: Mercier Press, 2005 edition) p. 78.

[104] Frank and Catherine Cahill-Fabiano, *Healing The Past, Releasing Your Future* (Kent: Sovereign World Ltd., 2003) pp. 41-42.

[105] Fabiano, p. 49.

[106] Fabiano, pp. 43-44.

Chapter Five

The Neurological Nightmare

I sought the Lord, and he answered me; he delivered me from all my fears (Ps. 34:4).

For the wisdom of this world is foolishness in God's sight. As it is written: "He catches the wise in their craftiness"; and again, "The Lord knows that the thoughts of the wise are futile" (1 Cor. 3:19-20).

Marcie: Losing Hope In A Psychiatric Ward

Several years ago I received a phone call informing me that Marcie was in the psychiatric ward of a local hospital. I had known Marcie previously from another church and knew that she had been receiving psychiatric medication. I also had the immense privilege of praying with her on a few occasions and watching Jesus bring deep healing to some of the most painful parts in her life. But I also knew that there was room for more healing. After the phone call, I visited her a number of times in the hospital. What really disturbed me was that she was totally convinced that she would die in the psychiatric ward; she had all but completely lost hope. She was also suffering from many drug-induced side effects, which in turn required more medication, which in turn caused more problems. Each time I visited the psychiatric ward, I sensed an overall gloom of despair and noticed how many of the patients appeared somewhat withdrawn, sometimes listless, even "numb and not there" in a few cases.

Marcie's most pressing problem was a recurring, intense, oppressive thought, a paranoia, which consumed her mind for several hours of every day and robbed her of most of her sleep and now required sleeping pills on top of the antidepressant medication. But the medication did not alleviate her immediate problem. On top of this, a drug-induced haze made it difficult to concentrate. Just to have someone there, to listen and empathize, was healing for her. After several visits, with her growing stated belief that she would die in the psychiatric ward, I prayed more earnestly, asking the Lord to reveal how to pray with her. Many believers in her church were interceding for her.

At about the sixth visit, when she was finally alert enough to respond to healing prayer, Jesus brought back three related memories, each of which clearly built upon the other, all directly tied to the paranoia. The memories came back slowly, and the associated feelings seemed to take forever to come back as well. It was obvious that the drugs were numbing her whole being and impeding her spiritual healing. But nevertheless, Jesus' gentle healing presence and His love dealt with the pain, bondage, and confusion of her mind. As a result, the paranoia ceased almost immediately. In a week she was out of the hospital and has since resumed an active life. It was obvious that her situation did not really improve until that time of healing prayer.

Are Psychiatric Drugs Relatively Safe?

Given that there is no biological or genetic basis for psychiatric drugs, you might still argue that they should be taken anyway since "they work" and one can benefit from them. You could be quite pragmatic about the whole thing—just because we really don't know how and why they work, take them anyway. Besides, getting help in the end is what counts. Since many authors state that you'll need these drugs like you need insulin if you are a diabetic, there may not be a lot of choice—at least, on the surface.

The issue of safety is paramount, of course. You would naturally assume that these drugs have been well researched, verified, efficacy proven, government approved, and administered by competent mental health professionals. Would you expect any less for your own health or for your loved ones? Yes, thalidomide was a drug nightmare that caused many birth defects and much human suffering—but surely the medical profession has learned its lesson since then. Are the risks minor? Are the costs worth it?

Psychiatric drugs for treating mood disorders "have been around for many years and have an excellent track record for long-term safety."[1] Drugs for depression and mood disorders offer "safe, effective treatment" for Christians.[2] Concerning the newer antidepressants, King wrote:

> These medications are safe in all ways: There are few if any side effects (minor, if any); the medications are not habit forming or addicting, and they are compatible with other medications. If a chemical imbalance is present, within several weeks the person will feel remarkably better and be functioning in keeping with his or her usual productive norm. If the symptoms were *not* biochemically induced, no harm will have been done; it is a "trial and see," not a "trial and error." [3]

It would appear, then, that safety is not a major concern when taking psychiatric drugs. Many other authors and writers would echo the same view as those quoted above, and all from their professional training and clinical experience. But not everyone would agree. The question merits deeper probing. Just how safe are psychiatric drugs? Should one worry about side effects at all?

Rabbit Syndrome and More

The apparent help from psychiatric drugs can come with a price. Beyond financial costs are the harmful side effects and possible permanent brain damage. Unfortunately, not every patient is fully informed of the risks.

The side effects of psychiatric drugs are much like the symptoms they purport to cure. Cohen is a professor of social work at the University of Montreal, where he teaches and researches in the field of psychiatric medication. Breggin and Cohen, in their highly acclaimed book, *Your Drug May Be Your Problem: How And Why To Stop Taking Psychiatric Medications*, describe symptoms which are experienced by those who take psychiatric medication. Depending upon the drug or drugs and your unique body chemistry, you will most likely experience at least one, if not more, of the following: weakened concentration, memory lapses, sluggish mental ability, confusion, less able to handle stress, increased anger and irritability, problems sleeping, fatigue, feeling like you have the flu, depressed mood, mood swings, reduced self-awareness or self-perception, "out of touch" with self and others, anxiety, euphoria, mania, acting out of character, neurological or muscular problems, headaches, nightmares, withdrawal effects which are often opposite the effects of the drug.[4]

While the occurrence of those symptoms are quite rare, it depends on the drug, its dose, and drug interaction, among other factors. For example, from 22 to 40 percent of people on lithium will experience confusion and disorientation, and over 32 percent will experience memory impairment.[5]

Medication-induced movement disorders include Neuroleptic-Induced Parkinsonism, Neuroleptic Malignant Syndrome (muscle rigidity, elevated temperature, or "other related findings" like changes in level of consciousness), and Neuroleptic-Induced Acute Dystonia (abnormal positioning or spasm of muscles of the head, etc.).[6] Ritalin, taken by children for ADD and ADHD, can cause permanent disfiguring tics and can suppress growth.[7,8]

A task force report of the American Psychiatric Association concluded that the risk of suffering from the frequently irreversible tardive dyskinesia (uncontrollable movement of face, including tongue, lips, mouth and cheeks, or hands, feet, arms, and legs) is an alarming 30 to 57 percent for those taking antipsychotic (neuroleptic) medication.[9] No surprise, since the brain seeks to compensate for the invasion of the psychiatric drugs and becomes distorted in its functioning. The brain

116

often takes a long time to recover and sometimes never does, leading to permanent brain damage.[10]

If you experience hardly any or none of the above symptoms of side effects, does this mean that you will be spared any negative effects? A lack of symptoms does not guarantee that the drug is safe for you. Concerning the side effects of drugs like Prozac, you could be experiencing "*silent brain damage* that does not develop overt symptoms."[11] While you think there is no problem or side effect, significant and silent brain damage that only surfaces later can be slowly developing. The aging process is quietly being accelerated, and the probability of Parkinsonism increases over time.[12]

Sexual dysfunction is experienced by 60 to 75 percent of people on antidepressants, based on more recent studies.[13] The dysfunction, for both men and women, includes loss of libido, difficulties in arousal, and problems in achieving orgasm.[14] The rate is almost 40 percent for the newer antidepressants, based on a study with 6297 people.[15] Children whose mothers took Valium or similar drugs while pregnant have "an increased risk of hyperactivity and learning disabilities."[16]

Psychiatric drugs can be addictive, with serious withdrawal syndromes, and thus you are effectively "held hostage."[17] For Prozac-type medications such as Zoloft, the five main physical withdrawal effects are disequilibrium (e.g., dizziness, feeling like you are spinning, difficulty in walking), gastrointestinal problems (e.g., nausea, vomiting), flu-like symptoms (e.g., fatigue, chills, muscle pain, lethargy), sensory disturbances (e.g., tingling, electric shock sensations), and sleep disturbances (e.g., insomnia, vivid dreams).[18] The main psychological effects are "anxiety-agitation, crying spells, and irritability."[19]

Probably one of the strangest, but quite rare, side effect of some antipsychotic drugs is "rabbit syndrome," which can cause a person to "mimic the chewing motions of a rabbit."[20] Rest assured, this discussion about "side effects" of psychiatric drugs is *not* a rabbit trail!

Even some non-psychiatric drugs can raise similar concerns. For example, isotretinoin, or Accutane, developed for people with severe acne but now used increasingly by people with mild or moderate acne, might lead to depression or suicide as well as even serious birth defects.[21]

In 1994 in the U.S., an American's risk of injury from car accidents was 2 in 100, while injury from prescription drugs, including psychiatric drugs, was 26 in 100.[22] All the negative effects of psychiatric drugs argue against the idea that they correct a biochemical imbalance in the brain in a specific manner. Psychiatric drugs are more like toxic substances that assault the brain. For some people, these drugs are a prescription for disaster.

Making Normal People Feel Weird

What happens when "normal" people with no mental illnesses take antidepressants? Could it be like someone ill from a vitamin deficiency being restored upon taking vitamins while most people won't notice a difference taking more vitamins? After all, antidepressants also supposedly correct a biochemical imbalance. Concerning antidepressants, Mullen, not unlike many others, wrote:

> They are not "uppers" or "happy pills"; they only restore normal mood and the ability to control one's thoughts. They do not create an artificial high or artificial personality and have no effect at all on a person with normal mood.[23]

There is, however, a body of research that indicates otherwise. Researchers since the 1990s have been reporting how antidepressants change personality, causing emotional blunting, emotional indifference, disinhibition, and more, to various degrees in normal people.[24] In one case, a woman's personality changed so much that she arrived almost naked at parties.[25] Healy conducted his own research trial with reboxetine and Zoloft on healthy volunteers and observed more and unusual side effects than expected, plus two cases of near suicide.[26] Healy's results were confirmed by other studies. In the 1980s, for example, Zoloft and Paxil "were shown to produce dose-dependent agitation and apprehension in healthy volunteers."[27] In fact, pharmaceutical companies *have know for decades* that SSRIs can have harmful, deleterious effects on normal people, since those companies actually conducted such research studies—but few of such studies were ever published.[28]

Using the results from trials with healthy people and data from Wales, it has been estimated that a healthy person with normal mood would be 2000 times more likely to commit suicide when taking Zoloft.[29]

Lithium has a numbing or dulling effect on *normal* people as well as on those diagnosed with mania, schizophrenia, or other mental illnesses.[30] The overall "blunting of various personality functions" and "slowing of cognitive processes" were typically observed. The obvious conclusion is simply that conditions in people different from mania or depression "respond" to treatment.[31] To claim that lithium corrects a chemical imbalance based on the "response to treatment" means that almost everyone has a chemical imbalance in one's brain, since almost everyone "responds" to lithium treatment in a similar fashion. So do we conclude that almost everyone is schizophrenic or manic?

Research with healthy volunteers completes the picture. People suffering from depression or other mental illnesses will experience the same serious side effects when taking antidepressants as normal volunteers. Some trials show that it is even worse for healthy volunteers, who may well "feel weird."

The conclusion that concurs with a lot of data and many research studies is simply this: ***everyone*** *can be harmed by psychiatric drugs, because they don't correct an imbalance for* ***anyone***—*they are always toxic substances in the brain that disable* ***everyone's*** *brain.* That certainly includes all people with normal moods.

Are You a Guinea Pig?

You might expect, as I did, that psychiatric drugs are thoroughly tested for safety and finally approved by some government agency after lots of clinical trials involving stringent regulations. After all, there are millions of people taking psychiatric drugs for years. Maybe you or one of your loved ones is taking one or more psychiatric drugs. Unfortunately, the drug testing and approval system has some problems.

Before a psychiatric drug can be approved for use, certainly by the FDA in the U.S.A., it must undergo testing for positive, significant treatment effects and hopefully few and minor side effects. The testing typically involves a randomized double-blind placebo-controlled clinical trial (RCT). Some trials will also test a newer drug against an older drug. *Double-blind* means that neither the patient nor the administrator of the drug knows who is actually receiving the drug. *Placebo* means a pill that has no effect, to test against the actual pill with a supposed effect. *Randomized* means that people are purely by chance (randomly) assigned to the group that will actually receive the drug or the other group that will receive the placebo. The goal is to determine if significantly more people have less depression from taking the drug, for example, as measured by some rating scale before and after the trial in comparison to the placebo group or a group on another drug. This all appears solid and scientific, but there are some serious limitations, and I will discuss only fourteen. Warning: the following may cause anxiety or insomnia, so please do not read this just before going to bed!

The clinical trials are short term only: I was somewhat shocked to discover that most trials to test a new drug last only six to eight weeks, or a few months at most, and therefore only consider *short-term safety*.[32] This gives an illusion of safety, because considerable evidence over decades has shown that serious hazards of drugs are often slow, insidious, difficult to uncover, and appear over many years.[33] This is a dilemma for people who take a drug for many months, if not years, which is common. Side effects that will take years to appear will not have been considered in the safety of the newly released drug. Effectively, everyone who takes a psychiatric drug long term is, unwittingly, a guinea pig.[34] This is even truer for people taking several drugs who will inevitably experience drug interactions.

Long-term hazards are mostly unreported: In the absence of clinical trials for long term safety, one would hope that the hazards, side effects, and warning signs for a given drug are duly reported as people take the drugs. After all, the health of millions of people is at stake. Unfortunately, "long-term monitoring is virtually nonexistent" and only around *one percent* of serious side effects are ever reported to the FDA."[35] This means that 99 percent of the picture remains unreported, undocumented, and unknown. Hardly reassuring.

The double-blind objectivity often breaks down: No one, not even the patient, is supposed to know if they are taking the new drug. When people taking the actual psychiatric medication report new symptoms like a dry mouth or insomnia or gastrointestinal problems, both the patient and the researcher then know who is taking a drug. Data can no longer be taken without bias; the patient will have an expectation of improvement; and the researcher will view the patient differently. A critical feature of the trial then falls apart. Researchers may well become blinded by subjectivity.

Potential conflict of interest: Drug companies that will benefit from the drug's release fund much of the research on its safety.[36] The trials are expensive, and since the 1970s in the U.S.A. it was decided that pharmaceutical companies must run the trials and provide the data. The potential conflict of interest is obvious, considering that a drug finally approved presents potential income in the billions of dollars. The pressure to approve a drug, and soon, can be enormous.

Rejecting trials where the new drug failed: When a clinical trial shows that the new drug is worse or no more effective than the placebo, the trial is considered "failed" instead of the drug.[37] Suppose ten clinical trials showed the new drug was no better, or even worse, than the placebo. Now another two trials happened to show a small but significant effect compared to the placebo. Rather than concluding that the new drug is not effective or doesn't warrant registration, it is approved, because at least two "pivotal" trials were successful.[38] In virtually every other scientific discipline, researchers would consider "failed" trails as overwhelming evidence that the treatment is probably ineffective. Why make a special exemption for pharmaceutical companies? There have been a number of drugs released through the 1990s, sometimes with only two out of six trials showing an improvement over placebo.[39,40]

Suppression of negative results: When the results of the trial are not what the pharmaceutical company expects, those negative results might be "sealed" or just never disclosed.[41,42] This is not surprising, since the clinical trials are contracted out and paid for by the pharmaceutical companies who then own the results and consider those results as their proprietary property.[43] Data cannot be shared among scientists, and "these rules of science are suspended when it is a pharmaceutical company that refuses access."[44] A similar practice is the publication of only selected results from trials.[45] Some pharmaceutical companies have suppressed "research results into the suicidal ideation of antidepressants."[46] The whole picture of a drug's effectiveness or hazards might never be known.

Biased rating scales: The rating scales, with simple checklists for symptoms and effects, are biased and look for predetermined effects. For example, using the Hamilton Scale for depression, only 5 percent of Prozac patients were observed to experience sexual dysfunction. But rating scales that were sensitive to sexual dysfunction from psychiatric drugs uncovered rates more like 70 percent.[47,48] You don't often notice what you are not looking for.

Inappropriate rating scales: When patient-based or quality-of-life rating scales are applied to clinical trials, the drugs tend to fail compared to placebo.[49] However, that information "has not seen the light of day" and is often left completely unreported.[50] If quality of life is important, then the wrong scales are being used. This is not complicated. Anyone who has ever baked knows that you use a measuring cup to measure volume and not a ruler. It's amazing what you can learn in a kitchen!

Evidence for wrong conclusions: RCT clinical trials for psychiatric drugs really don't prove what most people would think. They only prove that a drug had an effect and "did something," presumably positive, compared to a placebo. The trials do not answer whether the effects of SSRIs are good, will work in the long run, or whether other approaches such as psychotherapy would be equally good or better.[51,52] Those are the more critical, important questions.

Not applicable to people on several drugs: Of necessity, the clinical trials must involve people with only the disorder, like depression, and only the drug being tested. If some people had several disorders and yet others were taking some other drugs, the final results would be confounded and most likely inconclusive. But there are many people who take several psychiatric drugs and many more who have several disorders—that is the real world. Strictly speaking, the results from these trials don't directly apply to such people, certainly to the whole issue of complex drug interactions. This diminishes the value of the results from these trials.

Little concern for eventual outcomes: Drug trials should deal with eventual outcomes. Did a person with depression return to work? Did the patients in a hospital eventually leave?[53] Instead, clinical tunnel vision focuses on short-term results defined by predetermined symptoms. The outcome assessments reflect the interests of pharmaceutical companies and their need to have a new drug released to the market instead of the lives as a whole of those taking the drugs.

Ghost-writing: Up to 50 percent of articles published in leading psychiatric journals, with the names of well-known psychiatrists as authors, are not even written by the supposed authors.[54] The articles have actually been written by medical writing agencies, at times on contract from a pharmaceutical company that put out offers for an article.[55] For further reasons, this means there is "no longer any guarantee" that articles published in even the most prestigious journals of psychiatry faithfully reflect the true results from clinical trials.[56]

Researcher independence in doubt: Much of the above is symptomatic of university researchers being too controlled by pharmaceutical companies that contract the research. The issues are so critical that the International Committee of Medical Journal Editors (ICMFE) enacted a set of ethical guidelines. But unfortunately, as of 2002, most medical schools that engage in industry-sponsored drug research do *not* follow those ethical guidelines.[57]

Faulty logic on the final result: Generally, about 70 percent of people in clinical trials respond to antidepressant drugs, and about 35 percent of people respond to the placebo within two weeks.[58] Medical researchers then report such drugs as being more effective than the placebo. Most people would think that perhaps the drugs are twice as effective as the placebo. But this is faulty logic. Remember that of the

70 percent of the people given antidepressants, we don't know how many of them would have responded to the placebo as well. Thus, it would be eminently reasonable to suggest that 35 percent of the 70 percent given the antidepressant would have done just fine without it.[59,60] Therefore, only 65 percent of the 70 percent really count towards a response for the antidepressant, or 45.5 percent (assuming that I am not suffering from mathematics disorder). Now what is really more effective? If depression is really such a biochemical reality, then why do 54.5 percent of people in clinical trials get better without antidepressants but with simply a sugar pill (placebo) and attention and hope from being in a trial?

Biased selection of people: Before the clinical trial is conducted, a "mini-trial" is first done to identify people who would respond favourably to a placebo.[61] Such people are then excluded from the clinical trial, which obviously biases and distorts the final results.[62] Oddly enough, people who would respond favourably to antidepressants are not excluded from the trial. In all too many trials, people who drop out of a trial due to strong negative side effects or lack of effectiveness from the drug are excluded from the final results.[63] A recalculation of the data from some past trials, including all who dropped out for drug-related reasons, revealed that Prozac was effective for only 47 percent of people, not 70 percent.[64] Using the logic from the last paragraph, and a generous 70 percent, only about 33 percent of people really respond to an antidepressant. Some prominent researchers have seriously questioned the generally accepted 70 percent effectiveness of antidepressants, arguing that such a number is overstated.[65]

The Illusion of Safety

Even given the above, one often hears that the newer drugs are now safer and one should abandon the older, more hazardous, drugs, as if psychiatric drugs are getting safer all the time. Yet the history of drug development and use gives a different picture. A review of the history of psychiatric drugs reveals the following pattern: the new drugs are enthusiastically promoted as newer, better, safer drugs, which are increasingly prescribed by more doctors in response to aggressive marketing and presumed scientific claims. About ten years later, problems begin to appear, which are of course denied by the pharmaceutical companies that become paranoid about market share. Since long-term monitoring of drugs and side effects is only voluntary and spontaneous, it takes another ten years for enough evidence to accumulate to alarm enough health professionals. Then yet another ten years are required for regulatory agencies to enforce changes. This "10-20-30" year cycle, as documented by Glenmullen, is still true of the more recent SSRIs, with the time from "miracle to disaster" taking 30 years, and the more recent drugs believed safer "because their hazards are not yet known." [66]

The 10-20-30 pattern continues. Anyone who still doubts the above should recall the painful and personal human costs surrounding thalidomide, silicon breast implants, Valium, and Halcion, to name a few.[67]

Hardly any research is being done on the long-term toxic effects of psychiatric drugs on people's brains—not by the FDA or the NIMH and certainly not by the pharmaceutical companies.[68] Yet, many people take these drugs long-term, so this would be important research, the results of which may negatively impact drug company profits.

There is yet another problem for clinical trials, beyond those considered above. How does one "measure" emotions to show a statistical advantage for a new drug?

30.5 Units Of Depression?

Modern psychiatry requires its own measurements in order to appear scientifically credible with the medical model of diagnosis, disease, and treatment. A person might have a weight of 165 pounds, a blood pressure reading of systolic 120 over diastolic 79, a hemoglobin count of 157, a creatinine reading of 64, and so forth. Such objective numbers are a necessary part of science and medical research, frequently used in clinical trials for statistical analyses. But what would psychiatrists do for clinical trials testing psychiatric drugs for depression, for example? Pharmaceutical companies need some sort of numbers to prove a statistical advantage in clinical trials for a new drug. How about a measurement like "30.5 units of depression"? While this may strike you as odd, it is not far from what is done.

Psychiatric diagnoses, like medical ones in general, are based on observed symptoms. One facet of measurement is the number of symptomatic occurrences in a given time period. A diagnosis of anxiety disorder requires that at least four symptoms from a predetermined list of six symptoms must occur in the majority of anxiety attacks wherein at least six such attacks are separated by at least a week from each other.[69] The symptoms must not result from a medical condition, a life-threatening situation, or physical exertion.[70]

But if one had only three of the symptoms and met all the other criteria or five of the symptoms but separated only by six days, there would be *no* anxiety disorder. Add another day interval to the five symptoms, the disorder suddenly appears. Thus, the general, continuous emotion and feeling of anxiety is transformed into a discrete category or classifiable "mental illness" based on observed symptoms plus measurement by number and frequency. An emotion is now "quantified."

The next challenge is to quantify even more to prove a "treatment effect" in clinical trials and also the degree or severity of the supposed disorder. This certainly requires numbers for statistical analyses. Hence the numerous rating scales based on a checklist of questions with a numerical value for categories in each question in order to derive a total score. The widely used Hamilton Psychiatric Rating Scale for depression, for example (see http://healthnet. umassmed.edu/mhealth/HAMD.pdf), has seventeen or twenty-one items depending upon the version and takes about fifteen minutes. While researchers no doubt believe in the validity and utility of this scale, like other scales there are limitations and critical assumptions.

Items have equal weight: For example, if the interviewer observes the person as moving around and finding it hard to sit still, this has the same weight in scoring a 3 as with the patient having suicidal ideas or gestures. Would ideas of suicide not carry more weight? But if so, how much more?

Four, or 6.5, or 8.25? Does a preoccupation with one's health really score a 2, same as genital symptoms like a severe loss of libido? What if there is simply a genuine, though strong, concern for one's wellness and wholeness for the former? Then that would be as significant as severe sexual problems?

Items can have different effective impact or "weight" on different people: "Worrying about minor matters" as part of psychic anxiety may be present but not a huge reality for one person yet the tip of an iceberg for a sensitive but shy person.

Subjectivity: Since it requires the judgment of the patient and the interviewer, there will be subjectivity. For example, the interviewer must decide if there really is any "depersonalization and derealization" (item 19 on the twenty-one-item scale) from symptoms such as "feeling of unreality and nihilistic ideas," from mild to severe or even incapacitating. For agitation, the interviewer can score a 2 for "any clear-cut symptoms," almost an open-ended judgment call.

Items are not unbiased: Why the particular seventeen or twenty-one items on this scale? Those items "fit almost hand-in-glove with the profile of imipramine," an early psychiatric drug.[71] The items were predetermined by the need to test the effects of a specific drug, and hence the items would reflect the expected effects of the drug, not the effects and symptoms of depression on people alone apart from any drug. This presents a problem for testing other drugs that have different effects or people that have other different but important reactions that just don't appear on the checklist. The scale then serves the drug, not the person.

Total scores obscure complexity: The theoretical maximum score is 67 for twenty-one items or 54 for the seventeen-item version, probably never obtained by anyone. In practice, a score of 28 or more indicates severe depression while the low 20s indicates moderate depression.[72] Yet from the same score of, say, 22, one person could have strong feelings of suicide and acknowledged depressed mood while the next person may have almost no score on those two items. While such numeric scores appear scientific, they are quite subjective and confounded by each person's unique history, personality, gender and cultural background, also making comparisons between patients impossible.[73]

The widespread and almost unthinking use of the Hamilton and other rating scales results in many clinicians "flying blind" or operating in a "virtual world." [74]

Quantifying behaviour, or measuring the soul, has limitations and problems in spite of the widespread practice. Assigning a number to a person is not an exact science. Even if one trained clinician to the next gives a very similar score for the same patient, which appeals to the reliability of the measurements, that does not in itself validate the measurement and assure its meaning. It could simply mean that errors in measurement occur with high repeatable precision. If your bathroom scale is calibrated incorrectly, everyone in your household could be erroneously ten pounds heavier regardless of who records the weights.

Any attempt to measure the human soul or behaviour or feelings is limited and suspect because it does not measure up to reality.

Effective for Whom?

Mental health professionals and of course pharmaceutical companies that market and promote their drugs will attest to the "effectiveness" of their treatments for mental illness. Most people would think that "effectiveness" means that they would be able to function reasonably well and get on with their lives. However, the mental health world thinks primarily in terms of reduction or management of symptoms—partly a reflection of the rating scales.

Consider neuroleptics, commonly prescribed for schizophrenics. British researchers studied the published results of 2,000 clinical trials from 1948 to 1998, and discovered that *only 4 percent* of those trials even considered the drug therapy's impact on daily life and social functioning.[75] The studies were preoccupied with whether the drugs lowered the symptoms of psychosis and not what was happening to *people*.[76] When patients were surveyed in 1999, 90 percent replied that they felt depressed, 88 percent considered themselves sedated, and 78 percent claimed to suffer from poor concentration.[77] Efficacy seems quite different when determined by patients or mental health professionals. Since patients are the ones who actually have to live with the drugs, should not their assessment count the most?

Are neuroleptics effective? Relapse rates for schizophrenics in the U.S. have shown that people are better off with *minimal or no* neuroleptics as part of their treatment.[78] In case you were wondering, the newer "atypical" neuroleptic drugs are no better than the older drugs.[79]

Personal Testimonies vs. Clinical and Scientific Results

Many researchers discredit personal testimonies, writing them off as "anecdotal." Some people might not take the testimonies in this book very seriously since they are not the result of clinical trials. However, the foregoing in this chapter shows that the results of clinical trials and how they truly relate to life may be seriously questioned and challenged. The advantage of personal testimonies is that it is in the context of a person's entire life, and usually others who have known the person for years can also testify to real, true, positive, lasting healing and change. The final authority on a person's healing is the very person who has experienced it. While a testimony can have a limitation or bias, exactly and precisely the same is true of results from clinical trials. The testimonies and stories of people being healed, especially in the Gospels, is also anecdotal.[80] We dare not discredit what the Scriptures values! Testimonies of truly changed lives is the most compelling evidence of the gospel.

Just Like Taking Insulin?

Some time ago while I was in my doctor's office for a routine physical, I happened to notice a poster concerning depression and psychiatric drugs. The statement on the poster that bothered me most was the idea that taking a psychiatric drug is just like taking insulin. This notion appears often and is routinely made by many Christian authors as well.

Taking psychiatric drugs has been equated to taking insulin or heart pills, or wearing eyeglasses for life.[81] But this is simply untrue, for at least nine reasons.

Firstly, people who take insulin will adjust the dose based on their blood sugar level, which can be determined quite readily. Contrast this with psychiatric drugs where no one can determine the level of serotonin, for example, in your brain. There is no way to determine how much Prozac or Zoloft, for example, you should take.

Secondly, insulin is a natural hormone in the body, which regulates blood sugar levels. Psychiatric drugs are not natural substances of the human body; they are synthetic, toxic, foreign substances.

Thirdly, diabetics who take insulin don't have side effects from taking insulin, since it is a natural hormone of the body. If diabetics don't take the right amount of insulin regularly, they often experience negative effects. Contrast this with psychiatric drugs that often cause noticeable and sometimes serious negative side effects when taken at supposedly the correct dosage.

Fourthly, virtually all diabetics can take insulin with no or minimal problems. Not so with psychiatric drugs—a significant percentage of people simply can't take the drugs, because the side effects are too severe.

Fifthly, almost all diabetics who take insulin notice quick relief, especially initially. Contrast this with taking psychiatric drugs, which might take weeks to "have an effect," if they ever do.

Sixthly, insulin is very effective for almost all diabetics. Not so with psychiatric drugs; they are not effective for everyone and for some people only cause negative side effects.

Seventhly, almost all diabetics take just insulin. Contrast this with psychiatric patients, who are typically given a "cocktail" of psychiatric drugs, and sometimes secondary drugs for the side effects.

Eighthly, except for a miracle, diabetics take insulin for life, and if they stop, diabetic shock is inevitable. Not so with a significant percentage of people, including schizophrenics and those with clinical depression, who eventually get well without any more drugs or with no drugs in the first place.

Ninthly, diabetics taking insulin don't experience a "wearing off" effect of insulin such that it is no longer effective. But this happens to over 30 percent of people on Prozac-type drugs and is called "Prozac Poopout."

If a normal person takes insulin, he or she will soon experience a diabetic coma, since the blood sugar levels will drop significantly. If a normal person takes a psychiatric drug, he or she will often experience noticeable and negative side effects. In this respect, taking insulin and a psychiatric drug are similar.

So is taking insulin just like taking a psychiatric drug? Not at all, when you really stop and think about it. But as has been noted, few people in psychiatry and related professions really stop and think about things. Uncritical thinking leads to erroneous beliefs and uncritical practices.

Conclusion

Some lives have been helped or even saved through taking psychiatric medicine, while some lives have been lost. All too many people have found that the risks and costs of the supposed cure or relief end up being worse than the emotional pain in the beginning. If you are paranoid about taking psychiatric drugs, then you are normal.

The clinical testing and evaluation of these drugs has its own problems and shortcomings. Rating scales, though intended to be helpful, have serious limitations and are reductionistic. The testing for safety and effectiveness can be seriously questioned.

So is there a place for psychiatric drugs? Psychiatrists themselves have different opinions on this. Many psychiatrists prescribe drugs readily and often quickly. While some are concerned at just how many Christians are taking psychiatric drugs and wonder if this should diminish, it has actually been argued that *even more* Christians should be taking psychiatric drugs. For example, not only clinical depression should be treated with medication but even low-grade depression known as dysthymia (formerly called "neurotic depression") should also be treated with psychiatric drugs.[82]

But some advocate virtually no use of psychiatric drugs, including a number of Christian psychiatrists and authors. Others maintain that psychiatric drugs could have, at best, a limited role as part of a larger treatment plan involving non-drug therapy. The drug would be an adjunct to help for a short period of time, giving some energy and focus to function.

For people with suicidal tendencies, for example, it is often argued that antidepressants will help to stabilize a person. But the drug might take several weeks to have an effect. What happens in the meantime? Then, in the early weeks or months on an antidepressant, patients are actually at *increased* risk of suicide since the extra stimulation and energy might allow unprocessed anger to surface, causing suicide or violent behaviour.[83] Some people are very sensitive to such drugs, and a normal dose might be fatal. I remember praying with one lady who had been put on just 10 mg of Prozac, and several hours later she was rushed to Emergency. A lady with depression and no history of suicidal symptoms became suicidal on just 5 mg of Prozac daily.[84] You never know if you are sensitive until you take the drug, and then it could be too late.

The drug may well "numb" the soul and complicate a person's healing. Even with a reduced role, such drugs must be taken wisely, with full appreciation of their limitations.[85] About three-quarters of all people on Prozac-type drugs could have the dosage lowered significantly or the drug eliminated entirely.[86]

What of those who are violent, seemingly consumed by rage, apparently experiencing some form of psychosis? In the former days, there would be physical restraints and padded cells. Today, drugs might be forcibly used to subdue a person, like a chemical restraint or a chemical lobotomy. This is an ethical dilemma, given a person's dignity and worth in God's sight.

People who refuse any form of therapy, counselling, or healing prayer leave little choice for their physician or psychiatrist. Some people almost *demand* psychiatric drugs, pressuring doctors to prescribe an advertised drug to "get the effect," and 90 percent of doctors do so.[87]

With the focus on instant and quick solutions in our technological society, the use of drugs as a seemingly quick chemical solution to life's problems is rather alluring and tempting.

We must not lose sight of the struggles of real people with their unique stories. The next chapter is devoted to Jacqueline's true story, involving deep emotional pain, anti-psychotics, and antidepressants. Jacqueline's true story, written from the depth of her experience, is her "neurological nightmare."

Endnotes _____

[1] Grant Mullen, *Emotionally Free: A Prescription for Healing Body, Soul and Spirit* (Kent: Sovereign Word International, 2003) p. 62.

[2] Grant Mullen, *Moods: What Christians Should Know About Depression, Anxiety and Mood Disorders* (Orchardview Medical Media, 2004) p. 72.

[3] Neil T. Anderson, Terry E. Zuehlke, and Julianne S. Zuehlke, *Christ Centered Therapy: The Practical Integration of Theology and Psychology* (Grand Rapids: Zondervan Publishing House, 2000) p. 351.

[4] Peter R. Breggin and D. Cohen, *Your Drug May Be Your Problem: How and Why to Stop Taking Psychiatric Drugs* (Cambridge: Perseus Publishing, 1999) pp. 52-56.

[5] Breggin and Cohen, p. 63.

[6] A. Frances, H.A. Pincus, and M.B. First, *American Psychiatric Association: Diagnostic and Statistical Manual of Mental Disorders. Fourth Edition, Text Revision* (Washington, DC: APA, 2000) p. 735.

[7] Seth Farber, *Unholy Madness: The Church's Surrender to Psychiatry* (Downers Grove: InterVarsity Press, 1999) p. 46.

[8] Walker, S., *A Dose of Sanity: Mind, Medicine, and Misdiagnosis* (New York: John Wiley and Sons, 1996) p. 58.

[9] Farber, p. 124.

[10] Breggin and Cohen, pp. 46-47.

[11] Joseph Glenmullen, *Prozac Backlash: Overcoming the Dangers of Prozac, Zoloft, Paxil, and Other Antidepressants with Safe, Effective Alternatives* (New York: Simon & Schuster, 2000) pp. 57-59.

[12] Ibid.

[13] Glenmullen, p. 120.

[14] Glenmullen, pp. 106-121.

[15] Anon., "Sexual Side Effects Common, But Still Underestimated by Physicians," *Brown University Psychopharmacology Update* 13(6):1,6,2002, reported in http://www.medscape.com/viewarticle/434554, 2002.

[16] Walker, p. 67.

[17] Glenmullen, pp. 69-78.

[18] Glenmullen, p. 72.

[19] Glenmullen, pp. 72.

[20] Jennifer S. Hoy and Bruce Alexander, "Rabbit Syndrome Secondary to Risperidone," http://www.medscape.com/viewarticle/432398, 2002.

[21] Anon., "Isotretinoin Use Soars in U.S.," *J. Am. Acad. Dermatol.* 2002: 505-509 reported in http://www.medscape.com/viewarticle/433357, 2002.

[22] Bruce E. Levine, *Commonsense Rebellion: Debunking Psychiatry, Confronting Society* (New York: Continuum Publishing Group Inc., 2001) p. 98.

[23] Mullen, pg. 62.

[24] David Healy, *Let Them Eat Prozac: The Unhealthy Relationship Between the Pharmaceutical Industry and Depression* (New York: New York University Press, 2004) pp. 174-175.

[25] Healy, pg. 174.

[26] Healy, pp. 176-190.

[27] Healy, pp. 194.

[28] Healy, pp. 188-189,192-193.

[29] Healy, p. 190.

[30] Ty C. Colbert, *Broken Brains or Wounded Hearts: What Causes Mental Illness* (Santa Ana: Kevco Publishing, 1996) p. 47.

[31] Ty C. Colbert, *Depression and Mania: Friends or Foes? A New "Non-Drug" Model of Hope for Depression, Mania, and Compulsive Disorders* (Santa Ana: Kevco Publishers, 1995) p. 97.

[32] Glenmullen, p. 20.

[33] Glenmullen, pp. 20-21.

[34] Glenmullen, p. 21.

[35] Ibid.

[36] Walker, p. 64.

37 Healy, 2004, pp. 35-36,267.

38 Healy, 2004, p. 35.

39 David Healy, *The Creation of Psychopharmacology* (Cambridge: Harvard University Press, 2002) p. 308.

40 Healy, 2004, p. 35.

41 Healy, 2004, p. 38,126.

42 Doug Macron, "Drug Firms Control Over Data Raises Concerns—Lancet Article," http:/www.medscape.com/viewarticle/443862, Oct. 31, 2002.

43 Healy, 2004, pp. 246,277.

44 Healy, 2004, p. 277.

45 Healy, 2004, p. 126.

46 Glenmullen, pp. 177-178.

47 Healy, 2004, p. 56.

48 Healy, 2002, p. 373.

49 Healy, 2004, p. 128.

50 Healy, 2002, pp. 373,38.

51 Healy, 2004, p. 267.

52 Healy, 2002, p. 315.

53 Healy, 2002, p. 309.

54 Terry Lynch, *Beyond Prozac: Healing and Mental Distress* (Douglas Village: Mercier Press, 2005) p. 35.

55 Healy, 2004, pp. 112-116.

56 Healy, 2004, pp. 119.

57 Amy Norton, "Clinical Trial Contracts Found Lacking in Safeguards," http://www.medscape.com/viewarticle/443561, Oct. 24, 2002.

58 Colin A. Ross, *The Trauma Model: A Solution To The Problem of Comorbidity In Psychiatry* (Richardson: Gateway Communications, Inc., 2000) p. 94.

59 Ibid.

60 Elio Frattaroli, *Healing the Soul in the Age of the Brain: Becoming Conscious in an Unconscious World* (New York: Viking, 2001) p. 92.

61 Lynch, p. 23

62 Ibid.

63 Lynch, p. 126.

64 Ibid.

65 Lynch, p. 78.

66 Glenmullen, pp. 12-13.

67 Glenmullen, p. 24.

68 Glenmullen, p. 105.

69 Allan V. Horwitz, *Creating Mental Illness* (Chicago: The University of Chicago Press, 2002) p. 65.

70 Ibid.

71 David Healy, *The Antidepressant Era* (Cambridge: Harvard University Press, 1997) p. 76.

72 Glenmullen, p. 66.

73 Glenmullen, p. 206.

74 Healy, 2002, pp. 350-351.

75 Robert Whitaker, *Mad In America: Bad Science, Bad Medicine, And The Enduring Mistreatment Of The Mentally Ill* (Cambridge: Perseus Publishing, 2002) pp. 289.

76 Ibid.

77 Whitaker, p. 256.

78 Whitaker, pp. 183-186.

79 Whitaker, pp. 254,269-282.

80 Charles H. Kraft, *Confronting Powerless Christianity: Evangelicals and the Missing Dimension* (Grand Rapids: Chosen Books, 2002) p. 75.

81 Mullen, 2003, p. 62.

82 Mullen, 2004, p. 29.

83 Glenmullen, p. 141.

84 Glenmullen, p. 154.

85 Glenmullen, p. 338.

86 Ibid.

87 Elliot S. Valenstein, *Blaming The Brain: The Truth About Drugs And Mental Health* (New York: The Free Press, 1998) p. 231.

Chapter Six

Jacqueline: Bipolar Disorder, Depression, and Suicidal Tendencies

He heals the brokenhearted and binds up their wounds (Ps. 147:3).

Peace I leave with you; my peace I give to you. I do not give to you as the world gives. Do not let your hearts be troubled and do not be afraid (John 14:27).

I have prayed with a number of people who, when I hear their whole story, I am amazed are still alive. Such is the depth of pain experienced by people, including those who belong to Jesus. In some respects, Jacqueline's story is like that.

When I first met Jacqueline, I knew very little of her journey. It was a privilege to pray with her and see the Lord begin to heal the deepest places in her soul and spirit. I asked few questions during our healing prayer sessions, relying more on the Holy Spirit to bring revelation and truth in the presence of Jesus. Jacqueline received different diagnoses from psychiatrists and was told very clearly that she had a chemical imbalance. Among other things, she shares in detail the effects of a number of psychiatric drugs, including their effect on her mind and soul. This is her true story.

Early Symptoms in High School

I first started noticing symptoms when I was in grade eleven with my first major depressive episode. I had no clue what was wrong with me—I felt sad and confused. I never wanted to be with my friends; I just wanted to go home. I was in my second year at a private Christian boarding school, and it was odd, because I loved my school and my friends and during my first year I rarely wanted to go home, because I missed my friends. The first summer I counted down the days for two months until I could go back to school. But grade eleven was different. I felt like I was going through a spiritual mid-life crisis. I prayed and prayed and begged God to let me know what was causing me such inner turmoil. Suddenly I felt insecure and uncomfortable in social situations where I normally felt so at ease. I got everyone I could at my school to pray for me, but they didn't seem to think that anything was wrong. They thought that I was just overreacting when there was nothing to overreact about. I felt as though I never fit in anywhere and wasn't comfortable in my body. This lasted for about five months. Then it left, and I was back to normal.

My second episode was at the end of grade twelve and throughout the summer after I graduated from high school. I felt as though everyone at the camp where I was working didn't like me and was against me. I felt as though the directors didn't like me, even though they had really liked me the year before. I was tired all the time, and I couldn't focus on anything, including my spiritual life. I felt so alone and so isolated, and no one could understand why or help me to figure out what to do about the situation. Mostly, I was told to give it to God and to pray about it, which was even more discouraging because I had such a hard time praying.

First University Years: More Symptoms and Pain

And then it left, and I was back to normal again. I started university and made it through my first year. However, I was different from how I used to be. I was very needy and lonely. I cried a lot, and I missed my mom, after being away for three years. I lived six hours away, and I felt totally isolated.

After that, I had about seven months where I had a very normal, healthy life. I started a new job for the summer and lived at home. I looked after myself. I was capable, and I switched schools. I could handle the pressures in my life, and I wasn't second-guessing myself.

Then I moved to go to university. I was in my second year of a three-year English degree, and I was away from my boyfriend of two years. Still, I was doing fine. I started getting sick again in October, and my boyfriend and I broke up at the beginning of November. I started acting differently. I no longer cared about things I had always cared about. I started partying more and stopped going to church. I still always prayed and had my relationship with God, but it just wasn't enough to help me deal with what I was going through. I never went to class, and I rarely got out of my sweatpants. Everyone was always saying how lazy I was, and I believed them. I was just so tired all the time, and I could not make myself go to class. I was dating a very supportive guy at the time who was also my best friend. He wasn't a Christian, so I thought that was why I was getting sick. I thought it had to be something I was doing or not doing. I figured it had to be spiritual.

Finally I realized something was wrong when I was sitting on my friend's bed feeling absolutely hopeless. I felt like that a lot. I would just get an almost-nauseated feeling in my stomach. While I was sitting on the bed, her friend phoned her and told her that the friend's dad had committed suicide. It was two weeks before her sister's wedding. This really upset my friend, as it would any normal individual, and she began to cry. She knew her friend's dad well and had known the family for a good part of her life. When I heard that news, I couldn't see how my situation was any better than hers. Then I realized that I had a problem.

Encountering the Mental Health Centre and Psychiatric Drugs

I looked on the back of the phone book and called the mental health centre. I had to first see an intake worker, and they would decide if I needed to see a psychiatrist. It was around this time that I also began to have panic attacks. I had a longer than usual research paper to do, so I got my books from the library and tried to begin it. But I couldn't. Anytime I even tried to look at the stack of books, I would start bawling and feel tight in the chest. I couldn't breathe, because I was crying so hard. I got an extension on my paper. The intake worker said that I would need to see a psychiatrist.

I was diagnosed with major depressive disorder and panic disorder. I was started on 10 mg of Paxil, an antidepressant, but it didn't seem to help. That was in April. They continued bumping up my dose until I was at 40 mg; the maximum safe dose is 50 mg. I was living in what felt like hell. My boyfriend was beginning to tire of my moodiness and my neediness. I was living in a resort town and feeling completely isolated. I was doing what the doctor said, but nothing was getting better.

Then things suddenly got better. At the beginning of July, my mood lifted. I never needed any sleep, and I never really needed to eat all that much. I went out to the bar and drank excessively compared to what I had previously. I was gallivanting around the bar scene with a number of different guys and ended up breaking up with my boyfriend. I thought I was better, and I continued to take my medication as per doctor's orders. But I would still have times when I felt like my life was out of control, and I had terrible anxiety. I decided at this time that I would attend another university in another city.

More Pain and Self-Mutilation

I moved in September to begin studies at another university, where almost immediately I crashed severely. I was still taking my Paxil. I started smoking then and had no idea what to do or who to turn to. Many of my Christian friends left me at that time because they didn't know how to deal with me and felt like my problem was that I had strayed from God and I was being selfish. My non-Christian friends didn't leave me, but they also had no idea what to do with me, so they would take me out to the bar to get my mind off of my "troubles."

Around that time, I suddenly started thinking about cutting myself. I am terrified of needles, and I am very sensitive to pain. I would cry when I got a paper cut, so it was outrageous for me to think of cutting myself with a knife. It was my own thought, but it was very intense and very commanding. All I could hear was a pounding in my head. "Cut yourself; cut yourself."

I said, "No, I can't cut myself. That's insane." But it was very persistent. So finally I thought, "I will just try it."

I went in my room and took a knife with me. It had a serrated edge, and I just did it. It was a very addictive feeling. I felt sharp pain, but all the worry and sick feeling in my stomach left. All I could feel was physical pain. I did that for a while, and I didn't think there was anything wrong with it. I knew everyone else thought it was a really sick thing to do, but I felt like it was normal.

A New Psychiatrist and an Emergency Room Experience

Finally my roommates convinced me that I should see a doctor. I knew I needed a new psychiatrist, but I didn't know how to go about getting one so I just went to a walk-in clinic. They gave me a referral to a psychiatrist at the university, who happened to be one of the best in the city. But he also looked at my arm and sent me to the emergency room. I knew the cuts weren't bad. They looked a lot worse than they actually were. We left his office, and my roommate and a friend of mine made me go to the ER.

It was very humiliating. The nurses had a real attitude towards me because they didn't think I should be there. I had, after all, done this to myself. They asked me in a loud voice in front of the whole waiting room what I was there for, and I said that I was having some psychiatric problems. I even gave them the note that the walk-in clinic doctor had given me, but they still wanted me to say to them that I had cut myself. So I did. We ended up waiting eight hours in the waiting room that night. When I left, I was drugged up and no closer to help than when I walked in. They said that they would have liked to keep me in the hospital but they had no beds. So they asked me, if they let me go would I kill myself that night? I said no, and they let me on my way.

I went home drugged up—on what, I am still not sure. I was trying to hold down a job, and I had to quit university because I just could not bring myself to go to class. I could not go. I finally got in to see my psychiatrist in November. She conducted interviews with my brother and my mom and interviewed me. She diagnosed me as bipolar. I didn't believe her at first, because my first psychiatrist had thought I might be bipolar but then concluded that I was not.

Drug Side Effects, More Pain, Suicidal Tendencies

At the beginning of December I was put on Topimax, an anticonvulsant mood stabilizer. The drug made me very sick, and I missed a lot of work before I decided to go off it two weeks later. I felt like there was battery acid in my stomach. I was working in a hotel in banquets, and Christmas is a major moneymaker; then in January there is no work. So for me to miss work at Christmas was very expensive. I began to run out of money.

After Christmas things got worse. I went back to my doctor, and she put me on lithium. I started out at a low dose, and it took a lot of time to get my lithium level to a therapeutic level. During this time, I somehow began skipping doctor's appointments, so I was not being treated consistently. I was severely troubled and very depressed.

In March of the following year, I crashed again, even further than before. I thought, there is no way that I am bipolar. I have no mania. I started to get the same pounding thoughts in my head that had originally told me to cut myself. Now all I could hear, like a pounding headache, was, "Kill yourself; kill yourself." I wanted to kill myself, but I knew that wasn't the answer; I had to keep fighting.

I went to see my walk-in clinic doctor again because I could not handle how depressed I was. He put me on Celexa, 10 mg. I had taken two days' worth, or 20 mg, when I started cutting again, only the thoughts wouldn't subside like they used to when I would cut. Instead, after cutting myself, I would hear, "No—cut yourself deeper. That wasn't good enough."

There was no rest. Finally I went and bought myself an X-acto knife. Up until this point I had only cut myself when I was alone, and I would only cut myself superficially. This time all my friends were around. I had to go to the bathroom continuously and keep cutting in the same spot. Finally I looked at my arm the last time and felt like a monster. What had I done? My arm had a gaping wound right above my wrist. I showed a good friend of mine, and he said I need to get help. I knew I did.

I went to work the next day, and my good friend went upstairs and got me a bandage from the first aid kit so my shirt wouldn't brush against the wound. It was very painful by this point. Then we went upstairs and started our banquet's shift. We had a few moments alone to set up a room, and I told him I was going to the hospital. He said that I definitely should and asked me who was taking me. I said I had my brother's car and would take myself.

He said, "No. I will be done my shift half an hour after you. You go home and sit on the couch. Don't move. Just wait for me. I will be there in half an hour."

I said, "Okay." By the time I went home it was about nine o'clock. The antidepressants had already started to work against me, even after only two doses. When I drove home I was buzzing. I had to turn the radio up as loud as I could, and I wanted to speed. I wanted to just push the gas pedal down as far as I could and grip the steering wheel really hard.

When I got home, I phoned my mom. Normally I had always approached the subject of my cutting like I felt some small amount of guilt. I knew it was inappropriate, and everyone else thought so, so I pretended I felt guilty and bad about it. This time when I talked to my mom, my speech was rapid. I was talking loudly and telling my mom all about the large gash on my arm and telling her in detail about the incident. She agreed I should go to the ER.

My friend picked me up after a while and took me in. Again I felt humiliated and had to tell them with other people behind me why I was there. I waited for six hours, and once again it didn't get me any further ahead. They had no beds available. I promised I wouldn't kill myself. I was drugged up again and sent home.

When we got home, my friend and I watched a movie, and my eyes were open and I was watching the movie, but I don't remember a single bit of the movie. It was crazy. The next day my friend drove me the six-hour drive home.

Back Home: Mixed Episodes and New Pain

My parents then told me that I should move home. They said that if I didn't, I would be going against their wishes for me. I wasn't well, and I needed to be taken care of. I was very upset about that. I live in a town in the middle of nowhere with about six hundred people. I would have no money to even buy cigarettes or to go where I wanted to go. None of my friends lived there any more, so I would have to be by myself. It was hard, but I decided that they were right. I couldn't be by myself any more. It wasn't safe, and I didn't trust myself. I took a three-month leave of absence without pay and moved home.

For the first while, all I did was sleep. I went back to the city once a month for psychiatric appointments, and sometimes the psychiatrist would even phone me at home to check up on me. She was an excellent doctor, because she truly did care about me, and I could tell.

I was having problems with mixed episodes towards the middle of my summer at home. I would be extremely anxious and agitated to the point of pacing and smoking continuously. I had rapid speech and felt energetic, but yet I was tired sometimes too. I was unable to relax and sleep, but I was tired. I felt like crying a lot, and I was very irritable. My doctor prescribed Olanzapine, or Zyprexa, 10 mg per night. This immediately started causing weight gain, which was horrible because there was nothing I could do about it. I was also prescribed Lorazepam, sublingual 1mg, to take as needed and Zopiclone, 7.5 mg, for sleep. I was able to function after this, and I decided I would go back to school. I thought I was better.

Back To University: More Drug Side Effects

I enrolled in psych nursing at my original university that fall because I wanted to be able to help other people like myself who were suffering, and my psychiatrist was so good to me that it inspired me.

I started school, and my lithium level was up to 1500 mg/day. I was still taking Zyprexa, 10 mg per day, but I decided to stop the Zyprexa when I went to school. I started off strong in school, but I could not get over the depression and the horrible lows that I felt. I also slept a lot and began to miss my classes. Somehow I managed to keep my marks up. I also felt horrible anxiety, and I clung to my ex-boyfriend. I was extremely needy. I got a new psychiatrist, but he didn't seem to care about me one bit.

I was put on Risperidol in November. It didn't help at all; I simply gained ten more pounds. My normally 123-pound frame was now up to 150 pounds. I hated it. I hated that I had no control over my weight. I snapped at my doctor when I went back and stated in a very harsh voice that I would not be going on any more "fat" drugs. He agreed and put me on Lamictal, or Lamotragine, another anticonvulsant. This drug did not have any serious side effects for me, although 10 percent of people get serious skin rashes that leave scarring and 1 percent of people actually die from this rash. This seemed to work for me for a while; it seemed to relieve some of the insanity. However, I was still depressed.

At this time my new doctor went against what my former psychiatrist had said. He put me on antidepressants even though my previous doctor wrote in my referral that I could not tolerate antidepressants. He put me on Prozac, 10 mg, and I was to wait for a month to come back for another appointment. I was so depressed, and the pills weren't working. Knowing that the maximum safe dose was also 50 mg, I decided to take two pills a day at 20 mg instead of 10 mg. If I went back to my doctor and told him it wasn't working, he would have just told me to start taking two. So that is what I did without his knowledge.

145

Prozac made me very sick. I was literally insane. My whole body felt crawly, and my insides were racing. I felt almost tingly. I could not sit still; all I wanted to do was die. I could not live like this any more. I went over to my old boyfriend's room and felt like hell had entered my body. I told him I was desperate. I didn't know what to do with myself, and I thought I needed to go to the ER. He couldn't tell when I was seriously sick or when I was just overreacting. He was tired of my being completely dependent on him.

I went home and sliced my arm. I called my brother and told him that I wanted to cut myself. He told me to wait; he would be over in a few minutes. I panicked. I thought, "I have to hurry and cut or he will be here and I won't be able to." So I gave myself a small cut and went to leave the room to go and let him in my building. But I had to rush back in to cut myself again, and the last time when I went to leave I knew I had to get a really good cut in, because this was the last chance I would have to cut before my brother got there. I grabbed my knife and pushed on my arms as hard as I could. I was bleeding when my brother got to my place. He told me to sleep and held a paper towel on my arm the whole night to stop the bleeding.

The next day I went to the ER, my first time in this city. They were very curt with me, and they gave me a shot without me asking for it. They told me it was my fault because I shouldn't have taken two pills instead of one. They referred me to the crisis centre, so my brother drove me there. I couldn't stay there though. I panicked, and I had to leave. My brother drove me home.

I felt like the worst human being on earth. I felt as though I had let everybody down. I wanted to die, and that made me feel even more guilty. I was at the end of my rope. I just didn't realize how much rope was left until the end.

That summer I was offered summer employment with the federal government. I was glad, because I needed a good job that would pay well. This was the answer to my prayers; I was so glad. I moved out of residence and into a house with a girl, whose parents owned the house. I went through some severe depression that summer. I cut every once in awhile, and there were some weeks of work where I would get up, go to work, come home, and sleep until the next day. I was exhausted. Then once it got to be midsummer, I was going out to the bar all the time. I would go out and drink, and I didn't really care about my job or what anyone thought—it was a hard summer. I had no clue what to do with myself when I started getting sick. I just couldn't find any peace, and I didn't know why I would want to cut myself. I was on 1500 mg of lithium per day and 150 mg of Lamotragine. I also still took my sleeping pill every single night and Lorazepam whenever I felt I needed it. I also started taking Gravol, because it would relax me. I wasn't living; I was just existing.

My Lithium Nightmare

That fall, I started school again. I was taking anatomy and physiology, which is an extremely heavy course load. I was also taking a couple of other classes and still working part-time with the government. I could *not* study. I would just sit and cry. I went home for the weekends before my exams, but I just could not study. My mom had to sit with me and help me study, and I could not figure out why. Had I become stupid? I remembered when I was in my first year of university, learning three hundred Ukrainian words in one weekend. That was the same week I learned the alphabet in Ukrainian, so it was all totally new to me, but I thought this was the assignment, so I learned those words and what they meant. So I just could not understand why I couldn't memorize my anatomy. I felt stupid. Sometimes when I would get so sick during these times, people would hint that maybe I just couldn't handle university. I felt horrible. I knew I had to get through it and I knew I was smart enough to go to school, but what was wrong with me?

In November, after my second set of midterms in anatomy and physiology, I decided that it must be the lithium that was doing this to me. I still believe that it was God who showed me that, because it was just an idea that came to me. I never read anything about it or heard it from anyone that it could do that to you. I just knew. So I talked to my doctor. I told him I wanted off my lithium. My mom also talked to him and told him the same thing. He said, "Okay, stop taking it." I went from 1500mg/day to nothing. I didn't realize that such a sudden withdrawal might be dangerous; I had no idea. He was the doctor, not me. I noticed an improvement in my anatomy and physiology immediately. I passed the first term with a B.

I wasn't aware of the withdrawal symptoms that people who are going off lithium go through. One month after I went off my lithium, I went into serious hypomania. I mean, I was insane. That is the only word that I feel describes what I was going through. I felt like I had just drank an entire pot of coffee and then one hour later drank another. I was talking fast and thinking fast and had great ideas. I was extremely irritable and just didn't know what to do with myself. I knew better than to drink by this time so I didn't drink, but I took a lot of Gravol trying to calm myself down. I would stay up all night and then sleep during the day. I wasn't going to class hardly ever, and when I did, I felt irate. I hated dealing with the insanity all the time and then having to go to class and hear them discussing the same things and teaching people all the simple answers to what I was going through. I became very overbearing, and I would tell people I barely knew about my personal life and what I was going through.

More Pain, Desperation, and the Crisis Unit

I was feeling absolute desperation. I could not handle myself. Finally, I cut myself really deeply again. I had an exam the next day, and I just needed some relief from the insanity. So I went into my bathroom with a new knife and began to cut. I kept cutting, until finally I knew that I had a choice to make. I could either seriously injure myself or call for help. So I called the crisis unit. They came in their minivan to pick me up. I went to the ER and I noticed that when I went with the crisis team, everyone was nicer to me. They didn't pick on me or humiliate me. I felt taken care of.

I had taken three Gravols and two sleeping pills before I cut, hoping that it would calm me down enough that I wouldn't cut. But it didn't make me tired at all. Finally, after about one and a half hours at the ER,

I was interviewed by the crisis team. I felt exhausted and calmer. I told them that I promise I wouldn't cut any more that night and that I would check in with them in the morning but I really wanted to sleep in my own bed. I went home around 4 a.m.

The next day I called to check in, and I was feeling better. By the evening, however, I was back on the fast track to insanity. I was flying, but it was not a good feeling. I felt like I needed to do something, but I didn't know what. I was so fast. Everything about me was fast. My thoughts were racing. I couldn't hold onto a thought. I was loosely connecting things, and I was interrupting everyone and snapping at everyone. I was colouring a lot at that time. It seemed to be the only thing that kept me occupied and the only thing that held my interest for longer than two seconds.

Finally, on Wednesday, I gave in and moved into the crisis centre. I was absolutely insane. I went in there, and I felt nervous about being in there, but at the same time I felt relieved that I was finally going to be able to get help. I stayed in for a week. The second day after I was put back on Zyprexa, it exhausted me. Actually, the exhaustion was probably due to a mix of the medication and not sleeping for a month. During the month that I was sick, I also never ate. I just was never hungry—I never needed to eat. The Zyprexa began to bring me down immediately. One of my friends that I met while in the crisis centre said that he couldn't understand a single word I said when I first moved in. I spoke fast and went from thought to thought to thought, without ever completing the previous one. I remember sitting at the supper table and thinking all kinds of funny things in my head. I knew that no one else would think they were funny, but I couldn't help laughing out loud. I just couldn't stop myself. Everyone at the table just looked at me, since most of the people in the centre were in for depression and suicidal tendencies. It was super crazy.

Out of the Crisis Centre and into Hypomania

I left the crisis centre at the end of January and kept in touch with some of the friends I had made inside. I was struggling with mania, constantly now. But if I took the Zyprexa daily, it would drag me down too far. So I talked to my doctor, and he said I could take the 25 mg of Zyprexa as needed when I started to feel too high. I didn't like taking it until I needed it, because it would drag me out the entire next day. The day after I took it, I would sleep until four p.m. But when the hypomania was bad, I would get hyperactive again in the evening. Sometimes I would have to take it for three nights in a row.

I hated hypomania; it was not fun in any way. I might have been laughing more, but it was like a twisted version of happiness. It was sick. I felt restless and fidgety and uncomfortable. I would blink lots, trying to blink my thoughts back to a normal speed. Sometimes I would shake my head to try and shake some normalcy back into it. I remember one evening when I was experiencing this, I was supposed to go to my night class. I got in the car and I started driving. "I have to go to class. I have to go to class. Just drive to class and park; then I will go inside. But I need to buy finger paints. Yeah, I need to finger paint. Go to class."

Well, I got to class, and there was nowhere to park, so I got discouraged, drove around the parking lot, and kept on driving. I went to Wal-Mart and spent about fifty dollars on finger paints and poster paints and glue and crayons and markers. I got to the till with all my stuff and realized I didn't have my debit card. But this did not deter me from my plan. I just drove home, still focused on my plan, and picked up my debit card. I went back to Wal-Mart and picked up my stuff. Then I went back to my house and began desperately to work on a project. I began a collage. I spent about three hours working on it, and I didn't stop. It depicted perfectly what mania felt like. My friend came over, but I barely had time to acknowledge him, because I was too busy.

There were many times that I would get an idea and just couldn't stop thinking about it. This may sound funny, but when it is so intense that you can't ignore it, it's scary. I remember getting the idea that I wanted to paint a mural on my apartment walls. I could not stop thinking about how good it would feel to paint huge lines with a paintbrush on my white walls. I knew that as soon as I did it I would feel really stupid and that I would have to pay to paint the apartment. Plus I am not a good painter, so it would look stupid. So I decided it was time to take my Zyprexa. I took it for three days to get rid of that idea.

People could not handle me any more, and neither could I. I hated what I had become, and I didn't know how to fix myself. I was out of control.

An Encounter with the Powers of Darkness

In about mid-March, I had a very weird and scary episode that I still do not totally understand. I was over at a friend's place and came home in the afternoon. I didn't know what to do because I wasn't in an episode, but I felt a really dark and sinister feeling. I felt kind of scared, but I didn't know how to express what I felt so I just went home anyway. I started to colour really morbid pictures, and as soon as I got home I began to take my sleeping pills.

My roommate at that time came into my room to talk to me, and she said that she was scared as soon as she saw me. I wasn't myself. I was so focused on my morbid colouring that I could not even make eye contact with her. I wouldn't answer her questions really either. I would just nod or say a few words. Normally if I wasn't feeling well and someone asked about it I would tell them and try to figure out what was wrong. This time I couldn't. I told her I was going to take all my sleeping pills. I started in on Gravol as well.

She got scared and called my other friend over, so she came too. They both just sat on my floor, visiting me, scared to leave me alone but not knowing what to say to draw me out. It was very annoying for me because I was busy and their incessant chatter was starting to get to me. I wanted to be alone and figure out whatever it was I was figuring out. Even with them in the room I continued to take Gravol and sleeping pills.

I sat in my chair with my journal and began to write. I don't remember what I wrote, but I do remember sitting in the chair and writing. They got scared and phoned the crisis centre. The centre phoned me back and asked me how it was going. I told them, fine, it is going fine. They asked me if I had taken more medicine than I should that day. I knew instantly that my friends had phoned and told on me.

151

I was irate. I started yelling at my two friends and calling them the enemy. The crisis team phoned the hospital to make sure I hadn't taken enough pills to kill me. I hadn't. They made me give my medicine, all of it, to my friends.

I stayed up all night. I read over what I had written, and I was terrified. I don't remember writing what was written in my journal. I have truly never thought about killing myself, and I had never thought of taking all my pills before. When I snapped out of it, I was terrified. I thought, "Can Satan actually kill me?" I knew that something spiritual had happened but I didn't know what. I had to phone the crisis team in the morning before ten or they would call the cops on me. I called them and set up an appointment. I was scared of myself; I didn't trust myself. I threw out all my Gravol.

Back to the Crisis Centre

I moved into the crisis centre again. I was very confused and very scared. I took comfort in reading the Bible and knowing that God was protecting me. I just had to say the verses over and over in my head. While I was there, I had a very interesting conversation with a friend of mine on the phone. I began telling him that there was something inside of me that I hate. I did not know what it was, but that is why I cut. I had no idea how to figure it out. I was seeing a counsellor at the university at that time, and I discussed it with her as well. I knew that I would not find the answer to my troubles in drugs. I had to start really striving to understand what was truly wrong with me. Not surprisingly after that episode, my roommate decided it would be best if I didn't live there any more. I agreed. I moved out on my own to a wonderful apartment. I was a little apprehensive about living alone, but I knew I needed my space to figure this stuff out. I moved out in the first week of April.

Mental Illness and Chemical Imbalance as Theory: A Rude Awakening

To my great surprise, I passed all my classes, *even* anatomy and physiology. Then in May I started back at my government job. My mom had gone for prayer with Deeper Love Ministries and had been to one of their healing prayer retreats. She had had a lot worked out on that weekend and had been delivered from a lot of spiritual bondage. She kept telling me that I needed to go, but I was scared. I figured if I went and God didn't heal me, I would really give up and kill myself. I was scared that God wouldn't want to heal me and that I would be disappointed. For some reason, I was so apprehensive about it all, I just didn't want to go.

There was one class at school that really made me start to question all that was going on in my life, and that was individual counselling. My teacher was very straightforward and didn't sugar-coat anything. He started saying that mental illness was just a theory, that they don't actually know if these illnesses are actually chemical imbalances or not, and that the debate exists among professionals to this day. I was horrified that he would dare say that to me. What I had was real. I needed my drugs to live. I had a *bona fide* illness, and I needed drugs to help it. I would never be better, but I could manage with my drugs. Ever since I started getting treated, they had told me this. They had presented it like it was fact, like they could guarantee that this was true. When I started to question it, I really started to get confused.

Topimax Trauma

After my last trip to the crisis centre, my doctor added another mood stabilizer, Topimax. I had been on it before but I felt like I hadn't given it enough of a try. My doctor told me that I might have some weight loss on this drug. I was excited about it. I was sick of being larger than I was used to.

The first month was just as bad as I remembered it being. I felt like there was battery acid in my stomach or permanent heartburn. It was horrible. It felt like the acid was eating away at my stomach, and my stomach felt raw most of the time. Finally, after a month my stomach began to get used to the drug, and the stomach reaction went away. I was so glad. I felt pretty good. I was still battling against hypomania most of the time. But at least my stomach wasn't in pain. The day of my brother's graduation, however, I woke up and got up with my mom, who was in town for the grad. After being up for about an hour, I felt intense pain in my back. I thought it was a back spasm. Then the pain moved to my side. I could not do anything but lie on the floor and cry. It turned out to be a kidney stone. I wondered how I got the kidney stone, and I told all the doctors about the drugs I was on, but they didn't say anything about them, so I thought, "Well, it must not be the drugs then." I continued to take my drugs.

One of the side effects of Topimax that I read about on the internet was anorexia. I suddenly noticed that I was losing drastic amounts of weight and that I was not eating. I would eat one sausage and an egg, and that is all I would eat all day. I normally have a large appetite, but I couldn't eat any more. I went out with a friend for supper on his birthday. I hadn't eaten all day, but all I could eat were a few bites of mashed potatoes, two shrimps, and two pieces of ribs. I was starting to get really worried, and so were my friends and family. I was getting pressured to eat, but I just couldn't.

Encountering the Healing Presence of Jesus

I was feeling really fed up by this point, so I finally called Dieter to make an appointment with him to get healing prayer. I knew that I had to do it or I would never be better. My mom pressured me to go, and I am glad she did. Once I decided that I was going to go, I said that I would keep going back until it worked, even if it took ten times. I would keep going wherever I had to go. I knew Dieter was writing a book on psychiatric illnesses and that he understood a lot about them, so I wanted him to pray with me. I just couldn't live like this any more. I couldn't handle it. I didn't want to work; I didn't want to play. I didn't want to eat or do anything; I just wanted to smoke—and I barely wanted to do that. I just had to. My smoking was out of control; I was smoking an insane amount of cigarettes. I was having crying spells too. I could not stop crying and getting my feelings hurt over everything. I hated my job.

Finally it came time for me to go to Winnipeg for healing prayer. Before I got prayer, I threw up twice, once at the restaurant and once when I got to the church. I was terrified. I told Dieter that I was very analytical and didn't think the prayer would work for me.

My first prayer session was very different for me. After Dieter anointed me with oil and we waited on the Holy Spirit, I remembered that my dad had suddenly died from a massive heart attack when I was six years old. I thought that was probably where my sickness was coming from, something to do with that. When they started to pray for me, I had to renounce the vow that I had made when I was young that I didn't need anybody and that I didn't want anybody. Then as the Lord took me back to a key memory, Dieter's prayer partner, a lady, asked me where my dad was. I told her, but I also told her that I felt like I had dealt with everything from that tragedy in my life. I felt like I had already given it up to God and been able to let go. I had mourned when I was fourteen and didn't know what could possibly be left over. Dieter then asked me what bothers me the most or what hurts the most out of all my memories of my dad.

Suddenly, I felt terrified. I remembered my mom desperately phoning a neighbour of ours and yelling into the phone that something was wrong with my dad. I could feel how scary that had been for me, but I had never really felt the fear before. I started to bawl, and the lady praying for me hugged me. I could feel how out of control things had been that night and how scared I had been seeing my mom, who was never scared, so terrified. I bawled for about fifteen minutes, and finally I felt okay. Then Dieter said that God had something He wanted to give me instead of fear. He said God was going to show me what it was. Instantly I saw the word *peace*. I felt peace, too. It was awesome!!

That was when I started looking into my drugs more. I started realizing that they were not helping me, and Dieter gave me some books to look up on the Internet. I read as much as I could about my drugs and about going off drugs. I was feeling pretty sick by this point, because I wasn't eating. I had lost another six pounds. I am not a very large person to begin with and I felt horrible not eating.

So I looked up the drug on the manufacturer's web page. Topimax, I found out, was what had caused my kidney stone. It said that if you get a kidney stone you are to stop taking Topimax immediately. But since no one knew about the drugs I was on, no one told me about that. I was on Topimax three months and had a kidney stone after two. I had still been taking it for a month after the kidney stone.

I had had enough. I felt like an old woman who needed thousands of drugs. I realized that they were really playing with my brain chemistry and they weren't even sure how the drugs work. The Web sites for all the drugs I was taking said that *no* long-term testing has yet been done. I guess I was the test case. I called my doctor and told him I wanted off my drugs. I knew that only God could help me now and that the medications were just making my life worse. My doctor just told me to stop taking Topimax and that I would go off Lamictal in a few weeks. I had no intentions of going off my sleeping pill, because I liked it too much. I knew that the prayer was going to work, and I wanted to live again and live drug free.

The second prayer session I went to was with Dieter and another prayer partner on his ministry team. I wasn't sure what was going to come out, but I knew something would happen. I wasn't as nervous this time, but I was feeling extremely angry about being tricked by the provincial health authority. I felt like they had deceived me into believing what they wanted me to believe, even though it was all just theory. They presented it to me as though it was the truth and there was no other explanation. I believed everything they told me and trusted that they knew about these potent drugs they were giving me.

We started the prayer session, but I had no peace. I felt confused. They had to pray against that. Then I felt the intense urge to cut. I thought—no, I haven't had this in months. I didn't want to tell them because I was embarrassed, but I felt like I should. So I told them, and they prayed that God would show me why I was feeling this.

I started to think about my mom's relatives and her family. I started to remember my granny and how she never seemed to like my brother and me. It made me angry, even while I was sitting there. Then I started to realize that I knew I looked down on my mom's side of the family, and I knew I needed to ask forgiveness for that. Then I realized even more as God showed me, because there is no way I would ever be able to figure this stuff out by myself. I knew that it was because of my mom's aboriginal heritage. I knew also that this attitude was passed down to me. I prayed against it and acknowledged that aboriginal people are made in God's image and asked forgiveness for that attitude. I also forgave my dad for passing those attitudes on to me, even though it was not intentional.

Dieter's prayer partner got a picture of me trying to separate myself into two separate entities instead of embracing myself as one person. I was trying to keep only the heritage my dad gave me and get rid of the heritage my mom gave me. She asked me if this made sense to me. It totally did. I had been diagnosed as bipolar. Two separate poles—hmm. This was unreal. I then realized that if I looked down on my relatives for being Indian I must look down on my mom because she was also Indian, and also on myself because my mom passed that heritage on to me. Then I realized what it was that I hated in myself. It all made so much sense.

Finally: Healed and Restored!

After that prayer session, I just knew that I was different. People who knew me could tell right away that something was different. I went off all of my drugs, including my sleeping pill. I could not believe what a difference was made in my life.

There is no way that medicine could have helped me with this. Even if I had gone through extensive counselling sessions and figured this out, that wouldn't have healed it. It would have simply made me aware of what the problem was instead of healing it. I very strongly believe that Jesus is the only answer to mental illness. No matter what drug they put me on, nothing was ever fixed. I prayed and prayed for God to heal me from the bipolar disorder. But if He would have just taken my symptoms away, like I was praying for, the issue would still

157

come out. It would just be in some other area. My symptoms were from a deep issue in my soul, not a chemical imbalance in my brain. Maybe I did have an imbalance, but the imbalance was caused by the turmoil inside of me, not the other way around.

Chapter Seven

Relational Imbalances: Towards Healing The Soul

The Lord is close to the brokenhearted and saves those who are crushed in spirit (Ps. 34:18).

Create in me a pure heart, O God, and renew a steadfast spirit within me (Ps. 51:10).

Anita: Healed from Depression

Anita experienced a miraculous healing from depression through the ministry of healing prayer that relies on the intentional presence of Jesus and His Spirit. This is her story and testimony.

Six months ago I never thought that I would ever be writing about how I'm not depressed any more. I don't remember when I first became depressed, but I do remember that it had something to do with being teased at school. I remember standing in a field on the playground all alone with no friends and wishing that I wasn't there. I was only ten years old at the time.

I went through the rest of junior high thinking of suicide. But I knew that suicide was wrong, and so I thought the suffering would never end. Once I changed schools in high school, everything was happy again. I thought that maybe the depression was just a teenage phase like so many people told me it was.

I graduated and moved to Winnipeg, and for the first time in my life I had a lot of friends and was really happy. But the depression came back. Two people who I thought were my best friends betrayed me. One of those two people would put me down so often that I believed everything he said—though I now know it wasn't true. I was diagnosed with depression by a doctor and put on antidepressants. I believed, though, that the antidepressants would not cure the depression. I found that the anger I had towards my two friends was consuming me. But I didn't know how to just let it go. It got to the point where I was so depressed that I lost most of my friends, almost lost my job, and found that some days I couldn't even get out of bed.

One day I had just enough. I felt like this emotional pain was never going to end. I had tried everything I could. I tried moving back home with my mom to get rid of some stress—to sort of start over again. Nothing was working. I didn't want to go back to the way I felt in junior high. I felt there was no way out.

One day I just kept hearing every awful thing everyone had ever said to me. I decide to try and kill myself. So, I took a bunch of Tylenol. But I chickened out at the last minute and told my mom what I did. As a result, I ended up in the hospital for a week. But, even after talking to the psychiatrist in the hospital and to my family, I still felt the same. I certainly didn't think that what to me seemed like a lifetime of depression could disappear in one day.

My mom and sister asked me to sit down with my pastor we knew for some healing prayer. I was going to say no. But something made me think maybe I should. My pastor and his prayer assistant prayed with me for two hours. And what I lived with for a lifetime was gone in a mere two hours!

After that day I have felt happy in a way I never thought was possible. I no longer take my antidepressant after being on it for a year. During that time, if I missed even a couple of doses of the antidepressant I would be so depressed that I couldn't get out of bed. I stopped taking it completely after that day with my pastor (it was my decision entirely, he never advised me to do so) and Jesus and I have never had a problem.

Today I am happier than I have been in my whole life. My relationships with my friends and family are greatly improved, and I find that I can look to the future and realize that I can do anything I want. I don't hear all the mean things people said to me any more, because Jesus has blocked them from coming in and He has shown me that all those things are *not* true.

So I say to anyone who thinks that he or she can't be healed or that God doesn't listen or answers your prayers that *He does*. And when He does, He does it better than you ever thought possible.

Healing Without Psychiatric Drugs

The most convincing proof that the biochemical imbalance or genetic theory is flawed would be to demonstrate that people can be healed or recover from supposedly biochemically caused emotional problems *without any psychiatric drugs at all*. Such proof would be more direct than from logic or science. Is Anita's true story just an exception, a rare event? What of Jacqueline's story, in the previous chapter, given the claims about chemical imbalances in the brain? Could these examples of healing without drugs be more the norm than the exception? The history of psychiatry itself has some important lessons for today.

In the eighteenth century, in the very early years of psychiatry, "asylums" for the "insane" were founded in many cities. Unfortunately, people who were committed to an asylum were often chained, caged, forced to live naked in their own excrement, bothered by rats, and became the object of ridicule by the general public, who in some cases bought tickets to watch these people "perform."[1] That in itself would drive most of us insane!

Pinel (1745-1826), when he became the chief physician at a large insane asylum in Paris, believed that these "insane" people were actually normal people who had experienced severe and abnormal problems

161

and that treating people like animals was not terribly helpful—a radical concept![2] So, he had them unchained, treated them like real people, and spent many hours listening to their problems and comforted them. He was "endearing" with his patients and even calmed them down with warm baths.[3]

Esquirol, Pinel's student, developed the concept further and claimed that one needed a "therapeutic community" (another radical concept!) where even the physicians lived and ate with the patients. Edward Shorter, medical historian at the University of Toronto, wrote that Esquirol and his family even dined with patients in the asylum.[4] The result was that many patients recovered and were released.

William Tuke (1732-1822), a Quaker, attempted the same approach in England by moving people to a peaceful country estate to work, play, rest, pray, go for long walks, and talk over their problems.[5] The first such "retreat" by the Quakers was established in 1796, with a central belief that mental illness was not biological but the result of the pain and shock of life.[6]

This approach, soon called "moral therapy," became widespread and yet was opposed by many mental health professionals at the time.[7] The term *moral therapy* comes from the French *le traitement moral* where *moral* has more the meaning of "mental" in English[8] and hence "mental therapy" might be a better translation. Amazingly, "at least 70 percent of those hospitalized for a year or less either improved or actually recovered."[9,10] Other sources show that from 50 to 80 percent of the mentally ill at various insane asylums offering moral therapy and compassion were cured or recovered.[11] Such results are better than much of what psychiatry offers today. While some may criticize the results and records from moral therapy, modern historians conclude that the results were surprisingly good and "fairly quick recovery from an acute episode of psychosis was common."[12]

Love and the power of a healing presence were effective in curing mental "illness" and restoring the soul. But scientific biological psychiatry soon took over those institutions for a number of reasons, and it wasn't long before the discharge rates dropped to 20 to 30 percent.[13]

This was one truly promising era of early psychiatry. It was simple and effective but unfortunately also "unprofessional," "unscientific," and eventually overtaken by social, cultural, and scientific forces.[14]

Peter Breggin, as a Harvard freshman in the 1950s, was part of a program where untrained freshmen were paired up for a year with patients in a psychiatric hospital.[15] The director of the hospital was not in favour of the program, and in an attempt to discredit the idea that untrained volunteers could be helpful at all compared to trained mental health professionals and psychiatry, he arranged for each volunteer to be paired up with the severest cases—schizophrenics and psychotics in the hospital's back wards. Each volunteer simply came in once a week and visited with the same person, listening to their heart and their life story, walking with them, and showing understanding and compassion. Within one year, eleven of the fourteen patients recovered from their conditions and were released from the psychiatric hospital. Instead of drugs, it was love, care, and affirmation that healed those patients who needed other people more than pills. The hospital director's plan had backfired.

Soteria House was founded in 1971 by Mosher, clinical professor of psychiatry at the University of California at San Diego. Mosher embarked on a well-designed clinical research trial. Young people diagnosed as schizophrenics lived drug free in a residence with nonprofessional people trained simply to listen and care.[16] In fact, some of the staff were former mental patients.[17] The basic idea or hypothesis was that meaningful relationships are eminently more helpful than drugs in the treatment of mental illness.[18] At two years after admission, former Soteria House patients were doing significantly better than those were treated in psychiatric wards with neuroleptics.[19] This was accomplished *without any drugs,* and schizophrenia is considered a more difficult psychiatric problem.

But not surprisingly, modern psychiatry has totally disregarded Soteria House and others like it, presumably since it directly calls into question the core assumptions and practices of modern psychiatry.[20] There was such a resistance from the medical community that there were attempts to cut the funding and discredit the research, and eventually Mosher was removed as the principal investigator. Soteria House was later shut down.[21] Mosher's hypothesis was deemed "offensive" by the academic psychiatric community.[22] The results of Soteria House have been subsequently repeated in Switzerland and other places in Europe.[23] Could it be that modern psychiatry has an attention deficit disorder to certain research results or perhaps a mild case of oppositional defiance disorder towards certain types of research or researchers?

The San Joaquin Psychotherapy Center in the U.S. is one of only a few full-service centres that does not use any psychiatric medication at all. The centre admits people with some of the most severe emotional and behavioural problems, sometimes taking six to ten different psychiatric drugs.[24] Following the basic ideas of moral therapy (this author would not endorse some of the non-drug treatments and beliefs of this centre), the success rate has been consistent and high, with a readmission rate of *zero* after ten years.[25]

If all the above can be done without drugs of any kind, it directly calls into question the entire medical model of psychiatry and the belief that psychiatric drugs are required to correct neurotransmitter levels. Love, empathy, and caring are more powerful than Luvox, Effexor, and Clorazil. From a professional and clinical viewpoint, "even the most dramatic biological symptoms of mental illness often disappear quite rapidly once the patient feels he is in a safe, non-stressful, and caring environment."[26] One should never underestimate the power of a healing community.

Relational Imbalance and Neurotransmitters

While much research and speculation goes on to support the notion that different brain chemicals and their supposed imbalance affect behaviour and moods, there is considerable solid evidence to support the *reverse* view that external life experiences, relational issues, and stress can effect the body and almost certainly the brain. In fact, stressful life experiences—and even recalling them over time—can change brain structure, function and even brain anatomy.[27]

Psychosocial dwarfism, or stunted growth in children from a stressful home or a dysfunctional family, is an especially striking example. The height of such children will not respond to hormones, but when they are placed in a supportive, nurturing family, they often experience a growth spurt, while such children left with their family rarely (one in thirty-five in one study) catch up to their normal size. If children are returned to their dysfunctional family, they often stop growing once again.[28] Another study of twenty emotionally abused and neglected boys in their toddler years showed that their trauma held back their normal physical development and growth.[29] When the trauma stopped, their normal growth and development resumed. This then points to the incredible importance of love and nurture, affecting the whole person.

Physical touch is crucial in the development of neural pathways and even brain size. One research study showed that children who don't play much and are thus in a less stimulating environment or who are rarely touched have brains 20 to 30 percent smaller in size than those of normal children.[30]

Charles Whitfield, physician and psychotherapist, cited a growing body of scientific research since the 1980s that has been increasingly and conclusively showing that trauma (or significant woundedness) in life, especially in the early childhood years, can cause chronic physical illnesses.[31] Physical illnesses that are gastrointestinal, gynecological, respiratory, neurological, or musculoskeletal (chronic back or neck pain, for example) in nature might have been caused by past abuse or trauma.[32] Sixty-five studies published from 1984 to 2003 involving 61,150 people demonstrated a significant correlation between childhood trauma and subsequent physical illness.[33]

The causal link between trauma and physical illness is increasingly well understood, given the integration of one's body, mind, heart, and soul; thus this is not mere correlation. Childhood neglect, abuse, and other forms of trauma can cause brain damage along with the disruption and dysregulation of one's hormonal and neurotransmitter systems, eventually affecting the cardiovascular and other organ systems in the body.[34] This is all part of the wider picture of the heart-mind-body connection well known in the medical world and clear in the Scriptures, especially in the Book of Proverbs.[35]

Equally compelling is the scientific evidence that demonstrates the association and causation between childhood abuse, neglect, and trauma with varying forms and degrees of mental illness that may appear slowly or abruptly later in life. Since 1980, over 300 clinical scientific studies have demonstrated a "strong link between repeated childhood trauma and the development of subsequent mental illness—often decades later."[36] In fact, "nearly every study that has examined a potential relationship between repeated childhood and later trauma and mental illness has found it to occur to a statistically significant degree."[37]

Focusing on trauma—people's past emotional pain—and their varied and unique ways of expressing that is a much more scientific and rigorous therapeutic model than the diagnoses and explanations offered by psychiatry.[38] This view or model of emotional suffering explains the facts, and with much better prediction than does the psychiatric model.

For depression, for example, an important question is, does depression result from low neurotransmitter levels *or does the depression actually cause the low neurotransmitter levels, should they occur?* Do then the mind and spirit of a person affect the brain and its biochemistry? We must go beyond correlation and understand *causation plus its direction.* Considering the biblical unity of heart, spirit, mind, soul, and body, the "heart or spirit will always be represented or expressed in the brain's chemical activity."[39] We are primarily spiritual creatures. One is then more often better to treat depression by understanding life and relational issues than by adjusting brain chemicals. Is it a neurological deficit or a love deficit?

Under the Kitchen Sink

Most people have a garbage receptacle in their kitchen, often underneath the kitchen sink. Everyone knows that as food scraps and such are deposited into the garbage, it will eventually start to smell. Most people that I know will soon take the garbage out, preferably before the smell becomes intolerable. In fact, now that I think about it, everyone I know does that—I must be "well-connected!"

Logically, there are other solutions to this all too common problem. You could apply a powerful deodorant to the garbage so that you wouldn't smell it—I have even seem commercials where some chemical is sprayed in a room and the room is suddenly amazingly fresh with no more foul odours or stale air. Or, to really fix the problem, you could get a nose spray or a nasal operation to destroy your sense of smell.

We would all probably laugh at those "solutions," for any sane person knows that it is best to just remove the garbage before it starts to stink and rot. While few analogies are perfect, in this case taking psychiatric drugs is not much different from the kitchen garbage problem when you consider the toxic waste of the soul as one's inner garbage. Taking psychiatric drugs covers up and suppresses the toxic waste in one's soul—lies, shame, fear, woundedness, guilt, anger, rage, and so forth. Like being unable to smell the garbage, you can't feel your pain any more, and no steps are being taken to remove the toxic waste of your soul.

Daniel: Dyslexia, Shame, and Fear of Insanity

The Fabianos wrote about Daniel, twenty-two years old, who suffered from an extreme case of dyslexia, confused sexual identity, pervasive shame, uncleanness, and the fear of becoming insane or mentally ill.[40] During a time of ministry, the Lord took Daniel back to the time in his life when he had been sexually abused by his older brother over several years.[41] This incest caused all these feelings, not unlike the "desolation" experienced by Tamar from her brother Amnon (see 2 Sam. 13:20). As Daniel received prayer, the Lord took Daniel back to one of the times of the abuse and came in a powerful way, with a bright light and a commanding presence. The Lord directly dealt with all the evil spirits involved, showed His protection for Daniel, and released him from all the fears and shame. That night, Daniel was totally healed from dyslexia and has since enjoyed much wholeness and healing. The core of that time of ministry and Daniel's healing was the direct presence of Jesus and His Spirit. The "toxic waste" of Daniel's soul had been removed.

Molasses in Your Brains

How does it feel when one's brain is disabled? What is it like to take an antidepressant or an antipsychotic? While some Christian authors write almost glowing reports on how absolutely wonderful psychiatric drugs are—and some Christians have had a positive experience—there is another side to this story. For example, Farber wrote about Angela, who described her experience with antipsychotic drugs:

> They knock you out. They cause aches and pains all through your body. They make you apathetic. They stop the whole spiritual transformation process. It's like putting molasses in your brain. You can't even concentrate enough to read.[42]

Or there's Barbara, who under duress took Thorazine, an early drug. The drug caused her to have weird hallucinations plus burning sensations all over her body, and at times she felt like she was going to explode.[43] Many people on Prozac report that they find it difficult to cry or feel sad.[44]

By disabling the brain, healing is made more difficult, because you often need to be in touch with your emotions in order to experience healing. But you experience a dissociation from emotional pain.[45] It's like your soul has been numbed. Those who mourn will be comforted (Matt. 5:4; cf. Deut. 21:13), but what if you can't mourn or grieve no matter how hard you try?

Psychiatric drugs cause chemical imbalances and brain dysfunction, which "dull the emotions and judgment."[46] One's ability to feel emotional pain is now blocked, as well as the ability to experience joy. Feelings of sadness or suicide, for example, diminish and thus the impact of depression—but at a price. Nothing has been healed at all; your inner being has been "reduced"; your ability to feel has been compromised.

A person may seem more agreeable or "compliant" and senses much less anger, but that means alienation from one's true sense of being.[47] Psychiatric drugs often make it harder to think and especially to remember, which blunts revelation and understanding and compromises one's healing. I typically find that when praying with people who are on antidepressants, it takes more time for memories to come back.

There is also a sense of hopelessness, since if a biochemical imbalance is truly the cause and one really does need the drug, then why attempt anything beyond drug therapy? Why hope for anything better? The drug therapy route means that the healing process is now determined and controlled by mental health professionals and not by the patient.[48] Violation of the soul is really behind the emotional pain and disorders, and psychiatric drugs simply add to that violation.[49] Colbert, in his book *Rape of The Soul*, wrote:

> Psychiatric drugs do not heal. At the very minimum, they block out the awareness of the wounded soul. In millions of cases they bring about a more permanent emotional death of the soul.[50]

Indicators of the Soul

When I was a theology student, I drove an old eight-cylinder Pontiac station wagon, which my wife and I called "Big Red." Many times we drove through the Rocky Mountains in British Columbia, and on a few occasions, as we drove on the more demanding stretches of highway, the engine light came on. I immediately pulled over to the side of the highway, stopped, and after letting the engine idle for a half-minute or so, turned it off. When the engine had cooled down, I checked the radiator and the oil. I'm not a mechanic, nor a wrench jockey, so I looked for the obvious and hoped for nothing more complex. In each case, the engine was low on oil, so I went to my case of twenty-four (Quaker-State oil, not beer, in case you were wondering!) in the trunk and topped up the engine with oil. Obviously, the engine needed an overhaul, but like most theology students, I didn't have enough money to afford that.

So what would you do if your engine light came on while driving your car? Would you not also soon stop and investigate to see what the problem is? We all know that if you just keep driving in total disregard to the warning light, you could ruin your entire engine or even get into an accident. In the same way, there are indicators of the soul that tell us to pull over to the side in our busy schedules and see what is going on in our souls, in those deep places. Feelings of sadness, sorrow, shame, guilt, anxiety, and more are all indicators of a soul that often is crying out for healing and restoration. What is really sad is that many people appear to take better care of their cars than of their own souls. Many of us take our cars in for regular maintenance and tune-ups; why not do at least as much for one's soul?

Feelings of sadness and sorrow, for example, are often natural responses to life and relationships. Feelings of depression are signals of emotional pain that make us desire to uncover the source of our suffering.[51] To *not* experience depression would actually be abnormal. Symptoms of "mental illness," even the bizarre ones, are expressions of one's self, manifestations of one's inner conflicts.[52] Colbert wrote:

> Regardless of the symptomatology, whether we are talking about depression, mania, anxiety, compulsive-addictive disorders or schizophrenia, the symptoms are always present for one particular reason: *to protect the wounded selfhood.*[53]

No matter how bizarre or strange the behaviours or symptoms, they are purposeful, indicating a wounded soul ultimately crying out for love and healing.[54] For some people, there is so much shame, guilt, fear, sadness, sorrow, painful traumatic memories, and more—which are not always readily apparent—that they are spiritually overwhelmed, and the result is dysfunction and emotional pain. In some cases, one can become emotionally paralyzed or even catatonic. Communication, not medication, is the crux.

Kathryn: Languishing With Lexapro

I have had the privilege of ministering healing prayer to Kathryn, who has been on a long journey, as described earlier in this book. She is able to clearly describe what I suspect many other Christians are experiencing. Kathryn shares how an antidepressant has numbed her emotions. This is the next part of her story:

I have been prescribed an antidepressant, Lexapro, for my depression. This antidepressant keeps me going at a very fast pace, able to accomplish a lot, sleep less, and survive my days in a different way of "survival" than when I'm not using it. I feel like the Energizer Bunny— or a robot—wound up and going all the time but not living at all. It is a drug, and I feel that very keenly! I have been praying and asking God to show me how and when to stop using it. My reluctance is the memory of the pain that caused me to feel the need for medication.

I hate the medication. I am numb—no pain, but no real joy, either. I feel emotionally disconnected from people, and it is affecting my relationships. Without medication, I am a naturally compassionate and loving person. For the most part, I have lived like this long enough that I can almost "fake it" now. The real compassion and empathy that I normally feel for people is not completely gone—only by God's grace and mercy—but at a much lower level than when I am not on the meds. My behaviour is much more compulsive/addictive—I have to fight the temptation to smoke again, since it is very strong. I believe that is because I am so disconnected from people such that the smoking is, for me, a comfort that I picked up at a very young age. My mother actually taught me to smoke as a stress reliever.

I am addicted to work—I can go for ten to twelve hours without a break—and not in a healthy way. It's an escape. I have watched more TV in the past few months than I have in my entire life, and that is not an exaggeration. I am not naturally a TV watcher. I used to go for months without even turning on the TV, but lately I compulsively turn it on in the evening—again, I believe, for an "emotional connection" that my heart is longing for but the meds keep me from getting in the

171

way God intended. I use more caffeine, because the meds keep me in a "fog" for several hours after I wake up.

A big eye-opener for me was when I went to see The Notebook recently. My son had told me that it was a beautiful story about the love and commitment of a husband to his wife in her ailing years. It is a beautiful story—and I think I was the only person in the theater who was not crying at the end of the movie. Not good!

Believe it or not, I miss crying. I am a naturally empathetic person, easily moved to tears of joy or sorrow. I suppose that's just another way of realizing that I am numb!

If I spend an extended period of time in the Lord's presence (it is difficult to sit still for long because of this drug), I feel Him "break through" the meds, but not in the way that I knew Him before. My daily quiet time is almost non-existent—and that is the biggest reason that I want and need to get off this medication. My son says the one constant that he remembers from his childhood is getting up every morning and seeing me in my special chair, waiting on God. I'm not boasting but just giving an idea of how important my time with God has been to me over the years. I could not start a day without at least thirty minutes in His presence. Now I'm up and out the door. I long to sit in God's presence again and experience Him the way I used to. Now, when I think I hear Him, I'm not sure if it's Him or my brain on Lexapro. I tell God every day, "Please come and find me. I miss you!"

Kathryn's self-assessment of her emotions concurs with what many researchers have reported. It is not unusual for people on psychiatric drugs to feel "numb" emotionally, sometimes unable to cry even when they really want to, like at especially moving films where most people are in tears.[55]

Conclusion

The biochemical and genetic theories for mental illnesses have already been shown in previous chapters to be flawed. The most potent refutation of them would be to demonstrate the healing of people diagnosed as "mentally ill" without using any drugs. That occurred in the history of psychiatry, and there are examples today, including people healed through the ministry of healing prayer. But psychiatry is loath to accept this, since it brings into question its reason for existence, its revenue, and validity as a medical specialty.

Much scientific evidence points to nurture and past relational issues, sometimes traumatic or deeply painful emotionally, as affecting people physically or causing "mental illness." Truly, *"A heart at peace gives life to the body"* (Prov. 14:30). Research concurs with the "wounded soul" of the Scriptures but offers weak support at best for mental illness as a biological concept and psychiatric drugs as their solution.

The use of antipsychotics and antidepressants can short-circuit one's spiritual growth and in many ways can violate the soul and one's selfhood. Apart from truly organic causes of emotional suffering, there is a wounded soul that needs love and restoration.

And what of natural remedies, like herbs? The same principle applies: when it's really an issue of a wounded soul, natural remedies won't ultimately help. They may be safer and may or may not have any real positive effect.

Psychiatric drugs are prescribed for a psychiatric diagnosis. This is the "other side of the equation." But are such diagnoses valid?

Endnotes _____

[1] Ty C. Colbert, *Broken Brains or Wounded Hearts: What Causes Mental Illness* (Santa Ana: Kevco Publishing, 1996) p. 102.

[2] Ibid.

[3] Edward Shorter, *A History of Psychiatry: From The Era of The Asylum to The Age of Prozac* (New York: John Wiley and Sons, Inc., 1997) p. 12.

[4] Shorter, p. 13.

[5] Colbert, p. 102.

[6] Robert Whitaker, *Mad In America: Bad Science, Bad Medicine, And The Enduring Mistreatment Of The Mentally Ill* (Cambridge: Perseus Publishing, 2002) pp. 22-23.

[7] Colbert, p. 103.

[8] Shorter, 19-20.

[9] Colbert, p. 103.

[10] Ty C. Colbert, *Rape of the Soul: How the Medical Imbalance Model of Modern Psychiatry Has Failed its Patients* (Tustin: Krevco Publishing, 2000) p. 33.

[11] Whitaker, pp. 27-34.

[12] Whitaker, pp. 84,36.

[13] Colbert, 2000, pp. 34-37.

[14] Whitaker, pp. 34-38.

[15] Peter R. Breggin, *Toxic Psychiatry: Why Therapy, Empathy, and Love Must Replace the Drugs, Electroshock, And Biochemical Theories of the "New Psychiatry"* (New York: St. Martin's Press, 1991) pp. 9-11.

[16] Breggin, p. 354.

[17] Colbert, 2000, p. 105.

[18] Loren R. Mosher, "Soteria and Other Alternatives to Acute Psychiatric Hospitalization," *The Journal of Nervous And Mental Disease* 187:142-149, 1999. pp. 142-146.

[19] Ibid.

[20] Ibid.

[21] Whitaker, pp. 220-225.

[22] Whitaker, pp. 220-223.

[23] Mosher, p. 146.

[24] Colbert, 2000, p. 179.

[25] Colbert, 2000, p. 180.

[26] Elio Frattaroli, *Healing the Soul in the Age of the Brain: Becoming Conscious in an Unconscious World* (New York: Viking, 2001) p. 92.

[27] Elliot S. Valenstein, *Blaming The Brain: The Truth About Drugs And Mental Health* (New York: The Free Press, 1998) pp. 126-128.

[28] Valenstein, p. 139.

[29] Charles L. Whitfield, M.D., *The Truth About Mental Illness: Choices For Healing* (Deerfield Beach: Health Communications, Inc., 2004) p. 200.

[30] Frank and Catherine Cahill-Fabiano, *Healing The Past, Releasing Your Future* (Kent: Sovereign World Ltd., 2003) p. 79.

[31] Whitfield, pp. 199-214.

[32] Whitfield, pp. 199-200.

[33] Whitfield, p. 203.

[34] Whitfield, p. 206.

[35] Dieter Mulitze, Chapter 5, "Healing The Whole Person: Understanding The Heart-Mind-Connection," *The Great Substitution: Human Effort or Jesus to Heal and Restore the Soul?* (Belleville: Essence Publishers, 2003) pp. 141-167.

[36] Whitfield, p. 3.

[37] Whitfield, p. 8.

[38] Colin A. Ross, *The Trauma Model: A Solution To The Problem of Comorbidity In Psychiatry* (Richardson: Gateway Communications, Inc., 2000).

[39] Ed T. Welch, *Blame It on the Brain? Distinguishing Chemical Imbalances, Brain Disorders, and Disobedience* (Phillipsburg: P&R Publishing, 1998) p. 47.

[40] Fabiano, p. 133.

[41] Ibid.

[42] Seth Farber, *Madness, Heresy, and the Rumor of Angels* (Chicago: Open Court, 1993) p. 90.

[43] Farber, p. 75.

[44] Colbert, 2000, p. 71.

[45] Colbert, 2000, p. 145.

[46] Peter R. Breggin and D. Cohen, *Your Drug May Be Your Problem: How and Why to Stop Taking Psychiatric Drugs* (Cambridge: Perseus Publishing, 1999) p. 41.

[47] Joseph Glenmullen, *Prozac Backlash. Overcoming the Dangers of Prozac, Zoloft, Paxil, and Other Antidepressants with Safe, Effective Alternatives* (New York: Simon & Schuster, 2000) pp. 84-85.

[48] Colbert, 2000, p. 153.

[49] Colbert, 2000, pp. 149-153.

[50] Colbert, 2000, p. 160.

[51] Peter R. Breggin, *The Antidepressant Fact Book: What Your Doctor Won't Tell You About Prozac, Zoloft, Paxil, and Luvox* (Cambridge: Perseus Publishing, 2001) pp. 9,17,25.

[52] Frattaroli, pp. 110-113.

[53] Ty C. Colbert, *Depression and Mania: Friends or Foes? A New "Non-Drug" Model of Hope for Depression, Mania, and Compulsive Disorders* (Santa Ana: Kevco) p. 60.

[54] Colbert, 1995, pp. 59-114.

[55] Glenmullen, p. 213.

 Chapter Eight

Psychiatric Labels: Science or Invention?

Why are you downcast, O my soul? Why so disturbed within me? (Ps. 42:5,11;43:5).

Because of this I will weep and wail; I will go about barefoot and naked. I will howl like a jackal and moan like an owl (Micah 1:8).

Paulette and Bipolar Disorder

Paulette came for healing prayer. She was hesitant to share her needs, and it took a while to develop a comfort level with the healing prayer team. I could sense she was reluctant to tell us something. She first shared about many years of sadness and deep inner pain and of not being understood in her church or by many of her friends. She eventually sought counsel from her pastor, who concluded that she was probably mentally ill, and thus he referred her to a psychiatrist. The psychiatrist, she told me, diagnosed her as bipolar disorder I—basically someone with serious ongoing depression. She said she never liked that label and found it hard to live with that diagnosis, as if it was her new identity. Further, the psychiatrist stated that this would be her lifelong diagnosis and therefore she would need psychiatric treatment with medication for the rest of her life. I asked her how she felt about that, and she replied that it felt like a "sentence for life," with little room for hope.

Should We Take Psychiatric Diagnoses Seriously?

Should Paulette, and many others like her, simply accept psychiatric labels and live under them? What does it really mean to be diagnosed with schizophrenia, bipolar spectrum disorder, dissociative disorder, hypoactive sexual desire disorder, avoidant personality disorder, mathematics disorder, or attention deficit disorder, to name just a very few? Should Christians simply accept these diagnoses at face value? Are these diagnoses valid and scientific? Where did they come from?

A lady once contacted me about healing prayer for her bulimic teenage daughter. She asked me if I had had any experience in praying for people with such a problem. I replied that up until that point, I hadn't. I explained that the diagnosis of bulimia is a recent type of diagnosis and what is really at stake are issues of the soul and heart unique to her daughter's life. Her response was that, nevertheless, having experience in praying for that specific diagnosis was important. She never did come with her daughter for healing prayer. The modern diagnosis had become the all-important consideration for her. Was she right?

Psychiatric labels are hard to assess biblically since they appear so foreign to anything found in the Scriptures. The psalms talk of one's soul being downcast (Ps. 42:5-6;43:5), in anguish (Ps. 31:7), weary with sorrow (Ps. 119:28); sorrow in one's heart (Ps. 13:2); one's soul and body in grief (Ps. 31:9); one's heart grieved and one's spirit embittered (Ps. 73:21); having a wounded heart (Ps. 109:22), a broken heart (Ps. 147:3), a crushed spirit (Ps. 34:18); and so forth. But that's still far removed from modern psychiatry with its own technical world and terminology—or "shrink rap." Are Christians at a disadvantage because the Bible only uses "common terms" like *fear, anxiety, sorrow, madness, confusion of mind,* or *sadness*? To begin to understand this, we need a short history of psychiatry.

The Chameleon Complex of Psychiatry

You might be tempted to think that psychiatry always involved psychiatric drugs, given modern psychiatry's fixation with drug therapy. This was not always the case. Actually, there was a time when if you suggested that people needed drugs for their "mental illnesses," you would be considered strange and out of touch with reality. How times have changed!

The responsibility for the mentally ill originally belonged to the Church for centuries but was transferred to the state by the early 1700s.[1] State-run insane asylums, often with quite inhumane treatment of people, were staffed mostly by secular physicians. The Church expressed little interest in severely disturbed people unless they were possibly oppressed by demons.[2] It was then up to the secular world to care for the mentally ill or insane.

In the early 1800s, some researchers rejected the view that mental illness was caused by moral or supernatural causes in favour of brain diseases as the cause.[3] The first diagnostic classification of mental illnesses for people in insane asylums was compiled in 1838.[4] Researchers believed that a *whole person* had a disorder. So a whole person was, for example, declared insane. The new view of Esquirol, that a person could be only *"partly insane,"* implying that overall a person was normal but in at least one area of behavior had a "mania", was gradually accepted. This was a most crucial development, creating the "cornerstone" of the modern concept of depression where a disorder was no longer a disorder of the entire person.[5] This opened the door to many more categories and classifications, with the result that almost any symptom or behaviour could, in theory, become a disorder or "monomania," as it was then known. Hence pyromania (fear of fire), nymphomania (inordinately strong sexual desires and behaviour), and kleptomania (compulsion to steal), for example, soon appeared as disorders.

Debates went back and forth among researchers to refine categories of emotional suffering. But, as even the Greeks and Romans observed, not everyone fit into the classifications, especially people showing *both* melancholia ("lows") and mania ("highs"). To account for such people, between 1851 and 1854 Jean-Pierre Falret published on *folie circulaire* (circular madness, or folly) while Jules Baillarger proposed *folie à double forme* (a form of double madness or folly). The novel idea was that a person could cycle systematically from one pole (mania or melancholic mood) to the other, but yet be otherwise normal. That was later renamed as manic-depressive illness (psychosis) or bipolar affective disorder.[6] A milder form of this is known today as "mood swings."

Psychiatrists believed that malfunctioning brains caused mental illness. Thus, a psychiatric disorder was evidence of a disordered brain. Brain pathology and neuropsychiatry dominated the treatment of mental illness in the nineteenth century.[7] But major changes in psychiatry were afoot.

A new psychiatry, called "dynamic psychiatry," eventually arose. Like a chameleon changing colour, psychiatry went from a neurological approach to a psychoanalytical approach. A major figure was Freud, who linked neurotic behaviour with normal behaviour and blurred the boundaries between them, while still acknowledging psychotic behaviour.[8] The categories of neurotic behaviour were expanded. Dynamic psychiatry took into account a person's whole life, especially childhood issues, trauma, dreams, memories, and the like. More behaviours were then in the realm of psychiatry and involved patients outside of the asylums. Whereas it was earlier believed that symptoms were direct indicators of brain diseases, dynamic psychiatry understood symptoms as *communication*.[9] In that understanding of psychiatry, " ... symptoms were never *direct indicators* of underlying disorders; instead they were *symbolic expressions* of conflicts that involved the entire personality."[10] The focus then was on decidedly personal and relational issues and their seemingly unique manifestation for each person through symptoms that needed to be understood. But the symptoms were only a means to an end, a form of communication.

Minimal attention was given to the symptoms themselves, since people's types of communication are unique and varying; there are many different ways of communicating; and some ways could mask or confuse deeper issues. The goal was to inquire deeper into a person's life, to analyze one's personality, beliefs, and experiences. People had to disclose their inner thoughts, feelings, memories, and emotions—all of which took time. Dynamic psychiatry assumed that basic human emotions and behaviours were on a continuum with mental disorders, neuroses, and abnormal behaviour—it was just a matter of degree.[11] The primary focus was *disordered relationships instead of disordered brains*. In time, the scope and "clientele" of psychiatry went from mostly asylum patients to those outside of asylums facing everyday distressing problems.

Separation Anxiety and Identity Disorder of Psychiatry

Dynamic psychiatry was the dominant thinking behind mental disorders until the 1970s.[12] But then the chameleon complex struck, with diagnostic psychiatry once again dominating and a return to *disordered or diseased brains*. Psychiatric diagnoses went from being not very significant to being central and very crucial.

Allan Horwitz is a professor in the Department of Sociology and the Institute for Health, Health Care Policy, and Aging Research at Rutgers University. In his book, *Creating Mental Illness*, he wrote that when contrasted with the dynamic model of psychiatry "… diagnostic psychiatry defines diseases through the presence of overt symptoms, regardless of the causes of these symptoms. It regards diseases as natural entities that exist in the body and that generate the particular symptoms a person displays… The diagnostic model also seeks the primary causes of disorder in disturbed brains rather than in dysfunctional childhoods… "[13] Under the diagnostic model of psychiatry, therefore, a person's therapy or "treatment" no longer involves an understanding of the issues of heart and soul, or one's emotional woundedness, but rather the most direct recourse to medication. The goal becomes symptom management instead of healing.

What activated the chameleon complex once again? A major factor was that modern medicine was becoming increasingly scientific. Medical diagnoses use observable and fairly consistent symptoms to identify diseases, which are often treated with drugs. Case histories were de-emphasized in favor of experiments, more rigorous clinical trials, and medical research with statistical analyses.

In the face of these developments, "psychiatry would have to do likewise to maintain its credibility and authority and very existence."[14] Neurologists had accused psychiatrists of being "unscientific" in the battle over the right to treat the mentally ill.[15] Psychiatry had to emulate the modern medical paradigm of diagnoses, diseases, and the treatment thereof. From the 1800s onwards, a priority of many psychiatrists was to turn their discipline into a truly scientific enterprise, like the "hard sciences" of the biomedical world.[16]

Psychiatrists were facing increasing competition for clients from non-physicians, who could be just as effective in alleviating emotional suffering. Who really needs a medical doctor if one's pain stems from childhood trauma or the stress of divorce? But if supposed mental illnesses really do come from diseases and really do require expert diagnoses and drugs, then you really need a psychiatrist.

Psychiatrists thus needed to make their specialty a part of modern, scientific medicine in order to uphold their "professional legitimacy" and pre-empt competition.[17,18] But dynamic psychiatry claimed that mental illnesses were continuous rather than discrete, that symptoms were symbols rather than indicators, that therapy required deep inward reflection, and that it is not primarily an issue of disordered brains or diseases—which were all at odds with the disease model of medicine— had to be abandoned or *psychiatrists would be abandoned by the world.*

To avoid the inevitable feelings of separation anxiety and abandonment from modern science, psychiatry had to conform to modern medicine. Scientific respectability required a biological basis for their specialty.[19] From the 1970s to the 1990s, it was clear that "only a biomedical-oriented psychiatry could advance the prestige and legitimacy of psychiatric practice."[20] Modern psychiatry suffers from an identity disorder that it is attempting to alleviate by utilizing a biomedical paradigm.[21] Modrow, author and former schizophrenic himself, argued in his book, *How to Become a Schizophrenic: The Case Against Biological Psychiatry* that psychiatrists could not keep their identity and professional credibility without claiming that schizophrenia and mental disorders are not real diseases any more than "clergy could retain their identities as representatives of God while adopting atheism as their official creed."[22]

Psychiatry and Botany

Except for the truly organic *indirect* causes, there are no biological causes for emotional and behavioural problems. There are no reliable diagnostic tests to identify them either. It should be no surprise at all that psychiatric diagnoses are for description only. How could it be otherwise? *Psychiatric diagnoses do not attempt to understand the causes.* Psychiatry only "describes" a person's mental disorder, offering *no* explanation.[23,24,25]

The *Diagnostic and Statistical Manual of Mental Disorders, Fourth Edition* (DSM-IV), is *the* authoritative standard text of psychiatry. The manual states that the purpose is to provide diagnostic criteria that are descriptive but "neutral to any theory of cause"[26] and makes no assumptions about any causes.[27]

Imagine waking up one day with strange spots over your body. How helpful would it be if you were diagnosed with "General Spots Disorder"? Or if you felt pain in your neck and your doctor diagnosed you with "Neck Disorder"? In contrast, being diagnosed with diabetes or measles where the cause and development of the disease are known is indeed helpful. Some psychiatrists will attempt to understand a cause, like emotional pain from past wounds, but in the strict sense of psychiatry, uncovering the cause is not an objective.

Medical science, like science in general, requires classification. Psychiatry attempts to appear scientific like other medical specialties by using diagnoses, which are not much more than sophisticated descriptions of what patients already feel and experience. Unlike other medical diagnoses, those of psychiatry are only syndromes with related symptoms – not actually diseases—without any proof of origin or development.[28]

Diagnosis without causation means that many people with quite different causes will simply be lumped together in the same classification.

For example, people diagnosed with clinical depression might be suffering from unresolved issues from rape, or irrational guilt, or an empty spiritual life, or maybe even the effects of racism.[29] Such diagnoses become meaningless and obscure reality. Yet, all those people would be given the same or similar treatment regardless of the real cause(s).

This type of diagnosis is based on a philosophy known as "phenomenology," most notably from the German philosophers Husserl and Jaspers.[30] It is a "descriptive science" where you simply study the phenomenon or "signs," with little thought beyond that.[31] The "phenomenon" or checklist items from invented lists of disorders and syndromes are searched for in a patient, with "subjective and irrational" results.[32]

This all leads to a "mechanical" or operational approach to psychiatry, where symptoms are recorded, patients are classified, and then an algorithm is applied to make a diagnosis.[33] Put simply, psychiatrists diagnose people much like botanists identify flowers—not an exaggeration when you realize that the impulse to classify mental disorders followed the example of the classification of plant species by Linnaeus in the 1720s and the early classification of illnesses.[34]

Combustion Disorder

Imagine that one morning your car is suddenly running "ragged" and occasionally backfiring. Your neighbour and a few other folk notice the abnormal, obviously dysfunctional, behaviour of your car. So, like any normal person with proper expectations, you go to your automotive dealer or local garage to get it fixed.

After you explain the problem to the mechanic, he asks you still more questions about your car's dysfunctional behaviour. He pulls out a clipboard, and from a twenty-one-point checklist for the Tork-Weiler Rating Scale he asks you questions about your car's behaviour. Your anxiety begins to subside as you realize that your problem is being understood and that help is around the corner for your disordered car.

He then takes you to his office, and you take a seat. In fact, there's even a leather couch if you want to really relax. You notice the wall behind his desk, lined with shelves of books on automotive theory, diagnostics, and so forth. You also notice several certificates and diplomas on the wall, all attesting to your mechanic's proven competence. You remain confident in your mechanic's licensing organization, including the car manufacturer. You then rest, sublimely confident that you are in the hands of a true professional.

A few moments later, without even checking under the hood or running a diagnostic test on the car at all, but after consulting his detailed, 900-page desk reference manual on car diagnostics, he declares that your car is suffering from "Combustion Disorder." He then gives you an invoice for the half-hour consultation plus a prescription for ten liters of a fuel additive and instructs you to add a quarter liter in the morning and the same amount no later than eight each evening. He warns you that a side effect might be yellow exhaust and fluctuation in oil pressure but encourages you not to be overly concerned. He then directs you to the receptionist, who will book a return appointment for you to see about adjusting the amount of the additive or using a different additive or maybe even another fuel additive "on the side."

What would you think? Is that helpful? Most people would be appalled at such a mechanic. Why should anyone expect less for their own soul than for their car?

Into the Pigeonholes

What happens in practice when psychiatrists apply the labels and classify people? How consistently and correctly do people, with all their emotional pain, fit into the slots or "pigeonholes" created by psychiatry? Does the "system" work?

In one study published in 1971, psychiatrists from two countries viewed a tape of a patient being interviewed. About 69 percent of American psychiatrists diagnosed the patient as schizophrenic, whereas only 2 percent of the British psychiatrists did so.[35] Isn't it alarming to know that you could have a 3,500 percent higher chance of being diagnosed as a schizophrenic simply because you live in the U.S.? The DSM-IV has been revised to help correct this, but it shows that *psychiatric labeling is not an exact science.* The DSM-IV has "atypical" behaviours, "subtypes," and the loose, nebulous category of "other behaviours or effects not elsewhere specified." This reveals the difficulty of classification, and even the authoritative DSM-IV itself acknowledges that the boundaries for mental disorders won't cover all situations; not all people fit into boundaries the same way; and *the correct classification of people is a probability.*[36] This is the "imprecise and inaccurate pseudoscience of labeling."[37]

People cannot always be reliably fit into a pigeonhole created by psychiatry. So why not increase the number of pigeonholes? Predictably, this is just around the corner with bipolar disorder I and II, for example. Bipolar affective disorder was some time ago expanded to bipolar I and bipolar II. Psychiatrists have long known the difficulty of diagnosing people with this disorder, and now the evolving spectrum of bipolar disorders includes bipolar 1/2, bipolar I, bipolar I 1/2, bipolar II, bipolar II 1/2, bipolar III, bipolar III 1/2, and Bipolar IV, depending upon the presence, duration, and intensity of hypomania, cyclothymia, and hyperthymia with depressive episodes.[38] The growing number of these disorders demonstrates their limitations when describing human behaviour.

Consistent and meaningful classification requires that disorders are clearly distinguishable, but, "the most common forms of nonpsychotic disorders—depression, anxiety, phobias, obsession and compulsion, panic disorders, somatization, and so forth—are difficult to distinguish."[39] Furthermore, disorders often appear together (comorbidity), like depression and anxiety, which weakens the classification system.[40] Worse still, the diagnoses of many patients change over time, and of course the past diagnoses are then called "incorrect," and sometimes the diagnoses are actually changed to justify the prescription of another drug.[41,42] Does the change in diagnoses over time then mean that the supposed disease changes over time as well? It is like being diagnosed with cancer, then arthritis, then hypertension, while the cancer disappeared, and then diabetes, which will disappear in a few years. For these reasons alone, when the system of classification is applied consistently, it does not work for psychiatric inpatients.[43]

186

Different causes in a person's life could lead to similar symptoms. Or similar causes could lead to different symptoms. Or symptoms could change quite substantially from the same cause(s) over a person's lifetime. This is simply because each person's story is unique and people have different ways of expressing their inner pain and woundedness.

"Empty, Hollow, and Thud"

Perhaps the most alarming example of simplistic and biased diagnosing of people is the Rosenhan study.[44] In the mid 1970s, Rosenhan, a professor at Stanford University, and seven other pseudo-patients, who were professionals and quite normal people with no history of hospitalization, went to twelve different psychiatric hospitals to observe what happens there. To get admitted, they called up for an appointment, and when interviewed by psychiatrists at the psychiatric hospitals, they complained about hearing voices saying "empty," or "hollow," or "thud." On purpose, they pretended to have existential symptoms, since there was not a single report of existential psychosis in the literature; thus, there should be no basis for admission. Nevertheless, on the basis of only that "symptom," they were diagnosed as schizophrenic. Except for falsifying their names and occupations, they told the truths about their lives and, upon admittance, behaved totally normal.

They were hospitalized from seven to fifty-two days before release. While they took many notes on what happened in the hospitals, the other patients perceived them as being normal or even "plants." But none of the staff did. They ascribed the note taking directly to the patients' mental illness and even fit past facts of the patients to support their diagnosis of schizophrenia.[45] Worse still, the patients were all discharged as "schizophrenics in remission" and thus judged still mentally ill with a possibility of recurrence of schizophrenia.[46] This was one of a number of studies that showed that "there is nothing scientific about psychiatric diagnosis."[47]

But the story doesn't end there. Rosehan later approached a prestigious American teaching hospital and informed the staff that within ninety days a pseudo-patient would attempt to gain admittance to the psychiatric unit.[48] About 193 patients were admitted, and in forty-one of those admissions at least one staff involved alleged that the patient was in fact an imposter.

There was only one tiny problem: Rosenhan never sent any pseudo-patients at all. The obvious point was proven again— psychiatric diagnoses can often reflect what mental health professionals *want to see*, not reality, thus further undermining the credibility of such diagnoses. When the hospital did not expect imposters, many imposters were allowed in. When the hospital did expect imposters, many people were judged as imposters when in fact they were not. Rosenhan's second study is an example of extremely low-budget and innovative research.

You can't fit a round peg into a square hole. This is certainly true when psychiatry attempts to fit people into its artificial slots or pigeon-holes.

Prescription Tunnel Vision

A major purpose of psychiatric labels is diagnosis for the *prescription of a psychiatric drug*. This becomes *description leading to prescription, with little attempt to truly understand people and their lives*. The diagnoses are inherently biased towards drugs and pharmaceutical companies. At times one can actually deduce which psychiatrist is treating a patient by looking at the prescribed drugs, irregardless of the patient's mental problems.[49] PRIME-MD (Primary Care Evaluation Mental Disorders) is supposed to enable family doctors to diagnose 90 percent of all psychiatric complaints in less than 8.5 minutes.[50] This is even more alarming since about 80 percent of prescriptions for antidepressants are prescribed by primary care physicians.[51]

Imagine a woman found attempting suicide because, in fact, she had been raped years ago and had never been healed from the trauma. Now she is diagnosed as clinically depressed with suicidal ideation. Just giving her an antidepressant is not much different from "treating" someone with abdominal pain by giving him or her morphine, which would just mask the signs of a bursting appendix.[52]

188

This reminds me of a cartoon where a man is sitting in front of a computer and there is something on the computer monitor that he either does not like or is incorrect. So what does he do? He reaches for some whiteout and applies it to the screen.

So when you seek help from a psychiatrist and you leave the office not understanding any more than when you came in, except for a "label" and possibly a prescription, don't be surprised.

Masochistic Personality Disorder and More

Politics is a larger driving force than science behind the development of psychiatric labels. For example, it was politics that made the American Psychiatric Association in 1973 remove homosexuality as an official psychiatric illness or disease from the DSM.[53,54,55] That development began from the efforts of a gay activist group.[56] In case you are wondering, the exact vote was 5,854 for removal and 3,810 against.[57] However, a homosexual who does not like being homosexual is still considered to have the disease of homosexuality.[58]

Masochistic personality disorder was once proposed as a new disorder—in spite of no real evidence—to classify women who supposedly actually enjoyed suffering and wanted to be battered.[59] It was even proposed that women who denied having this disorder would be classified as "unconscious masochists."[60] It was later called self-defeating personality disorder, originating from three psychiatrists who invented the label while on a fishing trip and after one short study had it included in DSM-III-R.[61] Self-defeating personality disorder was later removed from DSM-IV by pressure from feminists.

Vietnam war veterans, not being able to collect on insurance claims, lobbied for "post-traumatic stress disorder."[62] Narcissistic personality disorder (self-centred people who often take advantage of others) was a DSM diagnosis until 1968, then removed, and later reinstated by a vote in 1980.[63] If one takes the DSM seriously, this means that this disorder suddenly disappeared from the U.S. for fourteen years, and since 1980 there are people who suddenly have the disorder again.

Imagine a group of medical doctors holding a meeting and deciding to vote cancer out of existence. Who would take them seriously? The rest of the medical community would probably laugh at them. And yet we are to believe that psychiatric diagnoses are really illnesses and diseases?

Paraphilic coercive disorder was proposed as a mental illness for those who attempt rape, or fantasize about it, or have sexual arousal or desires with it during a period of at least six months.[64] Apparently if that was true for someone for only five and a half months, the mental illness did not exist. Fortunately, the proposed mental disorder was defeated on the grounds that it would turn criminal acts against women into a disease.

Walker is a neuropsychiatrist and director of the Southern California Neuropsychiatric Institute. He summarized the critique of many professionals concerning the influential DSM in his book, A Dose Of Sanity by stating that psychiatric labels in the DSM originate far more from politics and panels of psychiatrists voting at meetings than anything to do with science or medicine.[65]

Horwtiz wrote similarly that "... the revolution in psychiatric classification in the DSM-III was not the result of any new scientific findings. Instead, political, social, and economic considerations led to the new classifications."[66] This again questions the supposed scientific basis of the DSM to the present day, and therefore the labels, diagnoses, methodology – indeed the entire profession – since so much rests upon this "Bible" of psychiatry.

Gary Almy is a Christian associate professor of clinical psychiatry at the Loyola University School of Medicine and associate chief of the medical staff at an Illinois hospital. He argues that psychiatric diagnoses based on subjectively experienced symptoms have "no scientific foundation or validity."[67] Furthermore, the disorders and syndromes have "no known cause, no predictable course of illnesses, no specific and reliable treatment, and no reliable response to treatment."[68]

Not only is the DSM not based on much scientific research, but worse still, when there is applicable research it has sometimes been either distorted or intentionally ignored for political and other reasons in the ongoing revisions of the DSM.[69]

Power and Money

The proliferation of labels partly reflects the desire of psychiatry for more power and prestige by defining and claiming even more phenomena as falling within its scope.[70] Psychiatry attempts to re-define human suffering and human problems as mental illnesses in order to claim *more patients and thus more revenue* from the treatments.[71]

Not so long ago, there were mostly mental illnesses; then there were mainly "disorders"; and now suddenly there are also "disabilities." There are so many psychiatric diagnoses today that almost everyone could be determined as "mentally ill."[72] This is not far-fetched—the later inclusion of "adjustment disorder" and even "unspecified adjustment disorder" means that the DSM-IV now could include almost any human behavioural and emotional problem.[73]

The DSM-I manual had 106 mental disorders; the DSM-IV now has, fifteen years later, almost 400 more than the DSM-II.[74] Is it really possible that 194 actual disorders or mental illnesses have suddenly appeared in fifteen years? Are we to really believe that on average one disorder appeared *every month for those fifteen years* and was adequately researched for its scientific basis?

The "learning disabilities" category was invented as a new disease and turned into a "growth" industry. Virtually nonexistent in 1965, the number of children diagnosed from 1976 to 1983 with a learning disability—which includes ADHD—in the U.S. went from around 800,000 to 1.8 million.[75]

Obsessive compulsive disorder (OCD) has increased a *thousandfold*, while social phobia, invisible until the 1990s, is now prevalent in epidemic proportions, with Paxil as the common anti-shyness drug.[76] Alarmingly, the thousandfold increase in OCD does not appear to surprise anyone.[77] Psychiatry also has its fads when it seems almost everyone is diagnosed with the latest diagnosis, such as MPD, OCD, and so forth.[78]

Clinicians and psychiatrists want to keep their clients, so it should be no surprise that the DSM included many billable conditions for many people. In fact, the very grounds "for inclusion of the conditions found in the DSM-II, and perpetuated in the DSM-III-R and DSM-IV, did not stem from either theory or research but from the need to maintain the existing clientele of mental health professionals."[79] The DSM-III was successful because it fulfilled the needs of insurance companies, pharmaceuticals, and regulators.[80] (But did it fulfill the needs of people with emotional wounds?) With the rise of government-funded health care and private health insurance, clinicians often needed diagnostic categories to obtain reimbursement for their services; thus "insurance forms, not the nature of symptoms, demand precise diagnoses."[81]

Psychiatrists in the U.S., on average, can make about $300,000 USD per year if they simply diagnose based on symptoms and then prescribe psychiatric medication. If they decide to minimize drug prescriptions and spend more time listening to people and understanding their pain, they will make only about $100,000 USD annually.[82] Typical fees per session for a psychiatrist in the U.S. in 1997 were from $100 to $175 USD.[83] Psychiatrists can charge as much as $250 U.S. for a fifteen-minute consultation to assess a patient's condition and possibly adjust medication.[84] Faced with this temptation, guess what happens most of the time?

Psychiatric hospitals can generate a considerable amount of revenue. In 1996, for example, a two-week stay in a private, nonprofit university-affiliated hospital in the New York City area would cost $23,100 USD just for the bed rate, at $1,650 per day.[85] The patient could easily be billed an additional $8,900 for say, ten ECT (electroshock therapy) treatments at $500 each and $1,500 for one MRI brain scan, for a total of $32,000, or $2,290 per day.[86] A longer hospital stay can cost $40,000 U.S. per month.[87] At least one for-profit psychiatric hospital in the U.S. actually decided to put their director of adult services on a quota system, which required the admission of a certain number of patients each month.[88] More admissions means more money.

Sometimes treatment plans are determined or influenced by the funding source rather than the real needs of the patient.[89] Therapists or clinics that advocate long-term psychotherapy too frequently can lose their contract with the insurance companies.[90] In the U.S. most insurance companies will only pay for drug treatment and limited psychotherapy instead of long-term psychotherapy, a trend determined simply by cost.[91] It is not uncommon for patients to be intentionally misdiagnosed or overdiagnosed—making the patient's diagnosis worse than the condition really is—in order to claim more billable services for a longer treatment plan.[92]

Clinical trials to test drugs for pharmaceuticals has become a lucrative business. In 1997, the average earnings for a community physician experienced at running clinical trials was $331,500.[93] For clinical trials with antipsychotics, a researcher could receive from $10,000 to $25,000 for *each* schizophrenic who volunteered for the trial.[94] Drug companies spend approximately $10,000 U.S. on each physician each year merely on education.[95] Mental illness is big business.

Labels end up claiming patients. For example, if Sally or Fred has a "clinical depression," it's assumed she or he must go to a clinic and be treated by a clinician or a psychiatrist. But what if Sally or Fred is having a "spiritual crisis"—would she or he not want to see a pastor or elder or someone gifted in healing prayer instead?

Every Problem Is a Psychiatric Problem?

With the number of psychiatric diagnoses increasing in order to increase psychiatry's influence, power, and wealth, almost every problem in life becomes a medical problem. When I was a theology student, I used to pull out the hairs of my rather sparse beard, which I have since shaved off. I did not realize at the time that I was suffering from a mental illness known as trichotillomania.

Psychiatric diagnoses for almost every area of life come with a billing code in the DSM-IV manual that psychiatrists can use for insurance or health care claims. People who write with grammatical and punctuation errors and incorrect paragraph organization may well be suffering from written expression disorder (315.2). Just a small sampling of billable mental disorders now includes the following:

coffee nerves (305.90), bad coffee nerves (292.89), shyness or Asperger's disorder (292.80), snobbery (301.7, subset of anti-social personality disorder), clumsiness (315.4), playing video games (362.2, part of malingering), histrionic personality disorder (301.50, need to be "life of the party," centre of attention), clumsiness (315.4), going cold turkey from tobacco smoking (292.0), snoring (780.59), and jet lag (307.45).

Selective mutism (313.23) is a mental illness in which someone hides information for at least one month, like a wife not telling her husband that she is going on private shopping trips.[96,97] Body dysmorphic disorder (300.7) occurs whenever a person is preoccupied with a defect in their appearance so that it causes a significant problem(s) in life. So, a woman bothered by the size of her breasts such that it leads to marital unhappiness or a man depressed about his long nose or baldness and a fear of remaining single all suffer from this mental illness. Dissociative fugue (300.13) occurs whenever someone, for example, suddenly leaves home and embarks on a journey, often after experiencing stress, for maybe hours or days.[98] People who feel a strong need to be taken care of, are afraid of separation, and show some desperation may well be suffering from a mental illness called dependent personality disorder.[99] People who cannot do mathematics as well as expected in their class or culture suffer from mathematics disorder (315.1).[100] Why not, by the way, art disorder, or history disorder, or interior design disorder, or quantum physics disorder, or music disorder?

Impulse control disorders have singled out hair pulling (trichotillomania), shoplifting (kleptomania), setting fires (pyromania), and gambling. Why not "vehicular speeding disorder, fast food over-consumption disorder, credit card over-utilization disorder, tattoo over-utilization disorder, or migratory bird excessive killing disorder"?[101]

Should you, the reader, have a "psychiatric problem" as determined by a psychiatrist or mental health professional and you disagree and refuse the treatment, you are thereby suffering from noncompliance with treatment disorder (15.18) This is no joke—if you don't believe me, look it up in the DSM-IV.

Effectively, almost all of life's problems become medical problems. Not only have more disorders and categories been added, but the boundaries of many have been lowered or extended to increase market share. Personality disorders tend to be just the exaggeration of normal character traits (angry, disagreeable, argumentative, selfish, deceptive, etc.) which then gives "patient status" to people, since they present trouble to others and their behaviour is thereby pathologized.[102]

Then there's the "not otherwise specified" category for many disorders. For example, anxiety disorder not otherwise specified (300.00) could include things like the fear of offensive body odour that causes you to avoid social contact.[103] (Don't "sweat it" if you have that concern!) "Lowering the threshold" of psychiatric diagnoses increases the "patient base" and often turns unhappiness into a disease.[104]

Even the very name given to a disorder or disability is chosen to make it more acceptable or marketable. Imagine meeting with your school counsellor and being told that your precious child has minimal brain dysfunction. How does that sound? Would you accept the diagnosis and the drugs? Not so readily, I expect. But if precisely the same condition is now called ADHD, would that be more acceptable, less onerous? Actually, ADHD went through over twenty-five name changes, including "restlessness syndrome," "brain-injured child," and "hyperkinetic reaction of childhood."[105]

Similarly, psychiatrists were increasingly concerned about the negative connotations with the term *neurotic depression*, widely used as a diagnosis that generated a lot of revenue. But revenue was going down. They therefore renamed this with the more clinical and socially acceptable term *dysthymia*, which was also moved from the personality axis in the DSM-III to the disease axis.[106] It's all in the "packaging."

I once saw a cartoon about a man concerned over the strange behaviour of his pet dog. So, like any responsible dog owner, he took his dog to the local animal psychologist. After analyzing the dog, the psychologist discussed the situation outside the office so the dog could not hear. The psychologist said that the dog was suffering from chronic low-grade depression with derealization and a partial dissociative disorder. And furthermore, the psychologist said, the dog is not able to find his "squeaky toy."

Wedding Night Psychosis and Masturbation Insanity

In order to label something as "abnormal," you need to know what is "normal." Many of the psychiatric diagnoses stem from what psychiatrists consider "unacceptable" or "strange" or "dysfunctional" or "culturally inappropriate." Yet "abnormal" has not yet been adequately defined, and therefore mental illness has not been perfectly defined either.[107]

In 1758, a Swiss physician published a clergyman's idea from 1710 that masturbation caused insanity.[108] The term *masturbation* comes from the Latin *manusturpation* or "defile by hand." As Szasz in *The Manufacture of Madness* wrote, this belief was held by medical authorities from 1800 until the 1930s, in spite of no evidence whatsoever.[109] It was actually believed that people who masturbated would have insane children.

Kraepelin's *Textbook of Psychiatry*, published from 1883 to 1915, included among other mental illnesses "wedding night psychosis" and "masturbation insanity."[110] I wonder, are those two disorders still in the DSM-IV?

A Louisiana physician in 1851 proposed "drapetomina," from *drapetes* (runaway slaves), as a mania of Negro slaves who had an uncontrollable urge to run away from their masters.[111] Dyaesthesia aethiopis was proposed as a mania for Negro slaves who were disrespectful, disobedient, and refused to work.[112] Is this not an example of turning racial tension and discrimination into mental illness?

Suicide and suicidal ideation is deemed a psychiatric problem in the U.S. During WWII, Japanese kamikaze (suicide) pilots flew directly into enemy ships, killing themselves instantly. In their culture, this was a high honour for their country and emperor. Yet there is no record of American kamikaze pilots. Are we to believe, then, that only people with psychiatric illnesses in America could be suicidal, while normal persons in Japan could commit suicide?[113]

What about cultures that regard people who experience paranoia, seizures, and trances as normal? Do they suddenly have a mental illness upon arriving in the U.S.? The Dobuans of Melanesia regard anyone who is always cheerful, happy, and outgoing as crazy.[114] Anorexia is found mostly in the U.S. and determined by American expectations about the ideal female body.[115] Is it even remotely true that some American women have suddenly developed neurotransmitter problems that cause anorexia?

"Normal" seems to be determined by culture, racial discrimination, and many other factors. With no agreement on what is "normal," psychiatry has yet another severe handicap.

The Liability of Labels

Psychiatric labels are harmful when they undermine a person's confidence and effectively become their new identity. Farber wrote about Ellen, who talked about her time in a mental hospital. She experienced a loss of dignity by accepting the diagnosis of manic depressive, which would mean all the benefits of the "sick role," the benefits of dependency, of being defined as helpless, incompetent, and needing to be taken care of.[116] Sadly, many of her friends in the mental hospitals could not cope with the loss of dignity and would commit suicide.[117] Psychiatrists have become, essentially, a "secular priesthood" that makes pronouncements over the lives of people.[118]

Psychiatric labels can distort the perception of both patients and therapists.[119] Once given a label, other therapists or psychiatrists typically see the person the same way and expect to see the symptoms for the supposed condition. The patient often sees him or herself that way, and the label can even become a "self-fulfilling prophecy." Mental health professionals are not immune from falling victim to their expectations and the blunders of categorical thinking.[120]

Conclusion

Psychiatric labels have some value and can help to identify a person's pain and distress. The diagnoses help psychiatrists share research results and communicate in their discipline through a common terminology.

Committed and caring psychiatrists find them useful to a degree. Some people are relieved to get a psychiatric diagnosis, since they feel "understood" or at least they now know what their problem is.

But the significance and value of psychiatric labels is diminished by being descriptive only, without a cause; not truly scientific, including dubious categories; not a "good fit for everyone"; subject to error; and not always correctly applied. The attempt to reduce life's mysteries and complexities to a label is intensely problematic. Terry Lynch concluded that "the process by which doctors diagnose 'mental illness' is fundamentally flawed."[121] Christians should not blindly accept these labels given their serious limitations.

When faced with psychiatric labels that seem so remote and alien from the Scriptures, many Christians feel at a loss in understanding and responding to psychiatry. Many feel compelled to "surrender." That would be a grave mistake. The biblical terms and descriptions of human emotional suffering are in no way inferior to those of psychiatry. Psalm 42, for example, is incredibly insightful concerning depression, and there are no less than forty-eight psalms that speak to grief, despair, and melancholy.[122]

The diagnoses of psychiatry should be questioned. Should we not be alarmed when normal human sadness and sorrow of previous generations suddenly become a depressive disorder of almost epidemic proportions?[123] Should we not be almost shocked when shyness or "social anxiety" becomes a pathology or a mental illness?[124] Should we not "ask the hard questions" when an entire nation is medicating unhappiness at an increasing rate?[125] Since more than science is involved in these labels, one should ask what assumptions, values, and motivations are behind them. The significance and relevance of the Word of God is in no way diminished because of an absence of such terminology in the Scriptures.

Given the involvement of politics and other questionable motives in inventing psychiatric labels, it is no small wonder that Jesus himself will one day expose the motives of men's hearts (1 Cor. 4:5, cf. Proverbs 16:2).

Endnotes _____

[1] Dan Blazer, *Freud vs. God: How Psychiatry Lost Its Soul & Christianity Lost Its Mind* (Downers Grove: InterVarsity Press, 1998) pp. 59-62.

[2] Blazer, p. 60.

[3] Blazer, p. 61.

[4] David Healy, *The Antidepressant Era* (Cambridge: Harvard University Press, 1997) p. 33.

[5] Ibid.

[6] Healy, p. 35.

[7] Blazer, p. 62.

[8] Allan V. Horwitz, *Creating Mental Illness* (Chicago: The University of Chicago Press, 2002) pp. 40-41.

[9] Horwitz, pp. 43-45.

[10] Horwitz, pp. 44-45.

[11] Horwitz, p. 51.

[12] Horwitz, p. 53.

[13] Horwitz, pp. 57-58.

[14] Horwitz, p. 58.

[15] Elliot S. Valenstein, *Great and Desperate Cures: The Rise and Decline of Psychosurgery and Other Radical Treatments for Mental Illness* (New York: Basic Books, 1986) p. 5.

[16] Roy Porter, *Madness: A Brief History* (Oxford: Oxford University Press, 2002) p. 183.

[17] Horwitz, p. 59.

[18] Stuart A. Kirk and Herb Kutchins, *The Selling of DSM: The Rhetoric of Science in Psychiatry* (New York: Aline De Gruyter, 1992) p. 10.

[19] Seth Farber, *Madness, Heresy, and the Rumor of Angels* (Chicago: Open Court, 1993) p. 144.

[20] Horwitz, p. 60.

[21] Colin A. Ross and Alvin Pam, *Pseudoscience in Biological Psychiatry: Blaming The Body* (New York: John Wiley & Sons, Inc., 1995) p. 86.

[22] John Modrow, *How To Become A Schizophrenic: The Case Against Biological Psychiatry* (Everett: Apollyon Press, 2nd ed., 1992) p. 221.

23 John Wilkinson, *The Bible and Healing: A Medical and Theological Commentary* (Grand Rapids: Eerdmans, 1998) p. 23.

24 Ed T. Welch, *Blame It on the Brain? Distinguishing Chemical Imbalances, Brain Disorders, and Disobedience* (Phillipsburg: P&R Publishing, 1998) pp. 12-14.

25 Gary L. Almy, *How Christian Is Christian Counseling? The Dangerous Influences That Keep Us from Caring for Souls* (Wheaton: Crossway Books, 2000) pp. 287-294.

26 A. Frances, H.A. Pincus, and M.B. First, *American Psychiatric Association: Diagnostic and Statistical Manual of Mental Disorders. Fourth Edition, Text Revision* (Washington, DC: APA, 2000) p. xxvi.

27 James Morrison, *DSM-IV Made Easy: The Clinician's Guide To Diagnosis* (New York: The Guilford Press, 1995) p. 8.

28 Joseph Glenmullen, *Prozac Backlash: Overcoming the Dangers of Prozac, Zoloft, Paxil, and Other Antidepressants with Safe, Effective Alternatives* (New York: Simon & Schuster, 2000) p. 193.

29 Peter R. Breggin, *The Antidepressant Fact Book: What Your Doctor Won't Tell You About Prozac, Zoloft, Paxil, and Luvox* (Cambridge: Perseus Publishing, 2001) p. 20.

30 Karl Stern, *The Third Revolution: A Study of Psychiatry and Religion* (New York: Harcourt, Brace and Company, 1954) p. 46.

31 Ibid.

32 Almy, p. 293.

33 Blazer, p. 31.

34 Healy, 1997, p. 33.

35 Elliot S. Valenstein, *Blaming The Brain: The Truth About Drugs And Mental Health* (New York: The Free Press, 1998) p. 157.

36 Frances, pp. xvii-xxi.

37 S. Walker, *A Dose of Sanity. Mind, Medicine, and Misdiagnosis* (New York: John Wiley and Sons, 1996) p. 34.

38 H.S. Akiskal, *Clinical Validation of the Bipolar Spectrum: Focus on Hypomania, Cyclothymia, and Hyperthymia*, 154th Annual Meeting of the American Psychiatric Association, May 5, 2001. http://www.medscape.com/Medscape/CNO/2001/APACME/Story.cfm?story_id=2248.

39 Horwitz, p. 109.

40 Ibid.

[41] Colin A. Ross, *The Trauma Model: A Solution To The Problem of Comorbidity In Psychiatry* (Richardson: Gateway Communications, Inc., 2000) pp. 27-29.

[42] Horwitz, p. 112.

[43] Ross, 2000, p. i.

[44] Robyn M. Dawes, *House of Cards: Psychology and Psychotherapy Built On Myth* (New York: Free Press, 1994) pp. 135-136.

[45] Farber, 1993, p. 124.

[46] Ibid.

[47] Ibid.

[48] Whitaker, p. 170.

[49] Ross, 2000, pp. 5-6.

[50] Valenstein, p. 183.

[51] Ibid.

[52] Elio Frattaroli, M.D., *Healing the Soul in the Age of the Brain: Becoming Conscious in an Unconscious World* (New York: Viking, 2001) pp. 32-33.

[53] J. Satinover, *Homosexuality And The Politics of Truth* (Grand Rapids: Hamewith Books, 1996) pp. 31-40.

[54] Walker, p. 20.

[55] Farber, p. 118.

[56] David Healy, *The Creation of Psychopharmacology* (Cambridge: Harvard University Press, 2002) p. 301.

[57] Paula J. Caplan, *They Say You're Crazy: How The World's Most Powerful Psychiatrists Decide Who's Normal* (Reading: Addison-Wesley Pub. Co., 1995) p. 56.

[58] Farber, p. 118.

[59] Caplan, p. 7.

[60] Ibid.

[61] Walker, p. 21.

[62] Valenstein, p. 162.

[63] Walker, p. 22.

[64] Bruce Wiseman, *Psychiatry—The Ultimate Betrayal* (Los Angeles: Freedom Publishing, 1995) p. 353.

[65] Walker, p. 19.

66 Horwitz, p. 68.

67 Almy, p. 290.

68 Almy, p. 291.

69 Caplan, p. 66.

70 Thomas S. Szasz, *The Myth of Mental Illness: Foundations of a Theory of Personal Conduct* (New York: Harper and Row, 1974) p. 39.

71 Farber, p. 32.

72 Caplan, p. 78.

73 Horwitz, p. 73.

74 Valenstein, p. 160.

75 Seth Farber, *Unholy Madness: The Church's Surrender to Psychiatry* (Downers Grove: InterVarsity Press, 1999) pp. 41-43.

76 Healy, 2002, p. 373.

77 Ibid.

78 Bruce Hamstra, *How Therapists Diagnose. Seeing Through The Psychiatric Eye* (New York: St. Martin's Press, 1994) p. 23.

79 Horwitz, p. 71.

80 Healy, 2002, p. 304.

81 Horwitz, pp. 74-75.

82 Modrow, p. xii.

83 Demitri Papolos and Janice Papolos, *Overcoming Depression* (New York: HarperPerennial, 3rd ed., 1997) p. 257.

84 Ty C. Colbert, *Depression and Mania: Friends or Foes? A New "Non-Drug" Model of Hope for Depression, Mania, and Compulsive Disorders* (Santa Ana: Kevco) p. 57.

85 Papolos, p. 301.

86 Papolos, pp. 301-302.

87 Frattaroli, p. 97.

88 Ty C. Colbert, *Rape of the Soul: How the Medical Imbalance Model of Modern Psychiatry Has Failed its Patients* (Tustin: Krevco Publishing, 2000) p. 179.

89 Hamstra, p. 15.

90 Hamstra, p. 16.

91 Scott Veggeberg, *Medication of the Mind* (New York: Henry Holt and Company, 1996) pp. 120-121.

92 Hamstra, pp. 19, 123,126-135.

93 Whitaker, p. 263.

94 Whitaker, p. 267.

95 Loren R. Mosher, "Are Psychiatrists Betraying Their Patient?" *Psychology Today*, Vol. 32:5, Sept./Oct. 1999.

96 Wiseman, p. 357.

97 Morrison, p. 1995.

98 Morrison, p. 322.

99 Morrison, pp. 463-464.

100 Morrison, p. 507.

101 Ross, 2000, pp. 203-204.

102 Shorter, p. 291.

103 Morrison, pp. 285-286.

104 Shorter, pp. 291-292.

105 Bruce E. Levine, *Commonsense Rebellion: Debunking Psychiatry, Confronting Society* (New York: Continuum Publishing Group Inc., 2001) p. 119.

106 Healy, 2002, p. 303.

107 Morrison, p. 7.

108 Szasz, p. 182.

109 Szasz, pp. 182-184.

110 Valenstein, p. 154.

111 Wiseman, p. 311.

112 Ibid.

113 Lawrence J. Stevens, *Does Mental Illness Exist?* www.antipsychiatry. org. 1995. pg. 4.

114 Horwitz, p. 7.

115 Hamstra, p. 25.

116 Farber, 1993, p. 22.

117 Ibid.

118 Farber, 1993, p. 113.

119 Hamstra, pp. 21-22.

120 Hamstra, p. 22.

121 Terry Lynch, *Beyond Prozac: Healing and Mental Distress* (Douglas Village: Mercier Press, 2005 edition) p. 175.

122 Frank Lake, *Clinical Theology: A Theological and Psychiatric Basis to Clinical Pastoral Care* (London: Darton, Longman & Todd, 1966) pp. 181-187.

123 Allan V. Horwitz and Jerome C. Wakefield, *The Loss of Sadness. How Psychiatry Transformed Normal Sorrow into Depressive Disorder* (New York: Oxford University Press, 2007) pp. 1-52.

124 Christopher Lane, Shyness. *How Normal Behavior Became a Sickness* (New Haven: Yale University Press, 2007).

125 Charles Barber, *Comfortably Numb. How Psychiatry is Medicating a Nation* (New York: Pantheon Books, 2008).

 Chapter Nine

The Demise of the Soul and the Rise of Mental Health

O Lord my God, I pray thee, let this child's soul come into him again. And the Lord heard the voice of Elijah; and the soul of the child came into him again, and he revived (1 Kings 17:21-22, KJV).

He restores my soul. He guides me in paths of righteousness for his name's sake (Ps. 23:3).

Grace: Healed From Acute Aloneness

For all of her life, as long as she could remember, Grace felt a deep "aloneness." This was a very strong feeling, at the "core of her being." This "aloneness" was associated with a deep sense of abandonment. She often told people, including her psychiatrists over the years, that she felt like she was "in a bubble." Because of this bubble she felt protected from the world; no one could get in, and no one could touch her. This is not what she wanted, since she desired, like anyone else, to truly connect with people. The aloneness did not go away even when she was with her friends or other people. Looking back over the years, she began to see how this aloneness and sense of abandonment with related feelings of being unloved was partly responsible for her attempts at suicide over the years. At the age of thirteen, she had overdosed with Actifed and then aspirin. Soon she was put on Haldol, and then for basically the rest of her life she has been on different antipsychotics and antidepressants. But in the midst of all this deep emotional pain, she did not know the root or origin of this aloneness that was in her soul.

After a worship service one Sunday morning, I met her at the front of the church, just to talk, not planning to minister healing prayer. She then happened to tell me that upon birth she was immediately placed in an incubator. She was four pounds and three ounces at the time and born two months premature. She was in the incubator for five weeks. That was in 1961, when parents could not touch their child while the child was in an incubator. It was a sterile existence, separated from Mom and Dad and any emotional bonding or physical touch that would convey love and nurture.

I asked her if she had ever received healing prayer for this, since that would have a major effect upon her life. I explained that upon birth a newborn needs to be held and cuddled, and the all-important bonding with Mother should begin in the first few hours and days of life. To not experience this can be quite traumatic and often has a major impact on one's adult life. She replied that she had never thought about that and had not ever received healing prayer for that part of her life. In fact, she had only recently remembered this, having forgotten about it for many years. I suggested that there was mostly likely a link between the deep sense of aloneness and her time in the incubator as a newborn.

As she was pondering this, she had a strong sense of Jesus' supernatural presence around her. Taking this as Jesus' direction that she was to receive healing prayer, I began to pray with her. I asked the Lord to heal that place in her soul that was affected from the time in the incubator. I prayed with her that Jesus would permanently heal her of that aloneness, as only He could as Lord of time and the One who restores the soul.

Grace first felt a warmth around her physical heart as I was praying that the Lord would fill her heart with the love, affection, and bonding that she missed while in the incubator. Jesus, who is also the Creator and great Physician, alone can do such a "surgery of the heart." Grace said that she also felt something "filling" or "pouring into" her heart while it felt warm, which we understood as the love that she had missed while in the incubator. She also felt Jesus actually holding her, embracing her, while she was in the incubator, and at that point the aloneness seemed to totally disappear. She exclaimed that Jesus was there; He was with her while she was in the incubator—she was not totally alone! In that moment, she felt a heaviness leave her being, as if a weight had been lifted off her. Jesus had taken her burden! She then saw a bright, comforting light come upon her, another manifestation of the supernatural presence of Christ that others have witnessed in healing prayer. Then she opened her eyes at the end of our prayer time. She remarked how everything in the church was noticeably clearer, brighter, and sharper.

Grace's healing, which involved an encounter with the living Christ, was real. The aloneness that she carried in her soul for over forty years is totally gone; she feels like a new person. The "bubble" has disappeared, and she is able to connect with people as God had intended. The Lord accomplished in less than ten minutes of healing prayer what over twenty years of psychotherapy and psychiatry failed to do. This is just another example of how Jesus can restore the soul (Ps. 23:3).

The Banished Soul

Psychiatry's fixation on neurotransmitters, genetics, brain chemistry, and drugs has basically "squished" the soul out of existence. Today's theologians are not comfortable with the concept either, as we shall see. The soul seems "banished" from science and even theology.

The prevailing view is that *soul* is just another way of referring to the whole person with a fully integrated body, mind, and soul (maybe even *spirit,* also!). But if each person *has* a soul, then scientific evidence must be reinterpreted and psychiatry can be challenged even further. If there is a separate, immaterial soul and even a spirit in a person, then the impact and relevance of psychiatric drugs is "squished down."

What is a scriptural view of *soul*? This is a fundamental question, a major "fork in the road" for any understanding on the nature of man.

Did the Lord really restore Grace's soul, or was she healed as a whole person? There is a difference.

From Old Testament times and among prominent Christians since the second century, it was believed that people are a "blended unity" or trichotomy of three components—body, soul, and spirit—which are different yet inseparable while each person is alive.[1] A similar main belief over the centuries was that people are a dichotomy, with only a body and soul, where soul and spirit are apparently used interchangeably in the Scriptures.[2] In both views, the body is believed to be of a different "substance" than soul or spirit, which are immaterial.

Biblical theologians for centuries debated the fine points about the relationship between soul, spirit, mind, heart, conscience, and so forth and whether man's nature or "constitution" is a trichotomy or dichotomy. That was the domain of biblical psychology proper, with its own history and methodology.[3]

Franz Delitzsh (1813-1890), a German Lutheran theologian and Hebraist, author of many commentaries of the Bible, wrote an almost 600-page treatise on the nature of man, entitled *A System of Biblical Psychology*. He defended a tripartite view of man while also exposing false tripartite views of man typically influenced by Greek thought. Spirit and soul are both immaterial, of the same nature, but different, with the spirit as primary and the soul secondary.[4] The soul is the "mediating link of the spirit and body" and "the spirit is the inbreathing of the God-head and the soul is the outbreathing of the spirit."[5]

A recent and now more predominant view among theologians completely denies the dichotomy or trichotomy of man.[6] Most biblical theologians today believe in "monism," that we are all one integrated being—one person, with heart, soul, mind, body, and spirit all rolled into one. One New Testament scholar wrote, "Recent scholarship has recognized that such terms as body, soul, and spirit are not different, separable faculties of man but different ways of viewing the whole man."[7]

Apparently now we are souls, while *body*, *soul*, and *spirit* are deemed just different aspects or ways of understanding people.[8] The centuries-old concept of the soul has been banished and discredited by many Bible scholars since 1925.[9] One main reason for this is the allegation that such views reflect Greek thinking, especially that of Plato.[10] This is evident in the authoritative *New International Dictionary of Old Testament Theology and Exegesis*. The Hebrew word *nephesh* is covered in just one single page, with the warning to not import any Greek thinking into this word, which occurs in over seven hundred times in the Old Testament and "seldom denotes a 'soul' in any full sense."[11]

This "prejudice" against the soul most readily shows up in Bible translations, with the Hebrew word *nephesh* translated as "soul" 533 times in the King James version, 220 in the RSV, 180 in the NRSV, 136 in the NIV, and only 88 times in the Living Bible.[12] The NIV Study Bible's footnote for Psalm 6:3 states that the soul is not a "spiritual aspect" different from the physical nor a reference to a man's "inner being" as opposed to the outer physical being; nor are there two "distinct" entities that constitute man. Rather, *soul* is another way of referring to the whole person.[13]

Were the NIV translators justified in removing the word *soul* all those 397 times—or in three-quarters of the occurrences of *nephesh*? Does Grace have a soul that was healed by Jesus, or was she just healed as a person "overall"?

Does Everyone Have a Soul?

Do people *have* "souls" that are distinct and possibly separate from a person; or *are* people souls, and hence *soul* is just another way of referring to the whole person? When we die and our physical bodies disintegrate in the grave (or are cremated!), what happens to our souls? If the soul is not separate from the body at all, then does the soul disintegrate as well? But if the soul can be separate from the body upon death, then, to be consistent, is not the soul a separable "part" of a person while living?

The Hebrew word *nephesh*, often translated as "soul," does at times refer to the whole person (a part standing for the whole, a *synecdoche*) or one's whole life or sons and daughters (Gen. 46:15,18,22,25,26,27;

Exod. 1:5;12:4,15,19;30:12,15;31:14; Josh. 11:11; 2 Sam. 19:5,6;23:17; 1 Kings 1:12, cf. Acts 2:43).

The original meaning of *nephesh* was probably "to breathe," clearly seen in verses like Genesis 2:7, where the Lord "formed the man from the dust of the ground and breathed into his nostrils the breath of life, and the man became a living being."[14] The KJV ends the verse with "and the man became a living soul." The soul is the vitality of life, the energy given by God. This explains its connection with the body's blood, for without it there is no life, just as when one ceases to breathe there is no life.[15,16]

While animals also have a soul (Gen. 1:21; Lev. 11:10; Job 12:10), man's soul is different, since the use of the Hebrew word *nesama* instead of *ruach* (wind, breath) signifies man alone as receiving the divine breath (cf. Gen. 2:7).[17] But there still is a distinct, separate soul in all people. Only people are created in the image of God (Gen. 1:27).

Two examples from the Old Testament are compelling. In Genesis 35:18-19, when Rachel was into hard labour and giving birth to Benjamin, the KJV reads more literally from the Hebrew "*And it came to pass, as her soul was in departing, (for she died) that she called his name Benoni, but his father called him Benjamin. And Rachel died, and was buried…*" The NIV reads "*As she breathed her last—for she was dying—she named her son Ben-Oni.*" The original text states that the soul parts from the body upon death (cf. Isa. 10:18,38:10).

Elijah's visit with the widow at Zarephath (1 Kings 17:17-22) is another important example. Her son became ill, stopped breathing, and died. The KJV, being more literal from the Hebrew, reads "*O LORD my God, I pray thee, let this child's soul come into him again. And the LORD heard the voice of Elijah; and the soul of the child came into him again, and he revived*" (1 Kings 17:21b-22a). The NIV renders it as "'*O LORD my God, let this boy's life return to him!' The LORD heard Elijah's cry, and the boy's life returned to him, and he lived.*" The NIV translation is correct if you believe only in one integrated, whole being. But the translation obscures evidence for another view on the doctrine of man.

Other verses give additional support for the soul being "within" someone. A person who experiences much adversity could have a soul that mourns within him (Job 14:22, KJV) or mourns for himself (Job 14:22, NIV). One's soul can be downcast (Ps. 42:5) or disturbed *within* oneself (Ps. 43:5). Hunger and dire thirst could cause one's soul to "faint" within oneself (Ps. 107:5, KJV) or one's life to "ebb away" (NIV). Some might argue that these are Hebraisms and figures of speech, but it depends upon your view *before* coming to the biblical text.

In the Gospels, Jesus said "*Do not be afraid of those who kill the body but cannot kill the soul. Rather, be afraid of the One who can destroy both soul and body in hell* (Matt. 10:28)." Jesus made it clear there is a soul at some point apart from the body. The Greek says "both," pointing to two types of existence. "This verse implies a body which is not the same substance as the soul, because the soul is capable of surviving the body after death."[18]

Paul wanted to "*depart and be with Christ, which is better by far; but it is more necessary for you that I remain in the body*" (Phil. 1:23-24). In 2 Corinthians 4:7 he referred to his body as a jar of clay, and echoes the same idea in 2 Corinthians 5:1-6, "*as long as we are at home in the body we are away from the Lord.*" He wrote about the outer nature wasting away and the inner nature being renewed daily (2 Cor. 4:16).

John wrote in Revelation 6:9, "*I saw under the altar the souls of those who had been slain because of the word of God and the testimony they had maintained.*" Although Revelation has a lot of symbolism, this verse can be taken literally. The souls called out in a loud voice, calling for eventual judgment and the avenging of their blood (Rev. 6:10). These were souls without bodies, and yet John saw the souls since his spiritual eyes were opened into the spiritual realm, just like today when people have their spiritual eyes opened and they see angels or demons with a definite, specific form. The souls were active and with emotion, crying out to the Lord (cf. Rev. 20:4). Once again, souls without bodies, yet having an existence. In the resurrection we will have *new* bodies, and we will reign on earth with Christ (Rev. 5:10 and Rev. 21:1).

The Scriptures do present evidence for a dichotomy or possibly a trichotomy of man. As a dichotomy, body and soul exist as an interactive, positive, and complementary dualism so that we are whole and integrated persons in this life, where we do *have* a soul as well as *being* a soul. In contrast to Greek thinking, the physical body is just as important as the soul, since the body is the temple of the Holy Spirit (1 Cor. 6:19), and all believers will have a resurrection body (1 Cor. 15:42-49).

Does Everyone Have a Spirit?

The Scriptures refer to a person's spirit as well as the soul. There is still more evidence that disputes monism and helps decide on dichotomy or trichotomy.

Jesus went to Jairus' house because the man's twelve-year-old daughter was dying (Luke 8:49-56). When Jesus arrived, the daughter was declared dead. It seems the delay in healing the woman who lost a lot of blood closed a window of opportunity for the little girl's healing. Jesus told everyone that she's just sleeping and to have faith, but everyone laughed at Him since they knew the child was dead. But Jesus took her by the hand and told her to get up. Her spirit returned, and at once she stood up (Luke 8:53-54). When the spirit is separate from the body, as the soul can be, the body is also dead and the person is not one "integrated being."

When Jesus died on the cross, He told the criminal who was crucified with Him and asked to be remembered that he would be with Him in paradise that day (Luke 23:43). The criminal's body was bludgeoned, dead, and soon in the grave, yet he was with Jesus in paradise that day. That is only possible if his soul and spirit had a separate existence from the body.

Jesus committed to the Father His spirit, which would be separate from His body while His body lay in the tomb (Luke 23:46; Matt. 27:50; John 19:30). When He appeared, He encouraged people to touch Him since a spirit does not have flesh and bones (Luke 24:39). In that verse, the Greek word is *pneuma,* typically translated "spirit," and not *phantasma,* which is translated "ghost." The NIV translation is incorrect.[19]

When Stephen was being stoned, he looked up to heaven. He saw Jesus and asked Him to receive his spirit since he was about to die (Acts 7:59). Although this passage refers to the spirit and not the soul, it still affirms the idea that our bodies are left behind and we are not integrated at the point of death (cf. Eccl. 12:7).

The Lord as creator forms the spirit of man that is *within* him (Zech. 12:1). It is our spirit within us that knows our thoughts (1 Cor. 2:11). A person's spirit can grow faint within a person (Ps. 143:4). If God takes this created spirit back to himself, everyone would perish (Job 34:14-15). The body without the spirit is dead (Jas. 2:26). The Word of God *"penetrates even to dividing soul and spirit"* (Heb. 4:12). If soul and spirit are really the same, then what is being divided?

One's interpretation and translation of Scripture for *nephesh* and *psuche* will be determined by whether one is a monist or at least a dichotomist. The monist will argue that 1 Thessalonians 5:23, *"May your whole spirit, soul and body be kept blameless..."* simply means the whole person. Dichotomists and trichotomists argue that this verse gives more support for their views. Delitzsch made a strong case for trichotomy.[20]

The difficulty in this debate is that the belief or bias of the interpreter of Scripture can determine the translation of the very Scripture that is supposed to determine the belief in the first place. It becomes a "hermeneutical circle." Word studies in themselves will not settle the issue. The passages considered above go beyond word studies to show that the recent concept of monism is incorrect, and we do have a soul, if not a spirit as well.

Are the Soul and the Spirit Identical?

The Scriptures use *soul* and *spirit* interchangeably at times, but both relate to the nonphysical aspect of a person. They overlap, but they are not the same. For example, *soul* can refer to a whole person, as in "twenty souls were saved." But *spirit* is not used the same way in the Scriptures. You never read that "twenty spirits were saved."

Soul and spirit have different emphases in the Scriptures. Soul focuses more on earthly and bodily aspects of the nonphysical person, including hunger, thirst, and appetites, and can even refer to unethical impulses, temptation, and sin.[21,22] The spirit of a person refers more to the connection with the indwelling of the Holy Spirit and one's relationship with God. The spirit is "diffused" throughout the soul, and the soul and spirit are both "diffused" throughout the body.[23] The soul is affected by both the body and the spirit and thus by the direction of the spirit and the desires or cravings of the flesh.[24]

Spirits may be in the air and around us; they may even be evil spirits; they can occupy one or more persons—yet none of that applies to the soul. Angels are never referred to as having a soul. Each person has a unique soul, a unique inner spirituality reflecting God's original creation. So while the soul and spirit of a person are similar in some respects and are used interchangeably by the Scriptures at times, the two are not the same. All people, Christian and non-Christian, have a soul.

In healing prayer, we must pray for and with the whole person and respect all of life's complexities and mysteries. In practice, healing prayer is almost always similar whether people are a dichotomy or a trichotomy. As led by the Lord, healing prayer might at times be focused on a person's spirit.[25]

When a person dies, their soul does not separate from their spirit. Whether the Scriptures talk about the soul after death, or one's spirit going to the Lord, it is irrelevant since where one is, the other is also found.

Does the Soul "Develop"?

Is the soul created "perfect" or "complete," or does it develop? This is a crucial question. If the soul originates as a "finished product," then how do we explain the sinful reactions that involve the soul, as numerous passages make abundantly clear?

What is the origin of the soul? Most scholars hold the creationist view, that God creates the individual soul and attaches it to the body of the created fetus at conception or sometime during pregnancy. God is intimately involved with our creation, right at conception and onwards. Isaiah wrote about the Lord who formed him in the womb (Is. 44:2,24) to be his servant (Isa. 49:5). The Lord said of Jeremiah, *"Before I formed you in the womb I knew you"* (Jer. 1:5). Job referred to the Lord who made him in the womb (Job 31:15). The Psalmist declared, *"you created my inmost being; you knit me together in my mother's womb"* (Ps. 139:13). The writer of Ecclesiastes declares this all a mystery, *"you do not know…how the body is formed in a mother's womb"* (Eccl. 11:5).

The creationist view, though basically correct, is incomplete. What happens upon the creation of the soul? A few scholars have studied this question for decades and give strong support for the developmental view. The soul is created as *potential* and develops in early relationships and bonding with mother and father. In other words, *souls come from families* and relationships.[26] This involves, unfortunately, all their sins and wounds, sometimes even abuse and trauma, sometimes experienced in the womb before birth. Therefore, the quality of human relationships in a child's family in the early years are crucial for the formation of the child's soul.[27]

The Lord has created us, but we also come from our families in terms of our body—DNA, for example—plus the subsequent *development of our souls within family relationships*. This view agrees with numerous studies in developmental psychology and makes better sense of verses like Exodus 34:7, Numbers 14:18, and Deuteronomy. 5:9—where the sins of the fathers will be "visited" upon the children of the third and fourth generation.

Once a family embarks on sin, it will be usually passed on by learned behaviour. With souls being formed in a family, it is almost guaranteed that the sin is passed on and becomes a part of the next generation. This is also because each soul, each child, has its own sin apart from the family, being conceived in a sinful, fallen world (Ps. 51:5). In Old Testament times it was not uncommon for three or four generations to live in the same house—they didn't have suburbs and apartments like we have today. Thus, family relationships and values and behaviours were strongly reinforced. By God's grace alone, sin is allowed to go only to the third or fourth generation.

The idea of the soul "developing" is alluded to in passages like Deuteronomy 1:39, where the Israelites rebelled against the Lord and were afraid to go into the promised land, fearing that their children would be captured. The Lord replied, "*And the little ones that you said would be taken captive, your children who do not yet know good from bad—they will enter the land.*" There is a stage in life where a child's soul, his or her "moral conscience," is not yet developed, so a very small child cannot be held accountable for his or her moral actions. Similarly, the Messiah as a child grew up to when He "*knows enough to reject the wrong and choose the right*" (Isa. 7:15-16). The soul is formed to completion over decades, especially the first one or two years, which involves all parental and family relationships.

But there is also spiritual formation, and the spirit's growth and development in turn depends on the growth and healing of the soul.[28]

For Christians, this involves a regenerated spirit and the indwelling of the Holy Spirit and therefore receiving the life of Christ (Ezek. 36:26-27; John 3:6; 2 Cor. 4:16; Rom. 12:2; Eph. 4:22-25; Col. 3:10).

Ralph: Healed from a Lifelong Burden

All of his thirty years, Ralph experienced life as a burden, requiring a lot of energy to get through each day.[29] During a time of healing prayer, the Lord reminded Ralph that his mother had laboured for twelve hours, and after much difficulty Ralph was finally born. "The long struggle to be born and the energy he expended in the process established a foundational pattern for Ralph."[30] The Lord took Ralph back to his time of birth (Ps. 22:9-10) and had him experience his birth the way the Lord intended it. Ralph experienced an "overwhelming sense of peace and security" from the Lord. From that day onwards, Ralph was free of the extra "burden" of life that drained his energy and could experience life like anyone else. The Lord had touched his soul and spirit at an early developmental stage in life.[31]

216

Emotions as Expressions of the Soul

If we truly have a soul, and emotions are expressions of the soul—and spirit as well—then anxiety, depression, fear, mood swings, and so forth must not be automatically considered as arising from brain chemistry. The *primary consideration* should be that they emanate from one's soul. This then determines a whole different course of "treatment." Rather than rushing to adjust neurotransmitters, we listen to the cry of the soul.

The soul is more than just breath or the animating principle of life in a person. The soul expresses itself through emotions, among other means, such as bodily functions and states. A wide range of emotions, and even very strong emotions, can emanate from one's soul and spirit. Over 120 passages in the Old Testament associate emotions with *nephesh*, the soul.[32]

The soul involves one's will and inner convictions. The soul as the inner volitional part of a person can sin (Lev. 4:2;5:1;5:17;6:2) or pursue evil spirits (Lev. 20:6). The soul can also lust (Deut. 12:15,20,21;14:26). With both heart and soul, one can decide to follow the commands of the Lord (Deut. 11:13;26:16;30:2,6,10; Josh. 22:5;23:14; 2 Kings 23:3,25; 2 Chron. 6:38; 34:31) or seek him (2 Chron. 15:12). With heart and mind and also soul, we are to obey and love the Lord (Deut. 6:5;4:9). In twenty-one occurrences, *soul* is used with *heart* to emphasize one's whole resolve and determination.[33]

Strong emotions are associated with the soul. Hannah was in bitterness of soul (1 Sam. 1:10), as was Job (Job 3:4), who also spoke in anguish of his spirit (Job 7:11). Those among David's men were *"discontented"* (1 Sam. 2:2, NIV) or *"bitter in soul"* (ESV). Bitterness of soul can lead to physical death (Job 21:25). Delilah vexed Saul's soul (Judg. 16:16; cf. Job 27:2,19:2). The Shunamite woman's soul was *"vexed within her"* (2 Kings 4:27, KJV); that is, she was distressed or anxious. When Job was terrified with nightmares and visions, his soul was inclined to choose death by suicide (Job 7:15)—or *suicidal ideation,* as some refer to it today. A *"languishing soul"* can lead to sorrow and despair (Deut. 28:65, ESV), or clinical depression. The soul can grieve (1 Sam. 2:33;30:2; Job 30:25). The soul *and* body can be consumed with grief (Ps. 31:9), be full of trouble (Ps. 88:3), or full of contempt and scorning (Ps. 123:4). The soul can be weary with sorrow (Ps. 119:28) or in anguish (Isa. 38:15; Gen. 42:21). Accordingly, one's spirit can grow faint (Ps. 77:3) and one's soul can refuse to be comforted (Ps. 77:2). A violent storm at sea can cause the souls of sailors to melt (Ps. 107:26, KJV) or to lose their courage (NIV).

One's soul can rejoice in the Lord (Ps. 35:9; Isa. 61:10), thirst after God (Ps. 42:1-3; Ps. 63:1-2; Ps. 84:2), and long for God's salvation (Ps. 119:81). Answered prayer can strengthen one's soul (Ps. 138:3). God's law brings life to the soul (Prov. 3:22; Ps. 19:7). When there is much anxiety, God's consolation brings joy to the soul (Ps. 94:19). Our inner being, our souls, should learn to rest in God (Ps. 116:7).

When Jesus was in the Garden of Gethsemane, His soul was overwhelmed with sorrow to the point of death (Matt. 26:38; Mark 14:34). Jesus' soul was troubled (John 12:27, KJV) or His heart was troubled (NIV). Sinful desires can battle against the soul (1 Pet. 2:11). One's spirit can also experience emotion, such as a brokenness that will effect one's health (Prov. 7:22). Nebuchadnezzar's spirit was troubled by a dream (Dan. 2:1). One's spirit can be despairing (Isa. 61:3), defiled (2 Cor. 2:17), or timid (2 Tim. 1:7).

Soul, Spirit, and Neurochemistry

The psychology of the spirit is complex. What about the mind, heart, will, conscience, inner being (1 Pet. 3:4; 2 Cor. 4:16), and so forth? Classical theologians have understood the mind to be the rational soul, the heart as part of the emotional aspects of the soul, and the conscious and subconscious in terms of the awareness of the soul. Some theologians have argued that the higher aspects of the soul relate more to the spirit of a person and the lowest aspects relate to the flesh and its desires. Others argue that the spirit is centered in the subconscious mind (Eph. 4:23; Rom. 7:22).[34] Oswald Chambers, who held to the concept of man as body, soul, and spirit, wrote that "the spirit expresses itself in the soul."[35]

The Puritan scholar John Owen related the heart to the soul as follows:

> The heart in the Scripture is variously used; sometimes for the mind and understanding, sometimes for the will, sometimes for the affections, sometimes for the conscience, sometimes for the whole soul. Generally, it denotes the whole soul of man and all the faculties of it...as they all concur in our doing good or evil.[36]

Chambers related the heart and the soul similarly, challenging the materialist view that the brain is the "center of thinking" with the biblical view that it is the heart which is the center of thinking since in the end, God judges people by their hearts and not by their brains.[37]

John Garrison, a Christian theologian, in *The Psychology of The Spirit* wrote that the soul and spirit are the "invisible forces" that sustain the body and keep it functioning.[38] If the soul is also life, as seen in Genesis, then it is the soul that drives the biochemical reactions in the body. While biochemical reactions can affect the soul, the soul-to-body direction of biochemical events is most certainly true and hugely significant. The spirit and soul of a person, and "not mere chemical or mechanical processes," explain why anyone has life.[39] Emotions, will, thought, behaviour, and more are first and primarily *outward manifestations* of one's soul and spirit.[40] Consequently, mental illness is viewed as "lower level disorders of the soul."[41]

But if you do not believe in an actual soul, you will focus on disordered brains instead of a disordered or wounded soul. In the absence of the soul, which cannot be scientifically measured or quantified, researchers focus on the brain and behaviour. Deep sorrow and anguish in one's soul, for example, becomes a debate about serotonin levels or other neurochemical reactions. Instead of hearing the cry of one's soul, there is a rush to tweak neurotransmitter levels. This is inevitable when you *turn a process into a thing,* a fundamental error.[42] So sexual orientation, joy, and aggression, for example, become localized in a person's brain chemistry or a spot on their chromosome.

Researchers have questioned the meaning and reality of dreams. Some researchers have claimed that "dreams were essentially the result of a rather random firing of large neurons in the brain stem that occur normally during certain sleep cycles."[43] Must we now believe that Joseph's dreams concerning the safety of the Christ child (Matt. 2:12,13,19,22) were just a "random firing of neurons"? Did the Lord appear to Solomon in a dream (1 Kings 3:5-15), or was it only overactive neurons?

With the soul and spirit "banished," materialism and behaviourism reign. Not a few researchers equate the mind with the brain. Many international experts in neuroscience seriously believe that we are just body and mind and the brain causes what happens in our minds and our thoughts.[44] We feel sad or "low" because serotonin is "low" in our brains. We think with compulsive, racing thoughts because the synapses are firing too fast.

For some researchers, mental events become merely products of physical events, which is decidedly materialist and gives priority to the brain rather than the mind.[45] This is seen in the view of Francis Crick, Nobel laureate and co-discover of DNA with James Watson, who once said that our emotions, memories, identity, free will and more can be attributed to our "nerve cells and their associated molecules."[46] If Crick truly believed this, he should have rejected the Nobel prize since it wasn't him but his nerve cells and their molecules that made the discovery. The discovery of DNA, then, and all the ambitions that drove the research can only be attributed to neurochemistry in the brains of two researchers. An uncomfortable application of reductionism? Meanwhile, secular scientists themselves have for some decades been calling into question this reductionism of the person.[47]

Imagine someone sending you a letter that encouraged your heart. What would you think of someone who claimed the letter was nothing more than paper and dried ink that could be analyzed chemically?

Or when a man embraces his wife, a scientist declares that moment can de completely described by hormones, neural pathways, the physiology of touch, and so forth? Does that not miss the entire point of love, emotion, and bonding? Isn't that what it really was all about? Those are examples of reductionism.

A considerable amount of scientific research is devoted to understanding mind and brain interactions and the nature of "consciousness." To avoid reductionism, some Christian researchers claim that brain and mental events interact in *both* directions and together in a correlated way.[48,49] *But there is a soul if not a spirit as well, in addition to the mind, which interacts with the brain.*

The Rise of the Mental Health Industry

So what happened when theologians banished the soul in the 1950s? Ever since then, people have still been wondering about their souls and asking the deeper questions about their inner being. For further reasons, psychiatrists won over the jurisdiction of healing people with emotional problems from the clergy.[50] There are hundreds of books being written about the soul, but the vast majority of them are written by New Agers, psychics, those in the occult and other religions. But sadly, few such books are written by Christians. People now go to mental health centres and psychiatry for help with their souls, since their practitioners address anxiety, panic, depression, phobias, and so forth. Pastors and priests are advised to send their parishioners to mental health experts when there are deep issues like clinical depression or schizophrenia.

Psychiatry and the mental health movement do not have a true, biblical concept of the soul. They would never suggest that the soul's formation has anything to do with seeking first the kingdom of God or denying oneself or becoming like a child to enter the kingdom. Sin, confession, and repentance are not great ideas there either.

Jeffrey Boyd is an Episcopal minister, prominent psychiatrist, and chairman of psychiatry and ethics at Waterbury Hospital Health Center in Connecticut. In *Reclaiming The Soul*, he showed how psychotherapy has triumphed over Christianity because of the loss of the concept of the soul from Christianity.[51] The vacuum created by the theologians gave rise to the mental health movement.[52] The mental health movement is more dominant than Christianity in North America, and it sets the agenda for today's problems. Boyd wrote:

> The problems are known as depression, anxiety, and attention deficit—not as human arrogance or sin. When human problems are defined in those terms, the Church doesn't have adequate answers and offers only second-rate solutions. Why? Because that list of problems reflects the mental health agenda. However, if the basic human problem were defined as arrogance or sin and the fact that it is pervasive throughout society (even mental health experts suffer from it), it would be clear that there is no solution but Christ.[53]

Conclusion

When the Church effectively banished the soul, it opened the floodgates for reductionism. Science reduced everything to the mind, which in turn is thought of as originating in the brain. In accepting modern psychiatry, the Church embraces the reductionism right along with it. It was only a matter of time until the mental health system usurped the Church's role in caring for the soul. With the rise of neuroscience, emotional problems are reduced to managing neurotransmitters. Could this be why psychiatrists are sometimes referred to as *shrinks*?

Confession has been replaced by the couch; prayer has been replaced by Prozac; Christ has been replaced by the chemistry of the brain; love has been replaced by Luvox; wholeness has been replaced by Wellbutrin.

Did the Lord heal and restore Grace's soul, that "component part" of her inner being that is highly integrated to her body such that it then changed her mental, emotional, neurochemical, and biological state? How deeply do we really believe in Psalm 32:3? Or were her neurochemical and biological functions altered so that she now feels better? Or was her mental and biological state improved only? Whether you believe that Grace *has a soul* instead of just *being a soul* makes all the difference in the world.

Not everyone will agree with the arguments from the Scriptures for a tripartite nature of man. One should avoid being too dogmatic about the psychology of the soul, since there is mystery in the soul and spirit. However, the bottom line in this chapter is that all people *have* a soul, which is immaterial and of a different nature than the physical body.

Endnotes _____

[1] John C. Garrison, *The Psychology Of The Spirit: A Contemporary System of Biblical Psychology* (Xlibris Corporation, 2001) p. 37.

[2] Louis Berkhof, *Systematic Theology* (Grand Rapids: Eerdmans, 1939, fifteenth printing, 1977) pp. 191-195.

[3] Franz Delitzsch, *A System of Biblical Theology* (Eugene: Wipf and Stock Publishers, 2003, previously published by T. and T. Clark, 1899) pp. 3-25.

[4] Delitzsch, pp. 103-119.

[5] Delitzsch, pp. 109,114,115,118.

[6] Garrison, p. 34.

[7] George Eldon Ladd, *A Theology Of The New Testament* (Grand Rapids: Eerdmans, 1974) p. 457.

[8] Jeffrey H. Boyd, *Soul Psychology: How to Understand Your Soul in Light of the Mental Health Movement* (Cheshire: Soul Research Institute, 1994) p. 9.

[9] Boyd, pp. 3-4,19.

[10] Boyd, pp. 3-4,10-11.

[11] D.C. Fredericks, article on *nepes* (# 5883), *New International Dictionary of Old Testament Theology and Exegesis, Vol. 3,* Willem A. VanGemeren, general editor (Grand Rapids: Zondervan, 1997) p. 133.

[12] Boyd, pp. 5-8.

[13] Kenneth Barker, general editor, *The NIV Study Bible, New International Version* (Grand Rapids: Zondervan, 1985) p. 791.

14 Bruce K. Waltke, article on nāpash, R. Laird Harris, Gleason L. Archer, and Bruce K. Waltke, *Theological Wordbook of the Old Testament, Volume 2* (Chicago: Moody Press, 1980) p. 588.

15 Garrison, pp. 50-51.

16 Delitzsch, pp. 281-292.

17 Victor P. Hamilton, *The Book of Genesis, Chapters 1-17: The New International Commentary on the Old Testament* (Grand Rapids: Eerdmans, 1990) p. 159.

18 Boyd, p. 27.

19 Garrison, p. 35.

20 Delitzsch, pp. 109-110.

21 Jeffrey H. Boyd, *Reclaiming The Soul: The Search for Meaning in a Self-Centered Culture* (Cleveland: The Pilgrim Press, 1996) pp. 74-76.

22 Garrison, pp. 58-63.

23 Garrison, p. 24.

24 Garrison, pp. 54-65.

25 Ruth Hawkey, *Healing the Human Spirit* (Chichester: New Wine Press, 1996).

26 Boyd, 1996, pp. 81-119.

27 Boyd, 1994, p. 117.

28 Garrison, p. 48.

29 Frank and Catherine Cahill-Fabiano, *Healing The Past, Releasing Your Future* (Kent: Sovereign World Ltd., 2003) pp. 55-56.

30 Fabiano, p. 56.

31 Fabiano, p. 55.

32 Malcolm A. Jeeves, *Human Nature At The Millennium: Reflections On The Integration Of The Psychology And Christianity* (Grand Rapids: Baker Books, 1997) p. 13.

33 Jeeves, p. 113.

34 Garrison, p. 24.

35 Oswald Chambers, *Biblical Psychology* (Grand Rapids: Discovery House Publishers, 1995 edition, first published 1962) p. 49.

36 William H. Goold, editor, *The Works of John Owen, Volume VI: Temptation And Sin* (Edinburgh: Banner Of Truth Trust. 1967, first published in 1850-53) p. 170.

37 Chambers, pp. 92-93, cf. pp. 99,113.

38 Garrison, p. 42.

39 Ibid.

40 Garrison, p. 20.

41 Garrison, p. 73.

42 Jeeves, p. 90.

43 Gerald G. May, *The Dark Night Of The Soul: A Psychiatrist Explores the Connection Between Darkness and Spiritual Growth* (New York: HarperSanFrancisco, 2004) p. 48.

44 Elio Frattaroli, *Healing the Soul in the Age of the Brain: Becoming Conscious in an Unconscious World* (New York: Viking, 2001) pp. 6-7.

45 Jeeves, p. 57.

46 Jeeves, p. 196.

47 Jeeves, pp. 56-57.

48 Jeeves, p. 57.

49 Ed T. Welch, *Blame It on the Brain? Distinguishing Chemical Imbalances, Brain Disorders, and Disobedience* (Phillipsburg: P&R Publishing, 1998) p. 29.

50 Stuart A. Kirk and Herb Kutchins, *The Selling of DSM: The Rhetoric of Science in Psychiatry* (New York: Aline De Gruyter, 1992) p. 10.

51 Boyd, 1996, p. 53.

52 Boyd, 1994, pp. 20,41-68.

53 Boyd, 1996, pp. 47-48.

Chapter Ten

A Theological Critique of Psychiatry

The hearts of men, moreover, are full of evil and there is madness in their hearts while they live (Eccl. 9:3).

"Who is this that darkens my counsel with words without knowledge?" (Job 38:2).

Bart: A Pastor Healed from Self-Rejection

Bart experienced some very painful pastorates, and was in the process of waiting for another settlement. But he was coping with a lot of self-rejection and feelings of failure and inadequacy. He was unemployed, not able to provide for his family, and felt he was a failure in his pastoral calling. After many months, as the feelings began to intensify, he came for healing prayer. This is his own account of how he was healed by the presence of the living Christ.

> As we were praying, the Lord brought to my mind an incident that is still clear even today. It takes place in our old house, and my parents were still married at the time. I am in an adjacent room but still within earshot. My mother is berating my dad for his religious "weirdness." She is quite angry because he apparently called in to work to say that he was staying home on

religious grounds. He was into Kabala, or numerology, and the numbers were "wrong" for him to go to work—or something like that. Because this was not an isolated incident, he lost his job. I can almost feel the emotion of that moment. The issues were religion and unemployment; both were looked upon with disdain.

"Why couldn't you just be a part of 'normal' religion?" By that my mother meant Anglican or Lutheran, which was their background. My dad was very defensive and also quite vocal.

I had struggled with both of my parents' disapproval, especially since I surrendered my life to Christ. There were also issues of acceptance/rejection, especially with regard to prophetic gifting and seeking people's approval. When we prayed to invite Jesus to come into the situation, He hovered over me protectively. His back was to my parents, effectively shielding me from all the verbal abuse that was going on. His right arm was extended, placed between my parents, seeming to break the flow of abuse. Then, as He looked squarely into my eyes, He said, "You already have my approval. I already love you. You have nothing to prove to gain my love and approval. I accepted you the moment you were born, and I rejoiced when you finally came to me for salvation. I am pleased with how you have grown. I am fully aware of what it has cost you to remain obedient and teachable."

I have never felt such a release. I now walk in full confidence that I have nothing to prove and that I am a person of worth and value, regardless of others' opinions and regardless of the circumstances. I know that He is always with me, that He will never leave me nor forsake me. Others have asked me what happened to me. They say that I carry myself differently; they have seen a "physical difference" in my walk and my demeanour. I know that it was Jesus who touched my life, and He has set me free.

Our prayer session with Bart was a blessing to us all. It was only seconds after we anointed him that the Lord directed him to this memory of an event early in his life. After he described what he felt and saw, we asked the Lord to speak His truth and heal him from the effects of that incident in his life. Suddenly he was silent, and for about three minutes tears trickled down his face.

We said nothing, sensing that the Lord was ministering to him directly. He then opened his eyes and shared what he experienced in the Lord's presence. Jesus spoke directly to the core issues in his life, and he was deeply healed. Affirmation directly from Christ was so overpowering that it changed his inner being. Truly, Jesus restored his soul in this part of his life.

Holiness or Symptom Management?

The goal of psychiatry is the management of symptoms so that one can enjoy a normal, functional life. This is commendable in itself. The result is a therapeutic self defined by the expectations of modern man. But a therapeutic self is not the same as a new self in Christ.

Up until about 1900, the goal in life for many people was to achieve holiness.[1] After 1900, the goal was to be adjusted to life, not alienated from one's self, not found with disorders or mental illness—"the quest for health began to compete with the quest for holiness."[2] But this is entirely different from being born again (John 3:16) and entering the kingdom of God. This is far removed from becoming like Christ, growing in holiness, and knowing the resurrection power of Christ and His sufferings (Phil. 3:10). The focus on the self is at odds with the call to deny oneself. Since the focus in psychiatry is not holiness and sanctification, it is not surprising that sin is missing from the therapeutic scene.

Goals determine strategies and means and will shape everything that follows.

Sin as Sickness: Downsizing Reality

Some psychiatric labels turn sin into mental illness or a disease. What can only and always be dealt with by the cross of Jesus now becomes a biochemical or neurological problem treated by drugs. Disease is confused with evil; psychopathology turns evil into illness.[3] One of the main reasons that the myth of mental illness is perpetuated is because many people would rather deny that people hurt one another than face the truth.[4]

Consider just a few examples. Transvestic Fetishism (billing code 302.3), cross-dressing by a male in a woman's attire, is listed as a sin in Deuteronomy 22:5. Oppositional Defiant Disorder, characteristic of youth who are negativistic, defiant, disobedient, and hostile towards those in authority, sounds a lot like the *"stubborn and rebellious son who does not obey his father and mother and will not listen to them when they discipline him"* in Deuteronomy 21:18. If the nation of Israel would reject the Lord, they would be cursed with *"madness, blindness and confusion of mind"* (Deut. 28:28), which would be diagnosed today as manias, disorders, and mental illnesses. Deuteronomy often refers to all those behaviours as indicators of what's in the heart, as evil that must be purged from among the nation (Deut. 13:5;17:7,12;19:19;22:22, 24;24:7), irreconcilable with any notion of mental illnesses.

Jesus' solution to Narcissistic Personality Disorder (billing code 301.81) would be to deny oneself and take up the cross (Luke 9:22-25; Mark 8:34-36, cf. Rom. 2:8;6:6). The apostle Paul describes people who have rejected God and are now given over to a depraved mind as being *"filled with every kind of wickedness, evil, greed and depravity. They are full of envy, murder, strife, deceit and malice"* (Rom. 1:29). That sounds like Oppositional Defiant Disorder, Conduct Disorder, Antisocial Personality Disorder, and more.

While it may appear blunt to declare some disorders as sin, remember that for all sin there is forgiveness and cleansing through the cross of Jesus by the grace and mercy of God. I realize the restraints of public medical practice, which is non-judgmental, and that many people do not in any way subscribe to Christian beliefs. Where sin is the issue behind emotional suffering (it isn't always), it is less than kind to diagnose real sin as mental illness and prescribe medication. This prevents people from experiencing joy from the release of guilt and pain underneath the "mental illness." People are thus robbed the opportunity of experiencing the grace of God.

This is also due to the language of sin being "lost" due to pluralism, modernism, and secularism, more so in the larger mainline churches.[5] A major consequence is that this biblical language, which so perfectly depicts the nature of man and the human soul, has been eventually replaced in both the Church and culture by the language of medicine and law.[6] Christians soon talk more about "pathology" than sin, "recovery" than repentance, "diagnosis" than judgment or discernment, "treatment" instead of penance.[7] Confession, forgiveness, and the power of the cross soon fade into the background. After all, who would expect anyone to repent of low serotonin levels?

But not everyone wants to face the possible issue of sin or woundedness in their past or their family. Family secrets may be exposed, reputations tarnished, and someone might actually have to repent. A biochemical solution appears less threatening with a "quicker fix" and no changes in relationships.

Neurochemical Glitch or Spiritual Crisis: Short-Circuiting Reality

When someone is coping with clinical depression, for example, it is typically seen as a negative, caused by some biochemical or genetic problem. Accordingly, drugs are prescribed to control the symptoms. But in many cases, the person is actually in a spiritual crisis, with symptoms as communication from a wounded soul or spirit.

I do not wish to minimize anyone's pain, emotional or physical and otherwise, that comes with depression or any other mental "illness." But psychiatric treatments can short-circuit spiritual growth and turn spiritual formation into symptom management. You might even end up with spiritual *deformation*. The "curse" of the health-care system is that the focus on finding relief is at the expense of understanding what's happening in people's souls.[8] Psychiatry typically misinterprets God's use of negative emotions, distress, brokenness, inner doubt and emotional turmoil in a person's spiritual development as spiritual failure or "nervous breakdown" treatable with drugs thereby " ... sealing off the attics and the basements of his mental life with pharmacological glue."[9]

What if "depression" today is at times the "dark night of the soul" where God is purging us of vices and worldly affections and attachments so that we will be matured and drawn to Him? The inability to enjoy life, no longer having former "spiritual experiences," feeling that God has basically "disappeared," loss of passion and motivation, a sense of inner dread and even some emotional pain, sleepless nights, and much more were understood as part of the spiritual journey for some.[10] Such things were no surprise to spiritual directors of the Church in ages past, such as St. John of the Cross (1542-1591). This could also be part of spiritual guidance[11] and spiritual mentoring.[12]

Addictions, Obsessions, and Compulsions: A Biology of Sanctification?

Obsessive compulsive disorder, by definition, involves actions and behaviours that are beyond a person's control—like compulsive handwashing. Addictions, and especially sexual addictions, are another example of an impulse or behaviour that has control over a person. Apparently neurological pathways are constructed in a person's brain so that these addictions become a biological problem, and then spiritual solutions alone are not effective.[13] When we experience pleasure, such as from sex, endorphins and enkephalins (brain chemicals) are released to the "excitement centres" of the brain, and repetition of the pleasure establishes neurological pathways in the brain.[14,15] Endorphins and enkephalins are opiate-like brain chemicals, discovered in 1974.[16]

A number of behavioural techniques are then required to re-program the brain by altering the neurological pathways.[17] For sexual success, men must learn how to recondition their sexual brain and thus overcome sexual addictions and other sexual problems.[18] A recommended technique for men is the use of a rubber band around the wrist, which a man flicks to cause pain each time he has a lustful thought, fantasizes, sees pornography, etc.[19] The brain is then progressively reconditioned, since it experiences pain and no longer sends endorphins or enkephalins to the "excitement centre," thus changing the neurological pathway through behaviour modification.[20] In spite of the apparent success of this technique and the presumed reconditioning of the brain, this whole approach raises some serious questions.

Was not a person's will involved in the temptation to engage in the initial stages of the addiction? What about cravings of the sinful nature, which can be the beginnings of compulsions and addictions (Eph. 2:3; 1 John 2:16)? A decision of the heart must have been involved to help develop the supposed neurological pathway changes. Does this not involve temptation? Otherwise, how could the Lord ever judge anyone for sexual or other addictions? There now comes a point where biology takes over; it involves a morally neutral brain. At what point does this happen? What and where is the "dividing line"? Does this "sin morphing into disease" really make sense?[21]

Even if we do accept the reality of neurological pathways in the brain that affect our behaviour (I do not want to discredit "good science"), I would argue that this is the biological expression of a spiritual reality. The Scriptures declare that "sin is self-reinforcing, leading to an ever deeper entanglement," and is often referred to as a "snare."[22] "Can the Ethiopian change his skin or the leopard its spots? Neither can you do good who are accustomed to doing evil" (Jer. 13:23). "Judah's sin is engraved with an iron tool, inscribed with a flint point, on the tablets of their hearts and on the horns of their altars" (Jer. 17:1). "The evil deeds of a wicked man ensnare him; the cords of his sin hold him fast" (Prov. 5:22). Such verses describe in general terms what neurological pathways (possibly) depict in specific terms—the power of habits, addictions, and compulsions in people's lives.

If a man is a slave to whatever has mastered him (2 Pet. 2:19), and if sexual addiction is sin, is he then ever a slave to neutral neurological pathways in his brain? Paul wrote, "For what I want to do I do not do, but what I hate I do" (Rom. 7:15), which is "another law at work in the members of my body" (Rom. 7:23). Is a sexual addiction then an issue of biology or sin living in a person (Rom. 7:17)? Did not Jesus Himself say that *out of the heart* come evil thoughts and sexual immorality (Matt. 5:19; Mark 7:21)? A change of heart is not the same as a change of neurological pathways. Did not Jesus also say that everyone who sins is a slave to sin (John 8:34)? Are we victims of neurology or slaves to sin? Is not addiction a form of idolatry?[23,24]

Reprogramming the brain has wider application that just sexual addiction. Milkman and Sunderwirth, lead researchers in the field, note that other types of "pleasure" include those of criminals such as rapists or serial killers, since the "excitement" of their crimes also releases endorphins and enkephalins into their brains to develop neural pathways.[25] Endorphins and enkephalins don't "know" the difference between forms of pleasure; whatever is perceived or experienced as pleasure will suffice. Sadomasochists who derive pleasure from pain or inflicting pain on others will develop new neurological pathways just the same. Some people crave or delight in evil (Prov. 2:14,10:23). Would the rubber band technique apply to such people? Or how about Christians who have a problem with materialism and have a love for money (1 Tim. 3:3;6:10; 2 Tim. 3:2; Heb. 13:5; 1 Pet. 5:2)? They derive pleasure from thinking about their investments, reviewing their portfolios, and are basically addicted to trading stocks, and so forth. Why not suggest that they also overcome their love of money via the elastic band technique? Is this even remotely what the apostle Paul had in mind when he encouraged us to "*take captive every thought*" for Christ (2 Cor. 10:5)?

Could changes in neurological pathways at times be an *expression* of the soul's effect on the brain showing up as "hardness of heart"? As people turn away from truth, reject God's grace and His ways, and increasingly follow sinful ways or idolatry, could this not in the end also change neurological pathways?

The Scriptures exhort us to be self-controlled (Acts 24:25; 1 Pet. 4:7,5:8; 1 Thess. 5:6) as a sign of spiritual maturity. We are called to avoid sexual immorality and to learn to control our own bodies in a way that is holy and honourable and without passionate lust (1 Thess.

4:3-5; cf. 1 Cor. 6:18). We are to say "no" to ungodliness and worldly passions and to live self-controlled, upright, and godly lives (Titus 2:12) and see that no one is sexually immoral (Heb. 12:16). A mark of godly Christian character is self-control (Titus 1:8;2:1,5,6; 1 Thess. 5:8), which is also a fruit of the Holy Spirit (Gal. 5:23). Among Christians there should not even be a hint of sexual immorality—which includes sexual addictions (Eph. 5:3). Our life in the Spirit means not gratifying the sinful nature, which includes sexual immorality, impurity, idolatry, fits of rage, and more (Gal. 5:16-21; Col. 3:5).

Sexual addiction involves giving up control to the power of the addiction. If it really is an issue of neurological pathways that require recently discovered techniques to reprogram the brain, then how could early Christians ever have obeyed God's commands concerning control over sexual addictions? The answer for the early Church, as for today, is Christ (Rom. 7:25), His divine power for our life and godliness (2 Pet. 1:3), and life in the Spirit (Rom. 8:9, 13,26,27) so that we may become like Christ (Rom. 8:29). If it is a matter of mastering techniques to reprogram the brain, we then enter works righteousness instead of living by grace. This also tends to be dehumanizing because we become reprogrammable biological machines. This all "smells" of secular humanism wherein man engineers himself.

What about good habits, or even strong virtues? Why not argue that they are largely a product of correctly programmed neurological pathways? Does the fruit of the Spirit (Gal. 5:22) become positively changed neurological pathways? What then happens to grace and the transforming presence of Christ if it is largely a matter of neurochemistry in the brain? Do we love others and do good mostly because of certain neurological pathways or because Christ is being formed in us and we are yielding more and more to the Spirit?

Instead of advocating techniques to change neurological pathways, one should look to the Lord and His transforming presence, in repentance and faith, to restore the soul, which will then ultimately result in neurological pathways changed for the better. The answer would be found in Jesus and His Spirit to overcome the power of sin and woundedness, which includes the ministry of healing prayer centred in the power of Christ's healing presence.[26] Christ's divine power has given us everything we need for life and godliness (2 Pet. 1:3), including victory over addictions, obsessions, and compulsions. We err by underestimating the power of sin and also the power of Christ and His Spirit to transform His people. If the power of sin is indeed such that it establishes new neurological pathways, then all the more reason to rely on divine resources to overcome the power of sin and thus alter the neurological pathways.

Serious problems arise when we suggest that neurological pathways are largely the problem in addictions and thus it is less of a spiritual issue. Sanctification then becomes more biological. Researchers in the field have already claimed that advances in science regarding "reward centers of the brain have led to a significant departure from the increasingly archaic spiritual and moralistic definitions of addiction."[27] The irony here is that Christian authors who appeal to such research give credence to the very researchers who would challenge the authority of the Scriptures and specifically the doctrine of sin. Science and theology here would be better integrated by holding that changed neurological pathways reflect a spiritual reality—issues of the heart—as an *expression of the soul and spirit.*

Howling like a Jackal, Hearing Voices, and Talking Donkeys

Imagine someone going around barefoot and almost naked, weeping and wailing, howling like a jackal and moaning like an owl. Does that sound "normal" to you? Almost any psychiatrist would have such a person treated with a drug or committed to an institution. But what if it is the prophet Micah (Micah 1:8)? Likewise, don't forget that Isaiah went around stripped and barefoot for three years (Isa. 20:3). Or what about a wife who told her husband to see a psychiatrist because he was convinced that God spoke to him, telling him to take their young and only son and drive in their half-ton pickup truck up to the summit of a nearby mountain and sacrifice their son on an altar? Nowadays, no explanation would prevent him from being declared as insane.[28] But that's the story of Abraham, except that he used a donkey to get up the mountain (Gen. 22:1-19).

Or what of people who hear the sound of marching in balsam trees (2 Sam. 5:24; 1 Chron. 14:15), or converse with a talking donkey (Num. 22:28-30), or claim that they actually heard an eagle call out in a loud, seemingly human voice (Rev. 8:13)? Might that be judged as psychotic, out of touch with reality?

Or what about the man who was convinced that God would judge New York City? Seems God told him to make a model of the city in his house and surround it with toy models of ancient siege equipment. He really believed that God was telling him to lie on his left side for 390 days, facing the model of the city, and then for 40 days lie on his right side, again facing the city. Initially, he could only use dried human excrement to bake his bread, but when he objected God told him that animal excrement would be also okay. Then, when it was all over, he took a sharp sword and cut off his hair and beard and used an electronic scale to make three equal portions of his hair. He burned one-third of his hair inside the model of the city (not causing a fire in his house), scattered another third around the model, and went down the street in his neighbourhood and threw the remaining third to the wind while waving his sword. What would most people think about such a person's actions? Probably insane, if not at least crazy and downright bizarre. But that's exactly what the prophet Ezekiel did (Ezek. 4:1-5:4), although he did not have an electronic scale—nor electricity.

Someone with such behaviour today would certainly be judged mentally ill by mental health professionals, yet we would see him as a man of God exercising the prophetic office in another time and culture. Remember that the authoritative DSM-IV states that delusions, hallucinations, grossly disorganized behaviour and such, as part of at least a brief psychotic episode for at least a day, cannot include a symptom if it is "a culturally sanctioned response pattern."[29]

Imagine your neighbour putting on a cloak made from camel's hair, refusing to eat anything except locusts and wild honey, and going around town telling people to repent because the kingdom of God was coming? I expect he would be committed to a psychiatric ward and declared mentally ill. But if it is John the Baptist doing the same things in a different cultural and historical setting (Matt. 3:1-4), any idea of mental illness vanishes. In reality, those who do not repent or take him seriously have a spiritual problem.

It is unwise for the Church to simply accept psychiatric diagnoses uncritically. The same system that defines bipolar disorder, delusional disorder, and psychotic episodes would ultimately undermine the Scriptures or negate part of the Word of God. This has been proposed for the prophet Ezekiel.

What about hearing voices, seeing visions, and the other seemingly strange experiences of Ezekiel? Halperin, a professor of religious studies at North Carolina University, proposed a psychoanalytical approach to interpret Ezekiel.[30] Ezekiel's act of digging through a wall (Ezek. 8:7-12) was a "symbolic representation of sexual intercourse."[31] Ezekiel exhibits a "frantic loathing of female sexuality" (Ezek. 8:7-12; Ezek. 16 and 23).[32] Ezekiel displays a "radical misogyny" or hatred of women.[33] Ezekiel went into a trance with repressed hatred stemming from his childhood, now projected onto those around him.[34] "Homosexual elements" are in Ezekiel's apparent hallucinations.[35] The wrath of God is just Ezekiel's own rage.[36]

Halperin concluded that the God of Ezekiel is a "creation of Ezekiel's own brain."[37] Ezekiel is a sick person with a mental pathology, whose thinking has helped the subjection and humiliation of women.[38] Halperin recommended that the book of Ezekiel be "expelled from the canon."[39]

Modern psychiatry would even call into question the sanity of Jesus Christ. *Such a system cannot decide on what is normal, real, and what it means to be truly human.* Farber, who practiced psychology professionally for sixteen years, concluded: "If Jesus Christ were to return today he would no doubt be considered mentally defective by mental health experts, as would Elijah, Elisha, Isaiah, or Jeremiah."[40] Remember that the apostle Paul was declared mad (Acts 26:24-25) and Jesus was considered "out of his mind" (Mark 3:21).

Psychiatric Diagnoses in the Scriptures

A careful reading of the Scriptures shows that the Bible quite adequately talks about the essence of some "disorders" of the mind. Pharaoh suffered briefly from Nightmare Disorder (Gen. 41:1-8) when he dreamt about the seven cows and seven heads of grain. King Nebuchadnezzar had the clear symptoms of Grandiose Disorder when he worshipped himself, declaring his own power and glory (Daniel 4:30;5:20) due to his arrogant heart and pride. Nebuchadnezzar was then reduced by God to insanity and a clear case of diagnosed Pica, eating a non-nutritive substance like grass (Daniel 4:32-33), repeatedly for more than one month (billing code 307.52) with animals. King David showed symptoms of Factious or Malingering Disorder (faking mental illness) when he deliberately faked insanity (1 Sam. 21:12-14, Ps. 34) to Achish king of Gath by making marks on the doors of a gate and letting saliva drool down his beard, in order to protect himself. Elijah was under great fear from Jezebel, so much that he prayed he would die (1 Kings 19:1-4), thus being suicidal.

Job understandably had strong negative emotions ("depression") from no peace, quiet, or rest, but only turmoil (Job 3:26), a loathing of life (Job 10:1), a broken spirit (Job 17:1), shattered desires of the heart (Job 17:11), no answer from God who seems absent (Job 30:20), internal churning in his spirit (Job 30:27), and yet not sinning (Job 1:22;42:7-8), with his unipolar depressive episodes.

Did Jesus have a unipolar major depressive episode in the Garden of Gethsemane when he said "*My soul is overwhelmed with sorrow to the point of death*" (Mark 14:33-34) and in deep anguish prayed with sweat dropping like blood (Luke 22:44)? Did the apostle Paul have Antisocial Personality Disorder when he uttered death threats against believers (Acts 9:1) and tried to destroy the Church by imprisoning men and women (Acts 8:3)?

Are we any further ahead in our understanding of the Scriptures with these psychiatric diagnoses and labels? All psychiatric labels are built upon the foundation of these common life experiences and feelings. It is the psychiatric edifice built upon all this, however, that can be questioned. Even though the Biblical descriptions are more common and not "scientific," they are no less profound or significant.

What if God Were a Psychiatrist?

Let's turn the proverbial tables around for a moment. If God were a psychiatrist, what might His disorders and diagnoses be? If Jesus were the standard for "normality," what would happen? How about the following?

Compassion Deficit Disorder:[41] Love is at the heart of the kingdom of God, and Jesus modeled much compassion. Yet, from God's view, there is a lack of compassion in this world and even at times within the Church. Type I Compassion Deficit Disorder is seen in those who see a need or hurt in others, feel something, but do very little about it. Type IV is seen where people have such hardened hearts that they feel almost nothing in the face of human tragedy or pain and are moved to do virtually nothing about it, or even cause others to suffer without any hesitation.

This disorder is clearly seen when people are treated less than with full dignity and empathy. Yet, some people are still drugged against their will and not listened to with sincerity, empathy, and respect.

Logic Disorder: This is an obvious disorder of biological psychiatry, given its numerous and systemic errors in logic as discussed throughout this book. Entire books have been written to document this seemingly chronic condition.

The logic and reasoning of modern psychiatry falls far short of the example of Christ in the Gospels. The thinking of Jesus was sharp, clear, crisp, and cogent.[42] Jesus used many *a fortiori* arguments (arguing from the accepted weaker to the stronger proposition), such as in John 7:21-24 and Luke 13:10-17 when he defended healing people on the Sabbath.[43] Jesus also used *reductio ad absurdum* arguments, like when he defended his identity (Matt. 22:41-46) and demolished the accusation that he drove out demons by the prince of demons (Matt. 12:25-27). Jesus often appealed to evidence and arguments in logical sequence known as *modus ponens* (way of affirmation), such as concerning his identity (Matt. 11:4-6; John 5:17-46). The logic of Jesus was also powerful when faced with the "horns of a dilemma"— as often occurs in philosophy—such as with the Sadducees and the afterlife (Matt. 22:23-32).[44] When faced with the dilemma of being accused of treason or being a traitor concerning paying taxes, Jesus replied with shrewdness and absolutely cutting logic (Matt. 22:15-22). Modern psychiatry would greatly benefit from following Jesus' example of using logic.

Learning Disorder: Logic disorders often lead to learning disorders. Faced with mountains of contradictory or opposing evidence, much of modern psychiatry does not want to learn, unable to correctly evaluate information. The effort to truly learn from the research is less when compared to other disciplines of research.

Truth Avoidance Syndrome: People who suppress truth, avoid the Cross, deny eternal realities, and argue against the Scriptures have this syndrome (Rom. 1:18-22). A strong diagnosis can be given when this syndrome results in broken relationships or negative behaviour in families or communities.

Spiritual Deficit Disorder: This is most evident when people reject God's love and consistently refuse to be filled with the Holy Spirit. The greatest deficit is not being born again and thus having entered into the kingdom of God (John 3:5-8). This disorder exhibits many types of behaviour throughout life that avoids receiving the abundant life that God has for all people. In some cases, it becomes a neurosis. Refusal to repent is a clear sign of being treatment resistant with Noncompliance With Treatment Disorder. This always leads to Borderline Personality Disorder, where people do not grow in the person and image of Christ.

Attention Deficit Disorder: Over 6,000 studies and thirty years of research have been unable to confirm the valid use of stimulants like Ritalin.[45] Nevertheless, psychiatrists are prescribing Ritalin in almost epidemic proportions for children in school. It appears that psychiatry is not paying attention to the cumulative research results and thus has an attention deficit disorder for the facts. This disorder is comorbid with Learning Disorder.

Chronic Disbelief Syndrome: This is the continued and persistent disbelief in Father God and His beloved Son. The major subtypes are agnosticism and atheism. The strongest form is that which consistently denies God as Father, and results in argumentative behaviour, criticizing those who have a personal belief in a loving heavenly Father, and whose critical behaviour impairs relationships in the workplace and especially professional and academic circles. An extreme form of this syndrome is seen in those who create or support whole movements or factions to promote their disbelief. In many patients, the onset of this syndrome begins in early university years. This syndrome is confirmed in patients with a score of at least 40 out of 70 on the Hardened Heart Rating Scale. Blinded minds (2 Cor. 4:4), corrupted minds (1 Tim. 6:5), and corrupted consciences (Titus 1:15) are indicators.

Specific manifestation of this syndrome is an argumentative behaviour that results in the allegation that belief in God comes from a need for security and strength, thus God is a psychological projection of one's needs.[46] However, a study of the psychology of atheism reveals that to a remarkable extent, "an atheist's disappointment in and resentment of his own father unconsciously justifies his rejection of God."[47] Almost all influential atheists in history had dead, absent, weak, or abusive fathers.[48] Research has shown that this is a typical root of this sort of behaviour, and thus the syndrome. In severe cases, the patient will have a neurosis of disbelief.

Authority Defiance Disorder: The disorder appears as the persistent refusal to submit to God's authority. This disorder is indicated by continued defiance against God's laws and commandments. Checklist indicators include sexual immorality or promiscuity, refusal to hear Truth, arguments and criticisms against the Church, even verbal abuse against the name and person of Christ. The disorder must continue for at least two years upon early adulthood, and with at least three occurrences per week. A firm diagnosis requires at least a score of 20 from the Jezebel Rating Scale. This disorder is often chronic, with many comorbidities throughout life. Those diagnosed with Authority Defiance Disorder typically have symptoms of Truth Avoidance Syndrome. People with an excessively high UDI (Universal Depravity Index as determined by the Sermon on the Mount) typically exhibit the Anti-God Personality Disorder.

Adjustment Disorder: This disorder is typical of those who refuse to adjust to the laws and ways of God and the kingdom of His Son. Behaviours include refusing to become part of a fellowship of a Church, and in more extreme cases (Adjustment Disorder IV), preventing others from doing so. The disorder progresses in life when a person avoids repentance ("treatment resistant") and baptism, consistently refusing to adjust to the ultimate reality of God's rule. Later stages of this disorder include avoidance of the topic of death, and in some cases even denial. A subtype is "Grace Disorder," wherein a person simply cannot adjust to living by grace but remains in legalism.

Speech Disorder: If pulling hair in one's beard is a disorder, then talking behind people's backs and spreading false rumours, or gossiping (2 Cor. 12:10; Eph. 4:31; Col. 3:8; James 4:11; 1 Pet. 2:1), can also be a disorder. People who gossip for at least a total of three hours each week, for at least three weeks out of every months for at least six months, should be diagnosed with this disorder. The Gossip Rating Scale will have a score of at least 40 when relationships at work or at one's church are significantly negatively impacted (cf. Prov. 16:28) by this pathological behaviour.

Delusional Disorder: This is the delusion that there is no final judgment or hell, the cross of Christ is irrelevant, and salvation in Christ is a non-issue. A milder form of this disorder shows behaviour that reinforces the belief that while Jesus is a way to God and a Saviour, He is but one of many. This delusion involves impaired thinking wherein those who hold to Relativism maintain that they are absolutely correct. Behavioural dysfunction appears as the continual avoidance of repentance, arrogant or proud attitudes that can lead to condescending attitudes of others, and the refusal to acknowledge and worship Jesus as the Lord of Kings. A frequent comorbidity is Worship Disorder.

Worship Disorder: One should only worship the Lord God, and have no other gods before Him (Deut. 5:9; Ps. 95:6;96:9; Matt. 4:10; Luke 4:7). The disorder is evident, and typically highly chronic, when people worship themselves, money, passions, and more. This results in disordered relationships and impaired views of reality, not to mention progressively hardened hearts. As the disorder progresses over time, people know and understand less and less (Isa. 44:18). Later stages of this disorder include delusions (Isa. 44:20). The common term for this disorder is *idolatry*.

The Simplicity and Wisdom of Jesus

One might be tempted to view the Gospels as slightly irrelevant when it comes to the technical and scientific discussion of neuroscience and psychiatry. After all, the Gospels don't talk about serotonin, rating scales, dysthymia, neuroleptics, down-regulation, reuptake inhibitors, synapses, and so forth. Of course, all like the foregoing were discovered or developed centuries later. This modern terminology and its concepts are like from another world, so different from the first century. We can easily get lost in a therapeutic jungle, a maze of academic jargon. One might even begin to wonder how this would all connect with the seemingly "simple" teachings of Jesus, the Great Physician who healed many people with all sorts of illnesses, diseases, pain, paralysis, seizures, and spiritual oppression (Matt. 4:24).

The teachings of Jesus cut to the absolute core of much more than we realize. His teaching and wisdom, inspired by the Holy Spirit, penetrate this entire discussion. The reason for most of the complexity is that the *real problem is not understood*. It is not an issue of biochemistry or genetics at all, in spite of the facade of scientific rigor. Endless discussions on neurotransmitter levels and psychiatric drugs obscure the issue by adding needless complexity. If we remove genetics, brain biochemistry, drug therapy, and all the flawed scientific reasoning, what are we left with? Clear the rubble, and we are left with a *wounded soul*.

It has been said that sometimes we can't see the forest for the trees. The complexity of brain biochemistry, psychiatric genetics, drug interactions, and so forth make for many trees, and we soon can get lost amongst them. But that's not the most serious problem. The most serious problem is that we are in the *wrong forest*. It is not biology; it is relationships and issues of the heart and soul. You can't solve a problem until you really know what the problem is. You can't give right answers until you know what the right questions are.

A huge and growing mountain of evidence shows increasingly that past trauma, wounds of the soul, and one's sin and sinful reactions are really behind emotional pain. Such emotional pain occurs when love was either withheld or distorted or there was hatred—in short, a love deficit due to a *relational imbalance*. People need a Shepherd who will restore their soul (Ps. 23:3).

The teaching of Jesus that we should love our neighbour (Matt. 5:43;19:19), one another (John 13:34;15:25;15:17), our enemies (Matt. 5:44) and of course God (Matt. 22:37; Mark 12:30) cuts to the absolute core of the entire issue. Lack of love wounds people, and therefore the experience of love will heal people. Our souls are crying out for healing and love. If a lack of love is the basic root cause of emotional pain, then a healing, caring, loving presence is the solution. That is why healing prayer in the supernatural presence of Christ is so powerful—it directly and dynamically addresses the *real problem*.

A considerable amount of research confirms that childhood trauma and wounds are often behind emotional pain and behavioural problems in the present. This does not rule out, of course, personal responsibility and one's own sin! But all too often sexual, verbal, or emotional child abuse is involved. Children should be loved as anyone else and never abused. Jesus welcomed and blessed children (Mark 10:13-16) and had incredibly harsh words for anyone who would cause them to sin (Matt. 18:5-6). Even the very thought of abusing a child is heinous to the living God. God considers it odious, wretched, and sinful when the weak and vulnerable, including children, are exploited or abused. Sadly, there are even so-called Christian families where incest occurs. I know, because I have ministered healing prayer to adults from such families. Imagine how much therapy, drug treatment, and emotional pain in the lives of people would never occur if there would be no such thing as child abuse? Ultimately, the seemingly simple teachings of Christ cut to the core.

Jesus taught about anger (Matt. 5:22; Mark 7:21; Eph. 4:26). This strong emotion is all too common and "most responsible for unhappiness and psychopathological behavior."[49] This is one major root of a lot of psychological and psychiatric problems. If Jesus' ways of dealing with anger—forgiveness, repentance, humility, experiencing His healing presence—were followed, much of today's "mental illness" would instantly vanish.

Jesus taught a lot about lust, adultery, and divorce (Matt. 5:28, 32,15:19,19:7-8,19; Mark 7:21,10:11). A considerable amount of research has also shown that divorce causes a lot of emotional pain and confusion in children, who then carry that into adult life. While Christ would not want people to live in impossible and sometimes even dangerous relationships, the sanctity and utmost honour for marriage should be upheld more than it is. Truckloads of emotional pain and wounds would simply disappear if divorce became rare and the vast majority of marriages brought deep love, nurture, and blessing into the lives of children. Again, the teaching of Christ cuts to the core.

Jesus taught that we must forgive others as God has forgiven us. Forgiveness was a major part of His teaching, for He knew that everyone would be hurt some time or other and the only hope for reconciliation would be through forgiveness (Matt. 6:12,14-15,18:21-35; Mark 11:25; Luke 6:37,11:4,17:3-4; John 20:23; Col. 3:13). Forgiveness would be like a spiritual shield preventing bitterness, resentment, anger, rage, hatred, and more from entering one's spirit and damaging one's inner being. Forgiveness would be a means to bring healing and release and to liberate us from many different types of emotional prisons. But psychology is only now beginning to appreciate what Jesus clearly and simply taught over two thousand years ago. Forgiveness has all but been neglected in secular psychology. Benner wrote:

> A computer search of over one thousand professional journals
> of psychology, psychiatry, and related fields identified only

fifty-five articles in the last fifteen years that even mentioned the word "forgiveness." Of these, only a small handful provide detailed consideration of the dynamics of forgiveness or its role in emotional healing.[50]

If the teaching of Jesus on forgiveness were fully followed, there would be an incredible amount of emotional and even physical healing today, as well as prevention of emotional and physical pain and wounds in the first place. Again, the teachings of Christ cut to the core.

People with anxiety disorders, panic attacks, addictions, obsessive-compulsive disorders, and more lack what is most essential—the peace of Christ (John 14:27). His peace is not of this world and provides the ultimate answer deep within our soul. The goal then is to connect with Jesus such that we experience His peace as well as His love and grace.

The above from the teachings of Jesus is only a small sample; there is much more that applies to modern psychiatry if we study the Gospels and listen first to the wisdom of Jesus.

Conclusion

Emotional suffering and pain are intensely spiritual issues. The Scriptures and in particular the teachings of Jesus, not psychiatry, provide the ultimate reference for the care of our souls. The attempts to turn sin, unhappiness, and life's crises into diseases and turn sanctification into biology must be resisted. What is "normal" must be defined by the spiritual realities of the kingdom of God. Life in the Spirit involves things that the natural man simply cannot understand (1 Cor. 2:14,1:20; Isa. 29:14).

The teachings of Christ stand above all the issues, no matter how scientific and technical, and are entirely and profoundly relevant. We devalue and diminish our souls to think otherwise.

Endnotes _____

[1] David Healy, *The Creation of Psychopharmacology* (Cambridge: Harvard University Press, 2002) p. 58.

247

2 Ibid.

3 Garth Wood, *The Myth of Neurosis: Overcoming The Illness Excuse* (New York: Harper and Row, 1986) p. 40.

4 Ty C. Colbert, *Depression and Mania: Friends or Foes? A New "Non-Drug" Model of Hope for Depression, Mania, and Compulsive Disorders* (Santa Ana: Kevco Publishers, 1995) pp. 55-56.

5 Barbara Brown Taylor, *Speaking of Sin: The Lost Language of Salvation* (Cambridge: Cowley Publications, 2000) pp. 24,21.

6 Taylor, pp. 31,53.

7 Taylor, pp. 38,54.

8 Gerald G. May, *The Dark Night Of The Soul: A Psychiatrist Explores the Connection Between Darkness and Spiritual Growth* (New York: HarperSanFrancisco, 2004) p. 6.

9 Frank Lake, *Clinical Theology: A Theological and Psychiatric Basis to Clinical Pastoral Care* (London: Darton Longman & Todd, 1966) p. xxvii.

10 St. John of The Cross, *Dark Night Of The Soul* (New York: Image Books. 1990 edition. Translated by E. Allison Peers, 1st edition, 1959).

11 Carolyn Gratton, *The Art of Spiritual Guidance: A Contemporary Approach To Growing In The Spirit* (New York: Crossroad, 1992).

12 Tad Dunne, *Spiritual Mentoring: Guiding People Through Spiritual Exercises to Life Decisions* (New York: HarperCollins Publishers, 1991).

13 Douglas Weiss, *The Final Freedom: Pioneering Sexual Addiction Recovery* (Fort Worth: Discovery Press, 1998).

14 Douglas Weiss, *Sex, Men, and God* (Lake Mary: Siloam, 2002) pp. 18-25.

15 Harvey Milkman and Stanley Sunderwirth, *Pathways to Pleasure: The Consciousness and Chemistry of Optimal Living* (New York: Lexington Books, 1993) pp. 83-120.

16 Milkman et al., 101.

17 Weiss, 1998, pp. 24-63.

18 Weiss, 2002, pp. 18-25.

19 Weiss, 2002, p. 109.

20 Ibid.

21 Edward T. Welch, *Addictions—A Banquet In The Grave: Finding Hope In The Power of the Gospel* (Phillipsburg: P&R Publishing Company, 2001) pp. 37-40.

[22] Jeffrey Satinover, *Homosexuality And The Politics of Truth* (Grand Rapids: Hamewith Books, 1996) p. 149.

[23] Satinover, p. 147.

[24] Welch, pp. 46-60.

[25] Milkman et al., pp. 96-97.

[26] Dieter Mulitze, *The Great Substitution: Human Effort or Jesus to Heal and Restore the Soul?* (Belleville: Essence Publishers, 2003) pp. 293-321.

[27] Harvey Milkman and Stanley Sunderwirth, *Craving For Ecstasy: How Our Passions Become Addictions and What We Can Do About Them* (San Francisco: Jossey-Bass Inc., 1987) p. 6.

[28] Karl Stern, *The Third Revolution: A Study of Psychiatry and Religion* (New York: Harcourt, Brace and Company, 1954) p. 244.

[29] A. Frances, H.A. Pincus, and M.B. First. *American Psychiatric Association: Diagnostic and Statistical Manual of Mental Disorders, Fourth Edition, Text Revision* (Washington: American Psychiatric Association, 2000) p. 332.

[30] David J. Halperin, *Seeking Ezekiel: Text and Psychology* (University Park: The Pennsylvania State University Press, 1993) p. 1.

[31] Halperin, pp. 2,117.

[32] Halperin, pp. 4.

[33] Halperin, pp. 218.

[34] Halperin, pp. 72,135.

[35] Halperin, p. 117.

[36] Halperin, p. 4.

[37] Halperin, p. 223.

[38] Halperin, p. 5.

[39] Halperin, p. 223.

[40] Farber, 1993, p. 38.

[41] Dieter Mulitze, *The Great Omission: Resolving Critical Issues for the Ministry of Healing and Deliverance* (Belleville: Essence Publishers, 2001) pp. 39-54.

[42] Douglas Groothuis, "Jesus: Philosopher and Apologist," *Christian Research Journal*, Vol. 25, no. 2 (Rancho Santa Margarita: Christian Research Institute International) p. 30.

[43] Groothuis, p. 50.

[44] Groothuis, pp. 47-48.

[45] Colbert, 2000, p. 119.

[46] Vitz, Paul C. *Faith Of The Fatherless: The Psychology of Atheism* (Dallas: Spence Publishing Company, 1999) p. 4.

[47] Vitz, p. 16.

[48] Vitz, pp. 17-55.

[49] Solomon Schimmel, *The Seven Deadly Sins: Jewish, Christian, and Classical Reflections on Human Psychology* (New York: Oxford University Press, 1997) p. 139.

[50] David G. Benner, *Healing Emotional Wounds* (Grand Rapids: Baker Book House, 1990) p. 134.

Chapter Eleven

Healing Prayer and Psychiatry: A Comparison

I pray also that the eyes of your heart may be enlightened in order that you may know the hope to which he has called you, the riches of his glorious inheritance in the saints, and his incomparably great power for us who believe (Eph. 1:18-19).

Jesus went throughout Galilee, teaching in their synagogues, preaching the good news of the kingdom, and healing every disease and sickness among the people. News about him spread all over Syria, and people brought to him all who were ill with various diseases, those suffering with severe pain, the demon-possessed, those having seizures, and the paralyzed, and he healed them (Matt. 4:23-24).

Charlene's Wall of Pain and Self-Rejection

Charlene experienced significant healing in the presence of Jesus. It was an immense joy to pray with her and see what the Lord would accomplish in her life. This is her account.

For about two weeks I had some very tense emotions, mostly sadness and deep anger. At any moment I could have started wailing. The people around me did their best to avoid me, since they never knew if I was going to lash out at them or not. I was easily offended and felt rejected at every turn.

One day when I was up in my bedroom crying out to the Lord, I realized that there was this huge wall of pain. It was such a strong wall of pain that I believe it was keeping love from getting through to me.

I was able to arrange a prayer appointment with Dieter and his prayer partner the next day. During the prayer time, God brought back a memory to me. It was one I have remembered many times, and I didn't think a whole lot about it. It happened when I was between seven and nine years old. I vividly remembered my mom sweeping the floor in the kitchen, with tears streaming down her face. I remembered wanting to help her, but I couldn't, knowing that I was so small. As we prayed into the memory, Dieter felt very strongly that this wall of pain that I have been feeling was *not my own but that of my mother's*. This was something that I had never thought of before; it had never occurred to me. As we prayed further into the memory, I started to remember how I felt. I had wanted to touch my mom or tell her that I loved her, but I knew she wouldn't receive it from me. So, I stood there and wished her pain on myself. I don't remember the actual words that I had spoken, but the Spirit confirmed that I had done so.

Dieter and his assistant then started to pray the pain off of me and the spiritual connection with my mom. I immediately fell on the floor crying and screaming. I don't know what else they prayed; all I know is that it didn't want to leave. Finally, the screaming stopped, and I sat up.

Another memory came to me. My mom told me this one, since I was a newborn when it happened. She had told me that the first two days of my life she gave me aspirin to put me to sleep at night because I was getting my days and nights mixed up. She was already trying to stop my emotions. She also told me that she had to stop nursing me because the five other children were curious. That spoke to my spirit that I was a burden.

The moment Dieter started praying for these things, I immediately got really heavy. I could hardly hold my head up. Dieter said that it was because I had taken on all my mom's burdens at that time. Dieter asked me to give these burdens to Jesus. I tried to do that, but I was so exhausted. Apparently I also took on all of my mom's exhaustion. All her pain, all her burdens, and all her exhaustion—no wonder I had been crying for weeks.

After they prayed these things off of me, I had a very peaceful release and rest. As we were leaving, there was a bubble of excitement rising within me. By the time we reached the car I couldn't contain it, and I talked all the way home.

During the two weeks after my healing prayer with Dieter and his assistant, I soon went through some more emotional pain. This time I could feel more strongly the pain of rejection. My mom's pain wasn't as painful as what I was feeling then. I spent a lot of my day doing trivial things, avoiding having to think about anything important. If I did, I would plunge into my pain and start crying. So, now it was my pain that I was feeling. I knew that I needed help again, so fortunately I was able to arrange a prayer appointment with Dieter.

In the prayer session, God revealed another memory. It was one where my dad had rejected me. Before this memory, Dieter got the word *self-rejection*. I knew it applied to me but didn't know why. My memory was from when I was ten or eleven years old. My friend Katie was over. We were in the basement playing with the balls on the pool table. My younger sister, Nancy, asked if she could play with us. I was going to say, "no, we don't want you," but I stumbled over my words and they came out that she could play. Nancy heard the tone of my voice and knew that I meant "no," and so she went and told my dad. Now, my dad had never, ever, taken an interest in or been involved with my friends and me. I guess my mom was gone that day. So, when my dad called me, I was shocked. He asked me why I wasn't letting Nancy play with us. I told him that I was letting her play. Then he just slapped me right across the face. This was my memory, and it was quite vivid.

As we delved into the feelings of the memory under the Spirit's direction, this is what was revealed. I was very angry with my dad since I felt he had no right to just waltz into my life when he had never been there before and suddenly discipline me. Unfortunately, we were raised with the view that it was a bad thing to be angry at your elders; it was a sin. So, I internalized all my anger and turned it into self-rejection. After all, I did lie to Dad in saying that she could play while in reality I didn't want to say that she could play. So I felt like a bad person.

We—my seven brothers and sisters and I—didn't have any rights to our feelings. We weren't allowed to be angry or emotional. That's how we were raised. Dieter said that with self-rejection it is difficult to receive love God's love since the self-rejection becomes a barrier.

It was a joy to pray with Charlene and observe Jesus and His Spirit at work. The first prayer session required quite a time of waiting on the Lord and listening for His direction. The first memory that the Lord brought to her mind was one that had recurred over the years, often a sign that the Lord had already been speaking to her. We had all assumed that it was her pain, but when it was revealed that it was her mother's pain and that she had wished it upon herself in order to help her mother, then there was progress. From our viewpoint, there were strong and intense manifestations of pain and also demonic influences, especially while she was on the carpet on the floor. The Lord severed those very real spiritual connections with her mother. A number of evil spirits were rebuked with minimal manifestations. Their power was immediately broken when Charlene confessed that all pain and burdens must be given to Jesus and that He alone is the Saviour and the One who atones for sin. After many intense moments, Charlene was overcome with the Spirit's peace. This memory revealed the root of the pain. Since that prayer time, that pain has totally vanished.

The memory about playing with a friend might seem trivial. However, it's all in how a person perceives and feels in the event. She agreed with us that when her own father, so totally unexpected, hit her in the face, the effect went deep within her heart and spirit. It was like her whole world changed in an instant. She obviously experienced rejection from her father. It was the self-rejection that went deeper still and has had such an effect upon her life—until coming into Jesus' presence in the prayer time.

The emotional pain that Charlene experienced was real and intense, affecting her relationships and her ability to function. A psychiatrist might have diagnosed her as depressed and prescribed an antidepressant. After all, the cause of her pain and crying were not obvious. She might have been even told that she had a severe chemical imbalance or perhaps a genetic disorder. This would have been unfortunate, since she simply needed to experience the healing presence of Jesus and the power of the Cross of Christ.

Psychiatry or Healing Prayer: Which Would You Choose?

There are many compelling reasons why healing prayer, centred in the healing presence of Jesus, is preferable to psychiatric interventions. This does not rule out in some cases psychiatry *and* healing prayer, but given the choice of initial or more psychiatric interventions as opposed to initial or more healing prayer, which would you choose?

In any case, one should always have a thorough medical checkup from a qualified and competent doctor to determine if there might be any truly biological reason for the emotional suffering. There is no contradiction between faith and medicine. God can and does heal through doctors and medicines, and we should be thankful.[1] I do realize that not all Christians believe in, or wish to experience, healing prayer as I have described in this book. I have seen many times first hand that coming into the healing presence of Jesus is far superior to anything that psychiatry, psychotherapy, or counselling can ever offer. The crux is the *Presence of a Person*, as opposed to the application of a method, analysis, or psychiatric medication. My reasons for this preference are as follows.

Ultimate goals: The ultimate goal in healing prayer is the formation of Christ in a person (Gal. 4:19), with increased holiness and sanctification. This involves learning to live by and within the kingdom of God, which is ultimate reality and was so important to Jesus. This is different from psychiatry where the goal is managing symptoms and behaviour patterns so that one might be functional and adjusted in life—certainly commendable to a degree. This distinction is crucial, since the ultimate goal or objective will determine everything else that follows. The final result will be either a child of the living God or one who functions and manages symptoms in the modern world as idealized by men. The mental health system effectively helps people conform to a world with values contrary to Christ.[2] The therapeutic self is not the same as the new self in Christ.

Psychiatry, and the mental health movement in general, have a pathological view of man. Life is viewed by "what is wrong," almost a negative view of health. In contrast, the biblical view of man has a positive final view—to become like Jesus, who is the one and only perfect model of humanity. Healing prayer helps people to become like Jesus, not just removing or suppressing negative aspects of life.

Ministering to the whole person: Healing prayer involves praying for the whole person, including body, soul, and spirit. Although some psychiatrists will engage in counselling or therapy, most focus on the body, especially brain chemistry. This leads to a materialistic and reductionistic view of people. Consciousness is more than molecules. Healing prayer involves ministering to one's soul and spirit and one's *whole life history*. This avoids the pitfall of reductionism.

Servanthood: Jesus came as the servant of many (Matt. 20:28; Mark 10:43). He came to heal, restore, save, and to take people's burdens. Healing prayer teams come as servants to those seeking healing prayer. This is unlike psychiatry, which in the end serves itself and the pharmaceutical industry more than the people it seeks to treat, as has been amply documented in this book.

Release from sin and guilt: Sin is a reality in this world and deeply impacts the human soul (John 1:29;16:8; Rom. 3:9,5:12-14;6:12-14). Through confession, forgiveness, and the Cross of Christ, people can be healed and released from the power of sin in their lives. Guilt is God's call to healing, a doorway to grace to experience the love of the Father; it is not a neurosis or compulsion. Much inner woundedness and pain involves having been sinned against and, at times, one's sinful reactions. Modern psychiatry, operating apart from the Cross of Christ, does not address this—a tragic, massive deficiency.

No labels: There is no need at all to find a "label" to "classify" a person. Such labels are designed to bring people under the control and authority of mental health professionals and psychiatrists; healing prayer simply seeks to bring hurting people into the presence of Christ. It is enough to know that each person is created in the image of God, a person in need of more healing, a person yet to experience more of the love of Jesus. There is no worry about getting the wrong label plus all the problems and assumptions that come with them. Each person's history and situation is unique; therefore no label or labels will fit well enough. It is enough to know and communicate the symptoms, the pain, the anguish of soul and spirit, and all that relates to one's life.

The biblical "categories" of bondage, worry, anxiety, shame, guilt, fear, bondage, oppression, and so forth from everyday terminology are entirely sufficient. Jesus was interested in healing individual people, not diagnosing and managing symptoms and behaviour. The Gospel accounts of the healings Jesus gave are in no way inferior to the supposed scientific sophistication of psychiatry.

Affirmation: The person receiving healing prayer is never considered mentally defective or labelled with a disorder. Instead, the person is of immense value (Matt. 6:26,30), created in the image of God, loved and cared for by Jesus. This is in contrast to psychiatry, which tends to use sophisticated labels and diagnoses that can define a person as defective, or strange, or difficult, or undesirable, for example.

Discernment: Discernment leads to true understanding, to the deeper reality in a person's life, so that the Lord's direction may be followed. Discernment comes by grace and the gifts of the Spirit and is unique to each person's situation. Each and every one of the gifts of the Spirit operates today,[3] and cessationism is unscriptural and totally erroneous.[4] Gerald May, a Christian psychiatrist, while affirming the accuracy of psychiatric labels, wrote that they reveal nothing "about the essence of a person" or the soul.[5] While diagnosis tries to analyze and overcome mystery in life, discernment aims to respond to that mystery "in accordance with God's will."[6]

Discernment is crucial in a person's spiritual life.[7][8] Is it "dysthymia" or "personality disorder" or a deep issue in the spiritual life? Is the demonic involved?

This is fundamental, since Christians want to know "what's happening?; why do I feel this way?" We can ask, as the Psalmist did, "*Why are you downcast, O my soul?*" (Ps. 42:11). This comes by waiting upon the Holy Spirit and using the spiritual gifts of wisdom, word of knowledge, and discernment.

When I pray with people, I fully expect Jesus and His Spirit to be present and reveal the cause(s), with no preconceived ideas on my part. The wisdom of God is required. Life is complex, often a mystery, and one cannot trivialize the human soul through scientific reductionism or rationalism. Rather than short-circuit understanding or blunt revelation due to altered consciousness from drugs, we immediately begin to understand.

Reliance on the wisdom of Jesus: Healing prayer does not rely on anyone's analytical cleverness. Rather, there is a conscious reliance on Jesus, in whom are hidden all treasures of wisdom and knowledge (Col. 2:3).[9] Jesus Himself is the wisdom and power of God (1 Cor. 1:24). Healing prayer takes this seriously and expects the wisdom of Christ, as He is present, to permeate the healing prayer session. While we can be thankful for the skill and insights of psychiatrists who truly care for their patients, psychiatry simply cannot match this.

No medication: Since there are no categories or diagnoses of mental disorders and no drugs are required, there are no side effects, long-term brain damage, or addiction or withdrawal issues. Given the very real negative side effects of psychiatric drugs and their documented and known hazards, this is not a small point.

Power to overcome oppressive spiritual forces: Healing prayer relies directly on the world view of Jesus, which includes the possibility of oppressive spiritual forces that can cause apparent mental illness or psychosis. The demoniac of the Gerasenes (Mark 5:1-16) was tormented by many evil spirits, shown in behaviour like violent rage and self-mutilation. In psychiatric terms, he would be diagnosed with manic-depressive psychosis or bipolar affective disorder.[10] Jesus delivered him of many demons, and he was "*in his right mind*" (Mark 5:15). This is a clear example of evil spirits causing behaviour that would have a psychiatric label. Today, such a person might be locked in a cell and put in strong shackles. The voices he heard were not delusions or hallucinations. This was a *normal* man in bondage to an evil and *abnormal* reality. Personality disorders, psychoses, hysteria, seizures, schizophrenia, delusions, hallucinations, depression, suicidal tendencies, and much more encountered in psychiatry may at times be caused by demonic oppression.[11] Similarly, involvement with the occult can cause severe mental disturbances of many forms.[12] John White wrote about his very clear, direct encounters with the demonic in his practice of psychiatry and believed that possibly many people suffering from mental diseases are demonized.[13] While Dissociative Identity Disorder (DID) is not the same as demonization, DID may well involve demonization.[14]

Psychiatry is impotent when faced with such realities. One must be prepared to confront all sorts of spiritual forces. The presence of evil spirits and many forms of spiritual oppression, when they are truly there, must be discerned and dealt with in the power of Jesus' name.[15,16] There are documented examples of people never responding to normal psychiatric treatment but instantly healed by healing prayer with deliverance from evil spirits.[17]

Psychiatric drugs are totally useless when encountering evil spiritual forces—only the power, blood, and authority of Jesus can deal with such realities.

Open to communication: The symptoms or presenting problems are understood as communication of deeper issues and are more than just signs for correct drug selection. The phenomenon or behaviour itself is not the problem but a sign of something else, something deeper. Instead of a disease or an illness, there is a spiritual need or crisis. This makes for a radically different comprehension.

Power to heal: People need actual, real healing, not just more analysis. Healing prayer seeks to minister actual healing in the Presence of Christ. Jesus is not only the "therapist" but the actual therapy. Physical, emotional, relational, or spiritual healing can happen in healing prayer in the presence of Christ and His Spirit. Often, the core is simply experiencing the love of Christ. At conferences and training seminars, I often refer to this as "spiritual open heart surgery." This is different from psychiatry focused on drug treatments that don't address the causes and underlying issues and don't offer direct healing. Removal or management of symptoms or regaining normal functioning is not the same as healing or the restoration of one's soul. Psychiatry seeks to make people stable or functional; healing prayer seeks the *transformation* of people.

Since healing prayer is intensely relational and not a "push button," not everyone is healed—or it takes a while—although each believer is loved by the Lord.[18] As John White wrote in *The Masks of Melancholy*:

> I believe divine healing is real. I believe gifts of healing are still practiced today. Yet I also believe that God in his sovereign purposes does not always grant healing and has never promised always to do so.[19]

But, in my experience, the majority of people receiving healing prayer are healed.

Dependency on Jesus and His Spirit alone: Depending upon the emotional or spiritual need, psychiatric intervention can delay resolution of life's problems, create a dependency on psychiatry and psychiatrists, and thus rob people of the opportunity to take responsibility. This undermines our self-respect if we can't take responsibility for our actions and behaviour. Rather, one should be dependent upon Jesus.

No or little expense: Healing prayer, as offered freely through the Church, will not incur expense as commonly found via psychotherapy or psychiatry. Not a few people, after considerable expense in counselling and psychiatry, received healing prayer on several occasions and began to experience significant improvement if not complete healing.

Kathryn: Further Healing

The first part of Kathryn's story appeared earlier in this book, as well as what she wrote about her struggles with Lexapro. As part of her journey in healing, she attended one of our healing prayer retreats. This is what she wrote.

I have to say in all honesty that I was skeptical prior to going on the retreat—believing that there was little hope of getting better and not needing the Lexapro any more. I have struggled with intermittent depression and anxiety for the better part of my adult life, using medication at times when it was most difficult, so how could one weekend retreat make a difference?

The unique quality of this retreat was that the focus and "life" of its program was not in prayer-filled methodologies, "360° feedback," or group therapy sessions, but rather waiting solely in the presence of Jesus, trusting Him to show up and bring truth to light and to minister healing to the deep places of wounding in people's hearts. We often act out our pain, not being consciously aware of or knowing its origin, but the One who created our hearts sees our pain, and He knows how, in what setting, and when to bring healing. I am so thankful today for those who have faith in His presence and are willing even to be "a fool for Jesus"—knowing that if He doesn't show up, nothing will change.

My story is one you hear often these days. I grew up in an alcoholic home. The verbal and emotional abuse escalated with my dad's increased use of alcohol, and I was his "punching bag." The words "I love you" were never spoken by either of my parents. I recall making martinis at a very young age and then doing whatever was necessary to avoid the angry outbursts that resulted as my dad became more and more intoxicated. In the morning, I served him coffee before he even got out of bed, after hearing him call to me from his room. "Hey, Dummy, where's my coffee?"

I became pregnant when I was twenty-five years old. I was engaged at the time, but my fiancé decided that he was not ready to be a father and told me that if I would not have an abortion, it was my baby. Through God's miraculous intervention, I became a Christian during my pregnancy and looked forward to the birth of my child, even though it seemed I would be raising him (or her) alone. I had a strong sense of God's presence during those nine months and felt in my heart that He would take care of us.

God's abiding presence notwithstanding, the years that followed were often difficult, as I lived out of a very wounded and shame-based identity, struggling emotionally and financially as a single mother. My son is almost thirty years old now. I never married, and the journey of faith during my single parenting years was filled with the unhealed pain of abuse from my childhood, along with the shame of being an "unwed mother" in a church that preached, but did not live out, the true message of God's forgiveness and unconditional acceptance.

As we entered into prayer that first day of the retreat, we waited in His presence. Neither the prayer ministers nor I had any desire to bring up issues just for the sake of discussion or some forced pseudo-healing. Having recently experienced a very painful betrayal in which I felt my heart "shut down" and more abuse from a "Christian" counsellor, I knew that conventional therapy would not bring the healing that could restore my broken heart. I needed Jesus.

Shame was the word that first came clearly to mind as we waited in silence. God showed me that this was the root of my pain and that I had been living with a shame-based identity for most of my life. I knew that before, but this time, I felt it rise up from deep within my being, and for the first time in months I wept. This in itself was a miracle since the Lexapro had kept me so numb that I was not able to cry at all for months.

In prayer, the Holy Spirit replayed a vision of what to me was a painfully recurring memory from my childhood. My father was sitting next to me at the dinner table, shaking his head as he looked at me, saying "Dummy, Dummy, Dummy... or his other line, which was "Damn, why couldn't you have been a boy?" As I watched this scene again in my mind's eye, I saw Jesus enter the room. He asked my father to leave the room, and He sat down in my father's chair. Jesus looked at me with eyes of tenderness and compassion and told me that I was a precious daughter. I literally felt a sense of relief at that moment, as if I had been carrying a heavy weight on my back that was suddenly removed.

Two verses came to mind during our prayer time. The first was Jeremiah 30:8 (AMP): *"For in that day, says the Lord Almighty, I will break the yoke from their necks and snap their chains. Foreigners will no longer be their masters. For my people will serve the Lord their God."* The next verse was Psalm 45: 10-11 (AMP). *"Hear, O daughter, consider, submit, and consent to my instruction: forget also your own people and your father's house; So will the King desire your beauty; because He is your Lord, be submissive and reverence and honor Him."* That makes me a princess.

Because of a recently discovered need to adjust my thyroid medications, I have not been able to discontinue the Lexapro at the time I am writing this. Even on the medication, however, and since the retreat, I have a new and deeper understanding of God's love and healing touch in my life, and I look forward to a day in the very near future when I will not be using an anti-depressant. One thing that I believe for sure is that the numbness and inability to emotionally connect with God and others that come from taking these medications is not the abundant life that is ours in Christ. It is a sad commentary that even in the Church we have come to settle for medicating the mind rather than healing the soul.

Shortly after the retreat, God spoke to me about my personal responsibility on this journey towards wholeness. One day in prayer, I heard Him say, "We have dealt with what initially caused your pain—your father's sin against you. Now let's deal with the choices you have made that have kept you there." I have since repented in a new way of my sinful choices, not the least of which included idolatry that resulted in codependency and self-forfeiture, asking God to continue to lead me into health and wholeness that will come with His healing presence *and* my co-operation.

As I reflect more on that weekend, I truly know that *I am different!* I have a new sense of boldness that I did not have before, and God has allowed situations that have proven it to be true—situations in which I would have been very intimidated a week ago. Also, the sense of shame is gone! I feel "lighter," and it's *nothing* that I have done; I feel like I've been "born again, again." I can't get enough of Jesus these days—I stop and worship Him anytime and anywhere now.

Endnotes _____

[1] Dieter Mulitze, *The Great Omission: Resolving Critical Issues for the Ministry of Healing and Deliverance* (Belleville: Essence Publishers, 2001) pp. 92-98.

[2] Seth Farber, *Unholy Madness: The Church's Surrender to Psychiatry* (Downers Grove: InterVarsity Press, 1999) p. 64.

[3] Mulitze, 2001, pp. 115-132.

[4] Mulitze, 2001, pp. 133-185.

[5] Gerald G. May, *Care of Mind, Care of Spirit: A Psychiatrist Explores Spiritual Direction* (San Francisco: Harper, 1992) p. 150.

[6] May, p. 153.

[7] Simon Chan, *Spiritual Theology: A Systematic Study Of The Christian Life* (Downers Grove: InterVarsity Press, 1998) pp. 1992-224.

[8] Thomas Dubay, *Authenticity: A Biblical Theology of Discernment* (San Francisco: Ignatius, 1997 revised edition).

[9] Dieter Mulitze, *The Great Substitution: Human Effort or Jesus to Heal and Restore the Soul?* (Belleville: Essence Publishers, 2003) pp. 311-316.

[10] John Wilkinson, *The Bible and Healing: A Medical and Theological Commentary* (Grand Rapids: Eerdmans, 1998) pp. 72-73.

[11] John Warwick Montgomery, editor, *Demon Possession: A Medical, Historical, Anthropological and Theological Symposium* (Minneapolis: Bethany Fellowship, Inc., 1975) pp. 223-279.

[12] Kurt E. Koch, *Christian Counseling And Occultism: A Complete Guidebook to Occult Oppression and Deliverance* (Grand Rapid: Kregel Resources, 1994) pp. 201-206.

[13] John White, *The Masks of Melancholy: A Christian Physician Looks at Depression & Suicide* (Downers Grove: InterVarsity Press, 1982) pp. 27-39.

[14] Charles H. Kraft, *Confronting Powerless Christianity: Evangelicals and the Missing Dimension* (Grand Rapids: Chosen Books, 2002) pp. 49-50.

[15] Mulitze, 2001, pp. 229-275.

[16] Mulitze, 2001, pp. 307-311.

[17] Montgomery, p. 271.

[18] Mulitze, 2001, pp. 101-107.

[19] White, p. 40.

Chapter Twelve

Conclusion

Do not associate with these nations that remain among you; do not invoke the names of their gods or swear by them. You must not serve them or bow down to them. But you are to hold fast to the Lord your God, as you have until now (Josh. 23:7-8).

See to it that no one takes you captive through hollow and deceptive philosophy, which depends on human tradition and the basic principles of this world rather than on Christ (Col. 2:8).

Jesus answered, "The work of God is this: to believe in the one he has sent" (John 6:29).

Jeannette: Walking in Newness

Jeannette, a committed Christian, came for healing prayer. Jeannette had a compulsion for overeating and was overweight. It was soon apparent that there were deep emotional roots behind the presenting issues. Jeannette experienced the healing presence of Christ, perfectly unique to her history and the deepest needs of her soul. Jesus brought healing from past memories; she experienced His love in very moving visionary experiences. There were moments of silence when Jeannette had many tears as the Lord healed her while she experienced His love in the exact places that she needed it. This is what she wrote:

> If I had to describe to you in one word what first comes to mind when I think about the Lord it would be His faithfulness. On this journey of faith I have been blessed to have received wonderful teaching, compassionate counselling, and hours of prayer. However, there was always a sense that there was *something missing*—I either wasn't grasping it or I wasn't worthy of receiving healing in certain areas.
>
> What was I doing wrong? After all these years as a faithful Christian, why was I plagued with the inability to move past some of my struggles? Over the last several years I really sensed that the Lord was longing to set me free so that I could be used by Him for His Kingdom. I knew that there were hurts in my life that needed to be healed so that I could fully live the life that He wanted for me. I believe that He always provides a way for us. For me, He provided the *ministry of deeper love* so that the Holy Spirit could come to heal me and set me free to walk in His newness.
>
> In my healing session with a Deeper Love Ministries team, I had shared with the prayer team that I have struggled with my weight since my early twenties. They suggested that I ask the Lord to show me if there had ever been a time when food had been withheld from me. Instantly, the Lord gave me a picture of when I was a little girl sitting in a small chair around a large kitchen table. One of the prayer team members asked me if the number "five" meant anything to me. In that moment I knew it was my fifth birthday party. Both my mom and dad were present and I saw my mom cutting my birthday cake into very thin pieces. I never got a piece of my birthday cake, because there wasn't enough to go around. At that moment, I felt insignificant. I wanted to be big; I wanted to be noticed. It was my birthday and I still wasn't important; I felt invisible.

Birthdays or any kind of events in our home were not tackled with excitement or love but simply as an event to get through. It was never fun—just an obligation. The prayer team then asked where Jesus was at my party, and I saw Him standing between my mom and dad. He lifted me off the chair, and He held me, with my head snuggled into His shoulder. I cried, and He comforted me. He then cradled me in His arms and told me how much He loved me. After He held me for a time, He put me down and told me to go and play and have fun. I ran happily along, turning often to ensure that He was still with me. (It should be noted that I had no memories of fun and laughter and play as a child, but I always had a memory of a little girl with her arms stretched up, wanting to be picked up.) And of course He was there strolling along and laughing and delighting in my fun. I love the sense I got that Jesus wasn't in a hurry and He was just happy to be spending time with me.

At one point I went through the gate of a chain-link fence, and I believe that picture represented the prison I had always been in. One of the prayer team members had indicated early on in our session that she saw the Lord massaging my heart. I believe with all the hurts and disappointments I had been through, my heart had become hardened. This was the Lord's way of showing me that He was bringing me back to life.

After coming through this gate, I ran into an open field with green grass and nothing but blue sky for miles. I then had a vision of flying a kite that was yellow, red, and green, and the Lord was holding it up with His breath. If you had asked me how to describe my childhood using a colour, I would have said grey. Therefore, the kite represented the colour that I never had in my childhood. Jesus then threw me up in the air, laughing and delighting in my happiness. I knew without a doubt that I was one of God's kids and that I was loved and I belonged.

At this point the prayer team asked me to confess the lie that I had always felt, that I needed to be big to be noticed and that I was insignificant and really not lovable. You see, the thread that had always been in my life was that I was alone and that, even though I heard the Lord loved me and that I was one of His kids, I never felt that way. I always felt like a fraud and that even the Lord wasn't really there for me.

I always remember wanting to be picked up and loved when I was a little girl, but my parents were emotionally unable to nourish me the way a little girl should be. So the lie had been planted, and it stayed with me until the Holy Spirit came in and revealed the lie. After I confessed the lie, I saw a picture of my head with a large slice of my head being removed. I then saw the top of someone's head where the hair is parted down the middle, and then suddenly I looked up into the eyes of Jesus—and it was me as a little girl, and that was the top of my head. That slice in my head was now gone, and the lie was gone forever.

The Holy Spirit wasn't finished yet, and He took me back to a time when I was a young girl of around ten or twelve. I was with a girlfriend, and we were exploring our bodies together. The Lord gave me a picture of this incident—it was very clear in my mind. At that moment of the memory I saw Him come into the bedroom and lift me from the bed. I had confessed any sin on my part. He carried me to a lake and washed me. Jesus then lifted me up from the water as clean and white as snow. We then strolled together, and for the first time in my life I felt clean and pure—very much like a lady. This incident had been revealed by the Lord, because I really had no memory of this event, even though it had actually happened. But all through my life I always felt unclean and I never knew why. When this was revealed, that sense of uncleanness and not being able to feel worthy was removed.

When I was growing up, my mother died when I was sixteen years old. My father was a workaholic. The only way my dad knew how to cope was to buy me things. But the only thing I wanted was my dad to pay attention, to be with me, to love me. He bought me a '63 Buick, baby blue with large wings out the back. Sixteen years old and my own car—wow, who wouldn't be happy! I wasn't; I just wanted my dad. So in one of my healing sessions, in a vision Jesus appeared in my '63 Buick, sitting in the passenger seat, once again delighting in spending time with me. The windows were down; the music was blaring (rock and roll—not hymns!). My hair and Jesus' hair was blowing in the wind, and we were having so much fun. When I thought I was alone and nobody wanted to spend time with me, Jesus had always been there.

This is just a "flavour" of my healing and how after years of struggling the Holy Spirit gave me such healing. The Lord has released me from that feeling of not belonging and not being loved, which manifested itself in so many areas of my life. I am healed and free from eating to fill up the emptiness, from seeking love in the wrong places.

Serving False Gods?

When Joshua was about to die, he challenged the nation of Israel to avoid the influence and idols of the nations around them and instead hold fast to the Lord (Josh. 23:7-8). He admonished the Israelites to never serve the gods of those nations nor ever bow down to them (Josh. 23:16).

Christians are generally very accepting of modern psychiatry. Incredibly, there are even committed Christians without an emotional problem who nevertheless want, even demand, a prescription for Prozac.[1] Many Christian authors advocate the use of psychiatric drugs for Christians, appealing to the supposedly scientific basis of psychiatry.

Meanwhile, many churches are *not* very accepting of the ministry of healing prayer. Only a minority of churches have trained, fully affirmed healing prayer teams, even though healing of the whole person is definitely part of the Great Commission.[2] Hardly any seminaries have courses on the ministry of healing prayer, while many seminaries offer courses on psychology, counselling, mental health, and "treatment plans" involving psychiatric drugs. I know of churches where the leadership is skeptical, if not even resistant, to healing prayer. But in those same churches, like others, many Christians will take Prozac or Zoloft with hardly a second thought. Isn't this all just a bit odd?

Many Christian authors advocate taking psychiatric drugs but with varying degrees of openness to counselling or therapy, in some cases healing prayer, and even in some cases openness to deliverance ministry. But nevertheless, it is repeatedly claimed that drugs will often play an important role because of the supposedly biological basis of emotional problems. After all, chemical imbalances in the brain and the genetics of mental illness are "established facts," with little room for doubt.

But as I have shown in this book, the supposed scientific basis of psychiatry is flawed, with numerous errors in logic, resting on "feet of clay." *Every Christian should know that the theory of chemical imbalances in the brain as a cause of "mental illness" is unproven, implausible, and incoherent and that the supposed genetics of mood swings and other emotional problems is simply untrue and unfounded.* Competent researchers have shown those ideas to be completely bankrupt. This is what every Christian should know. Anyone who doubts this indictment on the chemical imbalance theory should read *The Antidepressant Era,*[3] *The Creation of Psychopharmacology,*[4] and *Let Them Eat Prozac,*[5] all written by David Healy, a world-renowned historian of psychiatry, author, researcher, and academic.[6]

What is disturbing is that mostly non-Christian authors are the ones who take the time to point this out. This is not surprising, since evangelical Christians have *uncritically* accepted psychiatry, without any serious dialogue, and Christianity lost its mind in the process.[7] Many Christian intellectuals have uncritically adopted academic thinking and fallen for intellectual fashions that have become bankrupt.[8] What is more disturbing is that Christians are now for the most part misinformed, believing basically what the pharmaceutical companies want them to believe.

Depression as commonly known since the 1990s was virtually unknown as recent as thirty-five years prior.[9] When the first antidepressants were discovered, depression was relatively rare. What followed was the "invention of and marketing of depression."[10] In other words, a solution was accidentally found for a problem that was too small; therefore people had to be convinced that the problem is huge and universal in order to market the solution and generate billions of dollars in profits. Indeed, in just over a decade the number of diagnoses for depression increased one thousand times.[11] Did anyone notice? The marketing of depression has been very successful.

Books on psychiatry written by Christians must go well beyond simply quoting results from psychiatric journals, as many have done. Christians who read such books believe it is all authoritative and "proven," totally oblivious to the debate going on in psychiatry. Christians should know that there is another opinion on the matter.

As a research scientist myself who has published articles in international scientific journals, I have a high view of science. Being a Christian in science is as valid a calling as being a missionary or pastor. Christians conducting scientific research are actually "priests of creation" in the culture commission, while those in ministry are priests of redemption. Scientific research is a high calling and should move us to the highest scholarship and critical, careful reasoning for the glory of God and the sake of His people.

Yes, I am all for "All truth is God's truth." But I am not for uncritically, almost blindly, accepting the latest results from research in psychiatry. Before we accept something as "God's truth," we must first ask the question: is it truth?

What is really behind much of the research in psychiatry? Money, "market share," professionalism, power, and ideologies like scientific materialism, rationalism and reductionism. When you remove all the complex, long-winded arguments and reduce all those big words (my form of "reductionism"!), you are left with just the idols of mammon, power, and pride. I fully realize there are committed Christians serving within psychiatry, truly wanting to heal people. But I am talking about the larger picture, what the mental health "industry" as a whole has become.

How else do you explain researchers and company executives fabricating or burying research results? How else do you explain a drug company claiming that a new drug has proven effectiveness, is finally approved, and then when its patent protection expires it is suddenly reported as no longer effective by the same company while their next drug is now claimed as better and effective?[12] (And just when you thought planned obsolescence applied only to automobiles!) Scientific research is not conducted in pure academic isolation. Scientists also succumb to temptation and pride.

Too many Christian writers appear to have a simplistic, naive view of science. The gods of the foreign nations in Joshua's time have vanished. Idols of the mind and heart (Ezek. 14:3-7; Ps. 106:36; 1 John 5:21) have come to take their place, and they are far more destructive. Idolatry, a thoroughly biblical concept, provides the best framework for understanding our society.[13] Today there are idols of nature, mammon, history, power, religion, and humanity, influencing Christians in ways rarely noticed or understood.[14] We "bow down" and serve whatever forms our values, dictates our priorities and actions, and drives our motives. We cannot serve both God and money, for example (Matt. 6:24; Luke 16:13).

Unwittingly, as the Church has accepted modern psychiatry, it has embraced the idols that come with it. I fear that this has caused a spiritual stronghold within the Church. Modern psychiatry has become a Trojan horse in the Church. At the same time, the idols have put much of psychiatry in bondage, reflected in the fact that psychiatry has "lost its soul."[15]

As I mentioned at the beginning of this book, I am not against psychiatry *per se*. I am for a psychiatry, but a psychiatry true to its calling—the care of souls—and true to proper, sound research. I am also not against pharmaceutical companies *per se* either. There are drugs today that are useful and help promote healing, sometimes developed by committed, caring researchers. But I am for companies that appreciate a fair and just profit, still have a proper vision of truly helping people, and are not (largely) in bondage to the idols of mammon and power.

Christian Psychiatric Clinics and Mental Health Centres: A Real Alternative?

Are Christian-run psychiatric clinics and mental health centres much different from the world? Such clinics have been criticized for claiming to have a unique psychiatry when in fact there is nothing that makes them substantially different from secular psychiatry.[16] The exception is the use of Christian language, symbol, and ritual.[17] This is not to disparage any Christian clinics trying to be faithful to the Lord in all this.

Colbert expressed some reservation in dialoguing with one speaker from a well known Christian psychiatric hospital in the U.S.A.[18] The speaker claimed that his hospital, being a Christian one, kept drug use to "a minimum." When Colbert pursued the matter with the speaker, the speaker became defensive and evasive, and it was obvious that in actuality the drug use wasn't less than in other hospitals.[19] Colbert left the meeting irritated, feeling that the claim was made to convince ministers and therapists to send patients to that hospital.

Meanwhile, there are *secular* attempts to help people without drugs at all, in authentic "healing" communities like Mosher attempted with Soteria House. Such places exist now in Europe, for example. But since drugs are not used and psychiatrists are not needed and such a "treatment plan" is not easily billable by insurance companies or government health programs, funding is typically tight.

Some Christians advocate *both* psychiatric drugs and healing prayer of some form and, at times, deliverance ministry. This is certainly different from modern psychiatry's reductionism and fixation with drug therapy. As commendable as this view is, it leads to syncretism—mixing

275

truth with error and yet appearing acceptable. The pressures of the mental health system as a whole, professional liability, people's expectations for a "quick fix," the avoidance of personal responsibility and sin, and more basically force this view on Christians in the mental health system. But an entirely different matter is declaring to the Church that psychiatric drug therapy with healing prayer and deliverance is *the* accepted and biblical view—that view is indefensible and misleading.

Forsaking Living Water

An overwhelming mountain of scientific and clinical evidence proves that emotional wounds—a hurting soul—are the real causes of mental "illness." Past trauma, including child abuse, causes deep wounds in the soul and sometimes physical illness. Modern psychiatry does not look for or seriously consider the possibility of past abuse or emotional wounds in its patients, except for psychiatrists who take the time to do so. At one time psychiatry believed and taught that this was the case, when "dynamic" psychiatry was dominant. But in the "battle" over who gets to treat, and bill, for clients, psychiatry adopted the medical disease paradigm of suffering to make itself distinct from counsellors, psychologists, and therapists.

While there are hormonal and other physiological factors that can affect how we feel, the effect of past emotional pain and woundedness on the body—and even neurotransmitters if we could ever reliably measure them—must be fully and seriously taken into account. Yet psychiatric research resists this, since it would mean that drugs are not the solution. If drugs are not the solution, then who needs a psychiatrist? If it really is a love or relational deficit and not a neurotransmitter deficit, then therapy, and especially healing prayer, are needed.

There are mountains of books written on the effectiveness of psychiatric drugs as compared to counselling or therapy. Psychiatrists favour studies that show an advantage for drugs; therapists favor studies that vindicate therapy. Then another mountain of books compares different types of counselling and therapies, with confusing and inconclusive results when the dust settles after all the heated debates.

The Church has not only accepted psychiatry but also secular forms of counselling and therapy, simply "baptizing" them from the world.[20] As many Christian authors have documented, the Church has essentially adopted the methods and techniques of the world in healing and transforming the human soul.[21] Many pastors and counsellors use secular techniques when attempting to help people.[22] Instead of experiencing the healing presence of Jesus and His Spirit (John 7:37-38; 1 Cor. 10:1-4), as the true stories in this book demonstrate, the Church has largely gone to broken cisterns (Jer. 2:13).

On the one hand, the "usual spiritual remedies" won't really help, because they are adaptations of the world's thinking. Remember that there are even spiritual techniques, and the technical mindset has invaded spirituality and even the ministry of healing prayer.[23] So the "usual" things tried in the Church don't work that well, and believers are then more open to taking psychiatric drugs. But on the other hand, the drugs don't work that well either—no cause and no cure. (Sorry, I've run out of hands!)

Christians, then, are actually caught between two different inroads of secularism in the Church, coming from two different directions. Christians with real emotional pain and woundedness are "caught in the middle." It's like everyone moving between business and economy class on a plane that is about to crash.

As a result, the great majority of Christians on psychiatric drugs are being unnecessarily treated by those drugs and unnecessarily exposed to all the risks. There are Christians in psychiatric wards who need not be there at all. Marcie, whose story is earlier in this book, was one of them. This is *not* to shame anyone at all on psychiatric drugs, nor to question anyone's commitment to Christ. Those who have been helped by psychiatric drugs can still give thanks. But the Church has become a huge referral agency, providing a steady stream of clients and billable revenue to mental health professionals. Everyone knows this. Yes, people are being helped somewhat—but is that the best for people, and is that what God intends?

Joshua warned the Israelites that if they were unfaithful to the Lord, didn't fully obey Him, and compromised with the surrounding nations (Josh. 23:7,12,16), then the Lord would be angry with His people and they would perish from the land (Josh. 23:13,16). We see some similarities for the Church in the Western world. In the U.S. in particular, while more Churches close and others grow smaller, the number of therapists and psychiatrists and other mental health professionals *doubles about every ten years* and grows in influence and wealth.[24]

Riding a '63 Buick with Jesus

Jeannette's healing, as she wrote, was centred on the real presence of the living Christ. Healing prayer sessions can be quite different, and everyone's story is unique, so please don't think her story is "typical" of healing prayer. However, her story illustrates some of the things that Jesus can and will do. I am continually amazed by what I see Jesus do in healing prayer; He is so creative!

Jeannette received healing through recalling past memories and experiencing visions, not unlike Ezekiel's.[25] Jesus came to her birthday party when she was five, flew a kite with her, and rode a '63 Buick with her. Jesus in His wisdom knew where to go in her early years and exactly how to heal her soul. I witnessed Jeannette shed many tears as Jesus quietly ministered to her. This all looks "unscientific," "unprofessional," and just too plain simple. No complex talk of neurotransmitters or techniques to reprogram neurological pathways. Simply the Presence of Jesus and His Spirit. However, in less than several hours Jeannette was healed deeply and profoundly changed.

Dare I say a "miracle"? If the world and even Christian authors can write about miracle drugs and "magic bullets," why can we not talk about a miracle from Jesus? This type of healing prayer, based on a theology of The Presence,[26] is something the world cannot offer and does not have. Jesus Himself becomes the "therapy" and the "therapist"; we drink the living water only (John 4:14). With our burdens, we come directly to Him (Matt. 11:28). It is by His might and power that souls are healed and people are transformed (cf. Josh. 23:9-10). Must we not humble ourselves (Matt. 18:4) and be like a child to enter the kingdom of God (Mark 10:15; Luke 18:17)? Why make things complex when Jesus wants to make them simple?

Joshua reminded the Israelites why the Lord parted the Red Sea and the Jordan River, among other many miracles. *"He did this so that all the peoples of the earth might know that the hand of the LORD is powerful and so that you might always fear the LORD your God"* (Josh. 4:24). Similarly, healing prayer centred on the presence of Christ and His Spirit will show the power of the Lord among His people, and some people will fear the Lord. After all, Jesus is the power of God and the wisdom of God (1 Cor. 1:24). Jesus will come and accomplish what the world cannot, because the Church is then not using the methods and techniques of the world. Jesus will do awesome things in our midst if we are obedient (Josh. 3:5). Our work first and foremost is to firmly believe in He whom the Father sent (John 6:29). We must be sure we are not ashamed of the gospel (Rom. 1:16) or of Jesus and His words (Mark 8:38; Luke 9:26). We must always *"hold fast"* to the Lord our God (Josh. 23:8) and renounce all our idols (Josh. 24:14). Our hope and strength must be entirely fixed on Jesus, never distracted by ideologies or idolatries that make us turn *"aside to the right or to the left"* (Josh. 23:6).

A Lost Presence

For some Christians, stories of healing prayer like Jeannette's or Kathryn's (which follows) are almost out of their comfort zone or not in their "theological grid." This is partly because the felt presence of God, known and experienced in the Church over the centuries, has been diminished in much of the Church today. This is reflected in the practical atheism among many contemporary believers.[27] The main factors behind this, coming from our present modern culture, are "narcissism, pragmatism, unbridled restlessness, and the loss of the ancient instinct for astonishment."[28] Contemplation becomes difficult; sensing God's presence becomes almost impossible.

Theological language and theology in the Western tradition from the Middle Ages onwards has focused *less on experiencing God and experimental knowledge of knowing Him, and more on abstract thoughts, discussion, and debate about Him.*[29] Inevitably, spiritual theology that concerns the nature, growth, and process of the supernatural life in Christ by His Spirit[30] has been almost totally neglected in many seminaries.[31] By neglecting spiritual theology, the Church has become almost totally reliant on secular views of human growth and development.[32] In essence, the spiritual life is similar to the "life of human growth and development."[33] Since healing prayer is a part of spiritual theology, it then appears as foreign or strange to not a few Christians and parts of the Church. Experiencing and comprehending the healing presence of the living Christ then becomes difficult for Christians. As Leanne Payne, author and founder of Pastoral Care Ministries puts it, the idea of "listening to God and moving in the power and authority He gives to heal is strangely alien to many modern Christians."[34] Kraft has characterized this also as a problem plaguing the evangelical Church, wherein spiritual power has been ignored.[35]

Challenges for the Church

When Nehemiah heard about the deplorable condition of Jerusalem and the trouble and disgrace among God's people there, he wept, mourned, and fasted (Neh. 1:3-4). Like Nehemiah, leaders in the Church and Christians must be moved by the current situation and really see it for what it is. There are untold thousands of Christians with stories of pain and woundedness like those of Tanya, Jacqueline, Kathryn, Charlene, James, Marcie, Anita, Paulette, Grace, Bart, and Jeannette as described in this book. Some Christians have committed suicide while on psychiatric drugs; others today languish in psychiatric wards. Does that not move us to tears, to conviction, to action, to change? This is not an academic exercise; real lives are at stake here.

The Church needs to reclaim a biblical psychology of the soul and thereby counter the reductionism seeping in all around us. The temptation to reduce sadness and unhappiness to brain chemistry should be resisted. The pressure to redefine sin and sanctification in biological terms must be countered. Psychiatry's definition of what is normal and what it means to be human must be challenged. Psychiatry's ways of invalidating and devaluing people must be confronted.

A strong theology and sense of the Presence of Christ and His Spirit must be recovered and experienced in the Church, as is happening in some churches. This should be accompanied by experiencing spiritual power and authority. Every church should have one or more healing prayer teams. I know of one church that has over thirty active healing prayer teams. People who are called to this ministry are typically "energized" when they see people healed in the presence of Christ.

Churches should be safe, authentic healing communities, with no trace of Compassion Deficit Disorder. Instead of referring many Christians to secular mental health experts, including psychiatrists, Christians should normally first receive ministry within the Church, fully believing in the transforming power of Jesus and His gospel.

The hurting and the wounded in the world should be coming to the Church, inquiring and asking about this Jesus, whom they hear still does miracles, still even today heals the most deeply wounded and troubled of people. This is part of outreach and of evangelism. The Church needs to take back its authority to bring healing into the world, no longer eclipsed by the mental health system, fully recovering its ancient mandate for the care and cure of souls.

The greatest apologetic for the gospel is truly changed lives. This is the clearest, most tangible hope to the millions in this world who lead wounded, despairing lives, including those living behind masks of success. Friends, family, spouses, co-workers, and neighbours tend to notice when someone is truly changed. It creates a hunger for eternal life in Christ. Tanya, Jacqueline, Kathryn, Jeannette, and others who have shared their true stories in this book are examples of this. Always, the focus is only on the healing Presence of the risen Christ in our midst. When Jesus is lifted up, He will draw all men unto Himself (John 12:32).

So what do you do if you are taking psychiatric drugs and want to stop? Get the best medical advice possible to ensure that there is no truly organic cause behind your emotional suffering. Get the best healing prayer available, from a healing prayer team equipped in this amazing ministry rooted in the Presence of Christ and His Spirit. You might need several sessions. As the Lord begins to heal you, begin to slowly reduce the dose of your drugs until you come off them entirely—but always with the counsel of your psychiatrist or physician. Hopefully you belong to a caring community of believers to help you in your spiritual journey.

Kathryn: More Healing from Jesus

The core of healing prayer involves coming into the presence of Jesus with His Spirit. Typically, healing prayer ministry involves a healing prayer team that will pray with the person coming for healing. Sometimes, the presence of Jesus is more "direct and discernible" when Jesus appears in a vision not unlike he did to Paul (Acts 9:10-15;18:9;22:17;23:11), or Peter (Acts 10:9-17), or especially Ezekiel.[36]

Sometimes a person will be healed through a visionary experience *without* a healing prayer team present. That is what happened to Kathryn as she received still more healing through the supernatural, real, presence of Jesus. The Lord also brought back memories, gave her Scripture, and touched the precise places in her soul that needed His healing presence. Properly understood, this is simply part of Christian spirituality that is basically "the lived encounter with Jesus Christ in the Spirit."[37] Kathryn wrote the following:

> This morning I had an incredible healing experience in His presence. As I waited, the Lord brought me back to the time when I was eighteen years old, when my mom taught me how to smoke. I was working nights in a factory to save money for college, and the atmosphere there—a place full of "tough" men—was causing me a lot of anxiety. My mom said I would feel better if I smoked. The Lord brought me back to the time and place that we sat on the floor in my parents' bedroom and Mom showed me how to inhale. As I coughed and sputtered I saw Jesus come into the room and stand between my mom

and me. He reached down to take my hand and pull me towards Him. He embraced me and then said this was not what He had for me.

Jesus and I then went to the kitchen of that house and sat at the table. He told me that this was the place where my feminine spirit received the most damage. We lived there from the time I was seventeen to twenty-two years old, and those were the years that my dad was the most unhappy in his job and drank the most. I recalled my eighteenth birthday, when my dad took me to his favourite nightclub. He got very drunk that night. Looking back, I know it wasn't to celebrate my birthday that we went there but just an opportunity for him to drink.

That was also the year that my dad wanted my brother and I to attend the same Catholic high school—this memory came back as well. There was only one opening, and it was in the senior class, and I was then a senior. I recall sitting in the principal's office with my dad and my brother as Dad asked the priest, "Can you give Tim the spot instead of her?" He said they could put me in a different school. The priest apologized and told my dad the only opening was in my class and that there was not a possibility of making a switch. We never talked about it again.

As I waited on the Lord, Isaiah 26 came to my mind. I thought I knew what was in that chapter, but verse 14 was new to me. I read in my Amplified Bible, *"They [the former tyrant masters] are dead, they shall not live and reappear; they are powerless ghosts, they shall not rise and come back. Therefore You have visited and made an end of them and caused every memory of them [every trace of their supremacy] to perish."*

It seemed harsh when I first read it, and I said "Lord, was my father a tyrant?" I immediately thought of what a tyrant does—namely, using his power to rule with intimidation and fear, thus crushing the spirit of the people. In that sense, my dad was a tyrant. I know he had his own pain and that is what caused him to be that way, but that doesn't lessen the negative effect that his behaviour had on a daughter. I sense the verse was metaphoric as well—regarding sin as a tyrant.

Jesus and I sat at that kitchen table for quite a while as He told me the truth of who I was then and am today. I think there will be more memories, as I felt God was really focusing on that five year period as a time when a lot of who I was got "crushed," so to speak, by my father's misogyny that was directed towards me and the resulting choices that I then made in relationships with men.

From Lexapro to Abundant Life

Kathryn was finally able to come completely off Lexapro, and began to experience even more of the abundant life of Jesus. Enthusiastically, she wrote the following:

> It has been almost three months since the healing prayer retreat. I am completely off the antidepressant and feeling—honestly— a wholeness and sense of well-being that I have not known at any time in my life until now. There has not been even a hint of a panic attack, anxiety, or the depression that had previously plagued my life and kept me at best in only a survival mode. I know now that this is not an "illness" that runs in my family, but rather a brokenness that God desires to heal. Now I know in my heart that God loves me, and I experience a sense of His presence daily that I had not known before. Others comment on the change they have seen in me. I am so grateful to the ministry team for their encouragement and the hope they bring to millions who, like me, have suffered from depression, believing it is their lot in life. This simple faith in the healing presence of Jesus is the answer that disproves the methodologies and popular teaching of even so-called "Christian" psychologists, showing them to be nothing more than a mediocrity that we have been asked to settle for even as believers, when God is longing to give to us the abundant life for which Jesus died.

Endnotes _____

[1] Dan Blazer, *Freud vs. God: How Psychiatry Lost Its Soul & Christianity Lost Its Mind* (Downers Grove: InterVarsity Press, 1998) p. 112.

[2] Dieter Mulitze, *The Great Omission: Resolving Critical Issues for the Ministry of Healing and Deliverance* (Belleville: Essence Publishers, 2001) pp. 55-76.

[3] David Healy, *The Antidepressant Era* (Cambridge: Harvard University Press, 1997).

[4] David Healy, *The Creation of Psychopharmacology* (Cambridge: Harvard University Press, 2002).

[5] David Healy, *Let Them Eat Prozac: The Unhealthy Relationship between the Pharmaceutical Industry and Depression* (New York: New York University Press, 2004).

[6] David Healy, current staff Web site: http://www.cardiff.ac.uk/medicine/psychological_medicine/stafflist/personal_web_pages/david_healy.htm.

[7] Blazer, p. 4.

[8] Herbert Schlossberg, *Idols for Destruction: Christian Faith and Its Confrontation with American Society* (Nashville: Thomas Nelson Publishers, 1983) pp. 8-9.

[9] Healy, 1997, p. 4.

[10] Healy, 1997, p. 5.

[11] Terry Lynch, *Beyond Prozac: Healing and Mental Distress* (Douglas Village: Mercier Press, 2005) p. 85.

[12] John White, *The Masks of Melancholy: A Christian Physician Looks at Depression & Suicide* (Downers Grove: InterVarsity Press, 1982) p. 125,128.

[13] Schlossberg, pp. 6-7.

[14] Schlossberg, pp. 1-344.

[15] Blazer, p. 94-99.

[16] Blazer, p. 174.

[17] Ibid.

[18] Ty C. Colbert, *Depression and Mania: Friends or Foes? A New "Non-Drug" Model of Hope for Depression, Mania, and Compulsive Disorders* (Santa Ana: Kevco Publishers, 1995) p. 52.

[19] Colbert, p. 53.

[20] Dieter Mulitze, *The Great Substitution: Human Effort or Jesus to Heal and Restore the Soul?* (Belleville: Essence Publishers, 2003) p. 39.

[21] Mulitze, 2003, pp. 33-58.

[22] Charles H. Kraft, *Confronting Powerless Christianity: Evangelicals and the Missing Dimension* (Grand Rapids: Chosen Books, 2002) p. 8,55.

[23] Mulitze, 2003, pp. 169-204.

[24] Jeffrey H. Boyd, *Reclaiming The Soul: The Search for Meaning in a Self-Centered Culture* (Cleveland: The Pilgrim Press, 1996) p. 40.

[25] Mulitze, 2003, pp. 316-319.

[26] Mulitze, 2003, pp. 59-112.

[27] Ronald Rolheiser, *The Shattered Lantern: Rediscovering a Felt Presence of God* (New York: The Crossroad Publishing Company, 2001) pp. 17-27.

[28] Rolheiser, pp. 15-53.

[29] Tilden H. Edwards. *Spiritual Friend* (Mahwah: Paulist Press, 1980) pp. 6,31,196.

[30] Simon Chan, *Spiritual Theology: A Systematic Study Of The Christian Life* (Downers Grove: InterVarsity Press, 1998) pp. 17-18.

[31] Edwards, p. 196.

[32] Edwards, p. 32.

[33] Lawrence S. Cunningham and Keith J. Egan, *Christian Spirituality. Themes From The Tradition* (New York: Paulist Press, 1996) p. 49.

[34] Leanne Payne, *The Healing Presence: How God's Grace Can Work in You to Bring Healing in Your Broken Places and the Joy of Living in His Love* (Wheaton: Crossway Books, 1989) p. 38.

[35] Kraft, pp. 115-137.

[36] Mulitze, 2003, pp. 316-319.

[37] Cunningham, p. 7.

Appendix: Some Helpful Web Sites

The Web sites below are recommended for further study. I do not necessarily agree with everything you may encounter in these Web sites, but anticipate that each Web site offers something for your edification.

www.madinamerica.com

Robert Whitaker, author of *Mad In America*. This Web site lists the many positive reviews of his thorough and well-written book concerning the historical treatment of the "insane" or "mad," nowadays commonly identified as psychotic or schizophrenic. The Web site is also updated periodically with current research on schizophrenia, again supporting the arguments in his book.

www.healyprozac.com

David Healy, psychiatrist, researcher, renowned historian, and author of *Let Them Eat Prozac* and eleven other books and over 120 articles. This Web site has chapters 2 and 3 of *Let Them Eat Prozac*, a section on ghost-writing, issues in academic freedom, and much more. A number of downloadable articles.

www.socialudit.uk.org

A British Web site focusing on antidepressants—history, efficacy, ethics, drug hazards, and much more.

www.ICSPP.org

International Center for the Study of Psychiatry and Psychology, founded by Dr. Breggin. This is a non-profit international centre addressing the ethical and scientific issues in human research and services offered by psychiatry and psychology. This site is geared to professionals and has on its board and advisory council over 200 professionals in counselling, psychology, neurology, psychiatry, and other fields.

www.moshersoteria.com/soteria.pdf

The late Dr Mosher's Web site with a downloadable PDF published paper on the Soteria House project, with reference to similar projects now in Switzerland and other places in Europe.

www.critpsynet.freeuk.com

This is the Web site of the Critical Psychiatry Network in the UK. Psychiatrists, doctors, nurses, and mental health professionals who are willing to ask "the hard questions" are part of this network. This network hosts the Critical Mental Health Forum, which has monthly meetings of like-minded professionals who are willing to debate the many ethical and other critical issues in psychiatry. This is not an anti-psychiatry Web site; rather, a Web site from within psychiatry and mental health itself. You will find many useful links, recommended books, and articles to view. See especially Dr Joanna Moncrieff's "Is Psychiatry For Sale?" and "Psychiatric Imperialism: The medicalization of modern living."

Bibliography

Akiskal, H.S. *Clinical Validation of the Bipolar Spectrum: Focus on Hypomania, Cyclothymia, and Hyperthymia.* 154th Annual Meeting of the American Psychiatric Association, May 5, 2001. http://www.medscape.com/Medscape/CNO/2001/APACME/Story.cfm?story_id=2248.

Almy, Gary L. *How Christian Is Christian Counseling? The Dangerous Influences That Keep Us from Caring for Souls.* Wheaton: Crossway Books, 2000.

Anderson, Neil T., Terry E. Zuehlke, and Julianne S. Zuehlke. *Christ Centered Therapy: The Practical Integration of Theology and Psychology.* Grand Rapids: Zondervan Publishing House, 2000.

Arterburn, Stephen. *Hand-Me-Down Genes And Second-Hand Emotions.* Nashville: Thomas Nelson Publishers, 1992.

Barber, Charles. *Comfortably Numb. How Psychiatry is Medicating a Nation.* New York: Pantheon Books, 2008.

Benner, David G. *Healing Emotional Wounds.* Grand Rapids: Baker Book House, 1990.

Berg, Richard F., and Christine McCartney, *Depression And The Integrated Life.* New York: Society of St. Paul, 1981.

Berkhof, Louis. *Systematic Theology.* Grand Rapids: Eerdmans, 1939, Fifteenth printing, 1977.

Biebel, David B., and Harold G. Koening. *New Light on Depression.* Grand Rapids: Zondervan, 2004.

Blazer, Dan. *Freud vs. God: How Psychiatry Lost Its Soul & Christianity Lost Its Mind.* Downers Grove: InterVarsity Press, 1998.

Boyd, Jeffrey H. *Soul Psychology. How to Understand Your Soul in Light of the Mental Health Movement.* Cheshire: Soul Research Institute, 1994.

—. *Reclaiming The Soul. The Search for Meaning in a Self-Centered Culture.* Cleveland: The Pilgrim Press, 1996.

Breggin, Peter R., and D. Cohen. *Your Drug May Be Your Problem. How and Why to Stop Taking Psychiatric Drugs.* Cambridge: Perseus Publishing, 1999.

Breggin, Peter R., and Ginger Ross Breggin, *Talking Back to Prozac.* New York: St. Martin's Press, 1994.

Breggin, Peter R. *Brain-Disabling Treatments in Psychiatry. Drugs, Electroshock, and the Psychopharmaceutical Complex.* Second edition. New York: Springer Publishing Company, 2008.

Breggin, Peter R. *Psychiatric Drugs: Hazards to the Brain.* New York: Springer Publishing Co., 1983.

—. *Toxic Psychiatry: Why Therapy, Empathy, and Love Must Replace the Drugs, Electroshock, And Biochemical Theories of the "New Psychiatry."* New York: St. Martin's Press, 1991.

Breggin, Peter R. *The Antidepressant Fact Book: What Your Doctor Won't Tell You About Prozac, Zoloft, Paxil, Celexa, and Luvox.* Cambridge: Perseus Publishing, 2001.

Calbreath, D.F. "Aggression, Suicide, and Serotonin: Is There a Biochemical Basis for Violent and Self-Destructive Behavior?" *Journal of the American Scientific Affiliation* 53(2), 84-95, 2001.

Caplan, Paula J. *They Say You're Crazy: How The World's Most Powerful Psychiatrists Decide Who's Normal.* Reading: Addison-Wesley Pub. Co., 1995.

Carlson, Dwight L. *Why Do Christians Shoot Their Wounded?* Downers Grove: InterVarsity Press, 1994.

Chambers, Oswald. *Biblical Psychology.* Grand Rapids: Discovery House Publishers, 1995 edition. First published 1962.

Chan, Simon. *Spiritual Theology: A Systematic Study Of The Christian Life.* Downers Grove: InterVarsity Press, 1998.

Colbert, Ty C. *Depression and Mania: Friends or Foes? A New "Non-Drug" Model of Hope for Depression, Mania, and Compulsive Disorders.* Santa Ana: Kevco Publishers, 1995.

—. *Broken Brains or Wounded Hearts: What Causes Mental Illness.* Santa Ana: Kevco Publishing, 1996.

—. *Rape of the Soul: How the Medical Imbalance Model of Modern Psychiatry Has Failed its Patients.* Tustin: Krevco Publishing, 2000.

Collins, Gary R. *Christian Counseling: A Comprehensive Guide.* Waco: Word Books Publisher, 1980.

Cunningham, Lawrence S., and Keith J. Egan. *Christian Spirituality. Themes From The Tradition.* New York: Paulist Press, 1996.

Dawes, Robyn M. *House of Cards: Psychology and Psychotherapy Built On Myth.* New York: Free Press, 1994.

Delitzsch, Franz. *A System of Biblical Theology.* Eugene: Wipf and Stock Publishers, 2003, previously published by T. and T. Clark, 1899.

Dubay, Thomas. *Authenticity: A Biblical Theology of Discernment.* San Francisco: Ignatius, revised edition, 1997.

Dunne, Tad. *Spiritual Mentoring.* Ventura: HarperSanFrancisco, 1991.

Edwards, Tilden H. *Spiritual Friend.* Mahwah: Paulist Press, 1980.

Erasmus, Udo. *Fats that Heal; Fats that Kill.* Burnaby: Alive Books, 1986.

Fabiano, Frank, and Catherine Cahill-Fabiano. *Healing The Past, Releasing Your Future.* Kent: Sovereign World Ltd., 2003.

Falconer, D.S. *Introduction to Quantitative Genetics.* New York, Longman, 1981, 2nd Edition.

Farber, Seth. *Madness, Heresy, and the Rumor of Angels.* Chicago: Open Court, 1993.

—. *Unholy Madness: The Church's Surrender to Psychiatry.* Downers Grove: InterVarsity Press, 1999.

Frances, A., H.A. Pincus, and M.B. First, *American Psychiatric Association: Diagnostic and Statistical Manual of Mental Disorders. Fourth Edition, Text Revision.* Washington, DC: APA, 2000.

Frattaroli, Elio. *Healing the Soul in the Age of the Brain: Becoming Conscious in an Unconscious World.* New York: Viking, 2001.

Garrison, John C. *The Psychology Of The Spirit: A Contemporary System of Biblical Psychology.* Xlibris Corporation, 2001.

Glasser, William. *Warning: Psychiatry Can Be Hazardous To Your Mental Health.* New York: HarperCollins Publishers, 2003.

Glenmullen, Joseph. *Prozac Backlash: Overcoming the Dangers of Prozac, Zoloft, Paxil, and Other Antidepressants with Safe, Effective Alternatives.* New York: Simon & Schuster, 2000.

Goold, William H., editor, *The Works of John Owen. Volume VI: Temptation And Sin.* Edinburgh: Banner Of Truth Trust. 1967. First published in 1850-53.

Gratton, Carolyn. *The Art of Spiritual Guidance: A Contemporary Approach To Growing In The Spirit.* New York: Crossroad, 1992.

Groothuis, Douglas. "Jesus: Philosopher and Apologist." *Christian Research Journal*, Vol. 25, no. 2 (Rancho Santa Margarita: Christian Research Institute International).

Halperin, David J. *Seeking Ezekiel: Text and Psychology.* University Park: The Pennsylvania State University Press, 1993.

Hamilton, Victor P. *The Book of Genesis: Chapters 1-17. The New International Commentary on the Old Testament.* Grand Rapids: Eerdmans,1990.

Hamstra, Bruce. *How Therapists Diagnose: Seeing Through The Psychiatric Eye.* New York: St. Martin's Press, 1994.

Harris, R. Laird, Gleason L. Archer, and Bruce K. Waltke, *Theological Wordbook of the Old Testament. Volume 2.* Chicago: Moody Press, 1980.

Hawkey, Ruth. *Healing the Human Spirit.* Chichester: New Wine Press, 1996.

Healy, David. *The Antidepressant Era.* Cambridge: Harvard University Press, 1997.

—. *The Creation of Psychopharmacology.* Cambridge: Harvard University Press, 2002.

—. *Let Them Eat Prozac: The Unhealthy Relationship Between the Pharmaceutical Industry and Depression.* New York: New York University Press, 2004.

Horwitz, Allan V. and Jerome C. Wakefield, *The Loss of Sadness. How Psychiatry Transformed Normal Sorrow into Depressive Disorder.* New York: Oxford University Press, 2007.

Horwitz, Allan V. *Creating Mental Illness.* Chicago: The University of Chicago Press, 2002.

Jeeves, Malcolm A. *Human Nature At The Millennium: Reflections On The Integration Of Psychology And Christianity.* Grand Rapids: Baker Books, 1997.

Joseph, Jay. *The Gene Illusion: Genetic research in psychiatry and psychology under the microscope.* Ross-on-Wye: PCCS Books, 2003.

Keller, Evelyn Fox. *The Century of the Gene.* Cambridge: Harvard University Press, 2000.

Kirk, Stuart A., and Herb Kutchins. *The Selling of DSM: The Rhetoric of Science in Psychiatry.* New York: Aline De Gruyter, 1992.

Kluger, J., "Is God in Our Genes?" *Time Magazine, Canadian Edition,* Oct. 25, 2004, Vol. 164:17, pages 44-52.

Koch, Kurt E. *Christian Counseling And Occultism: A Complete Guidebook to Occult Oppression and Deliverance.* Grand Rapid: Kregel Resources, 1994.

Kraft, Charles H. *Confronting Powerless Christianity: Evangelicals and the Missing Dimension.* Grand Rapids: Chosen Books, 2002.

Ladd, George Eldon. *A Theology Of The New Testament.* Grand Rapids: Eerdmans, 1974.

Lake, Frank. *Clinical Theology: A Theological and Psychiatric Basis to Clinical Pastoral Care.* London: Darton Longman & Todd, 1966.

Lane, Christopher Shyness. *How Normal Behavior Became a Sickness.* New Haven: Yale University Press, 2007.

Levine, Bruce E. *Commonsense Rebellion: Debunking Psychiatry, Confronting Society.* New York: Continuum Publishing Group Inc., 2001.

Lewis, Howard R., and Martha E. *Psychosomatics: How Your Emotions Can Damage Your Health.* New York: The Viking Press, 1972.

Lewontin, R. C. *Biology as Ideology: The Doctrine of DNA.* Concord: House of Anansi Press Ltd., 1991.

—. *It Ain't Necessarily So: The Dream of the Human Genome and Other Illusions.* New York: Review Books, 2000.

Lockley, John. *A Practical Workbook For The Depressed Christian.* Milton Keynes: Authentic Publishing, 1991.

Lynch, Terry. *Beyond Prozac: Healing and Mental Distress.* Douglas Village: Mercier Press, 2005.

Mason, Mike. *The Gospel According to Job.* Wheaton: Crossway Books, 1994.

Matthews, D.A., with C. Clark. *The Faith Factor: Proof of the Healing Power of Prayer.* New York: Viking, 1998.

May, Gerald G. *Care of Mind, Care of Spirit: A Psychiatrist Explores Spiritual Direction.* San Francisco: Harper, 1992.

—. *The Dark Night Of The Soul: A Psychiatrist Explores the Connection Between Darkness and Spiritual Growth.* New York: HarperSanFrancisco, 2004.

Meier, Paul, S. Arterburn, and F. Minirth. *Mastering Your Moods: Understanding Your Emotional Highs and Lows.* Nashville: Thomas Nelson Publishers, 1999.

Milkman, Harvey, and Stanley Sunderwirth. *Pathways to Pleasure: The Consciousness and Chemistry of Optimal Living.* New York: Lexington Books, 1993.

Minirth, Frank B., and Paul D. Meier, *Happiness Is A Choice: A Manual on the Symptoms, Causes, and Cures of Depression.* Grand Rapids: Baker Book House, 1978.

Minirth, Frank, Paul Meier, and Stephen Arterburn. *Miracle Drugs.* Nashville: Thompson Nelson Publishers, 1995.

Modrow, John. *How To Become A Schizophrenic: The Case Against Biological Psychiatry.* Everett: Apollyon Press, 2nd ed., 1992.

Montgomery, John Warwick, editor. *Demon Possession: A Medical, Historical, Anthropological and Theological Symposium.* Minneapolis: Bethany Fellowship, Inc., 1975.

Morrison, James. *DSM-IV Made Easy: The Clinician's Guide To Diagnosis.* New York: The Guilford Press, 1995.

Mosher, Loren R. "Soteria and Other Alternatives to Acute Psychiatric Hospitalization." *The Journal of Nervous And Mental Disease* 187: 142-149, 1999.

Mulitze, Dieter. *The Great Omission: Resolving Critical Issues for the Ministry of Healing and Deliverance.* Belleville: Essence Publishers, 2001.

—. *The Great Substitution: Human Effort or Jesus to Heal and Restore the Soul?* Belleville: Essence Publishers, 2003.

Mullen, Grant. *Emotionally Free: A Prescription for Healing Body, Soul and Spirit.* Kent: Sovereign Word International, 2003.

—. *Moods: What Christians Should Know About Depression, Anxiety and Mood Disorders.* Orchardview Medical Media, 2004.

Papolos, Demitri, and Janice Papolos. *Overcoming Depression.* New York: HarperPerennial, 3rd ed., 1997.

Payne, Leanne. *The Healing Presence: How God's Grace Can Work in You to Bring Healing in Your Broken Places and the Joy of Living in His Love.* Wheaton: Crossway Books, 1989.

Pearson, Mark A. *Christian Healing: A Practical And Comprehensive Guide.* Grand Rapids: Chosen Books, 1995.

Porter, Roy. *Madness: A Brief History.* Oxford: Oxford University Press, 2002.

Rolheiser, Ronald. *The Shattered Lantern: Rediscovering a Felt Presence of God.* New York: The Crossroad Publishing Company, 2001.

Ross, Colin A., and Alvin Pam. *Pseudoscience in Biological Psychiatry: Blaming The Body.* New York: John Wiley & Sons, Inc., 1995.

Ross, Colin A. *The Trauma Model: A Solution To The Problem of Comorbidity In Psychiatry.* Richardson: Gateway Communications, Inc., 2000.

Sandford, John Loren, and Mark Sandford. *A Comprehensive Guide to Deliverance and Inner Healing.* Grand Rapids: Chosen Books, 1992.

Satinover, J. *Homosexuality And The Politics of Truth.* Grand Rapids: Hamewith Books, 1996.

Schimmel, Solomon. *The Seven Deadly Sins: Jewish, Christian, and Classical Reflections on Human Psychology.* New York: Oxford University Press, 1997.

Schlossberg, Herbert. *Idols for Destruction: Christian Faith and Its Confrontation with American Society.* Nashville: Thomas Nelson Publishers, 1983.

Shorter, Edward. *A History of Psychiatry: From The Era of The Asylum to The Age of Prozac.* New York: John Wiley and Sons, Inc., 1997.

Stevens, Lawrence J. *Does Mental Illness Exist?* www.antipsychiatry. org. 1995.

Stern, Karl. *The Third Revolution: A Study of Psychiatry and Religion.* New York: Harcourt, Brace and Company, 1954.

St. John of The Cross. *Dark Night Of The Soul.* New York: Image Books. 1990 edition. Translated by E. Allison Peers, 1st edition, 1959.

Szasz, T.S. *The Manufacture of Madness.* New York: Harper and Row, 1970.

—. *The Myth of Mental Illness: Foundations of a Theory of Personal Conduct.* New York: Harper and Row, 1974.

Tapia, A.T., Barshinger, C.E., and L.E. LaRowe. "The Gospel According to Prozac. Can a Pill Do What the Holy Spirit Could Not?" *Christianity Today*, August 14, 1995.

Taylor, Barbara Brown. *Speaking of Sin: The Lost Language of Salvation.* Cambridge: Cowley Publications, 2000.

Towns, Elmer L. *Fasting For Spiritual Breakthrough.* Ventura: Regal Books, 1996.

Tracy, Ann Blake. *Prozac: Panacea or Pandora? Our Serotonin Nightmare.* Salt Lake City: Cassia Publications, 2nd ed., 2001.

Valenstein, Elliot S. *Great and Desperate Cures: The Rise and Decline of Psychosurgery and Other Radical Treatments for Mental Illness.* New York: Basic Books, 1986.

—. *Blaming The Brain: The Truth About Drugs And Mental Health.* New York: The Free Press, 1998.

Veggeberg, Scott. *Medication of the Mind.* New York: Henry Holt and Company, 1996.

Verny, Thomas, M.D., with John Kelly. *The Secret Life of the Unborn Child; How you can prepare your unborn baby for a happy, healthy life.* New York: Dell Publishing Co., 1981.

Vitz, Paul C. *Faith Of The Fatherless: The Psychology of Atheism.* Dallas: Spence Publishing Company, 1999.

Walker, S. *A Dose of Sanity: Mind, Medicine, and Misdiagnosis.* New York: John Wiley and Sons, 1996.

Weiss, Douglas. *The Final Freedom: Pioneering Sexual Addiction Recovery.* Fort Worth: Discovery Press, 1998.

—. *Sex, Men, and God.* Lake Mary: Siloam, 2002.

Welch, Ed T. *Blame It on the Brain? Distinguishing Chemical Imbalances, Brain Disorders, and Disobedience.* Phillipsburg: P&R Publishing, 1998.

—. *Addictions—A Banquet In The Grave: Finding Hope In The Power of the Gospel.* Phillipsburg: P&R Publishing Company, 2001.

Whitaker, Robert. *Mad In America: Bad Science, Bad Medicine, And The Enduring Mistreatment Of The Mentally Ill.* Cambridge: Perseus Publishing, 2002.

White, John. *The Masks of Melancholy: A Christian Physician Looks at Depression & Suicide.* Downers Grove: InterVarsity Press, 1982.

Whitfield, Charles L. *The Truth About Depression: Choices For Healing.* Deerfield Beach: Health Communications, Inc., 2003.

—. *The Truth About Mental Illness: Choices For Healing.* Deerfield Beach: Health Communications, Inc., 2004.

Wilkinson, John. *The Bible and Healing: A Medical and Theological Commentary.* Grand Rapids: Eerdmans, 1998.

Wiseman, Bruce. *Psychiatry—The Ultimate Betrayal.* Los Angeles: Freedom Publishing, 1995.

Wood, Garth. *The Myth of Neurosis: Overcoming The Illness Excuse.* New York: Harper and Row, 1986.

Wright, Henry. *A More Excellent Way: A Teaching On The Spiritual Roots of Disease.* Thomaston: Pleasant Valley Publications, 5th edition, 2002.

Index

V

V2 rockets, 62, 63
vaginal spotting, 5
Valenstein, Elliot, 34, 35, 64, 80–82, 84, 136, 174, 199, 200–203
Valium, 117, 125
value, of people, 258
Vehicular Speeding Disorder, 194
Verney, Thomas, 109
Viagra, 67
visionary experience, in healing, 282
Vitz, Paul C., 250
VMAT2, 100, 101

W

Walker, S.A., 22, 133, 134, 190, 200, 201
Watson, James, 220
Weiss, Douglas, 32, 37, 248
Welch, Ed T., 175, 200, 225, 248, 249
Wellbutrin, 68, 222
Whitaker, Robert, 34, 35, 83, 108, 136, 173, 174, 201, 203, 287
White, John, 31, 36, 37, 81, 259, 260, 265, 285
Whitfield, Charles L., 81, 82, 107, 110, 111, 165, 174, 175

Wilkinson, John, 200, 265
Wilson's disease, 18, 89
Winnipeg, 155, 160
wisdom, of God, 258, 279
of Jesus, 18, 247, 258
Wiseman, Bruce, 201, 203
withdrawal effects, 75, 117
womb, 8, 62, 93, 98, 106, 107, 215
Wood, Garth, 248
World War II, 63
worldview, of Jesus, 259
Worship Disorder, 243, 244
Wright, Henry, 22
Written Expression Disorder, 193

Z

Zarephath, in 1 Kings, 210
Zilpah, in Genesis, 61
Zoloft, 14, 80, 83, 117–119, 125, 130, 133, 175, 200, 272
Zopiclone, 144
Zuehlke, Terry E. and Julianne S., 35, 80, 133
Zyban, 68
Zyprexa, 144, 145, 149, 150, 151

About The Author

Dieter K. Mulitze completed a Master of Christian Studies degree, with a concentration in spiritual theology, from Regent College, Vancouver, BC. Dieter holds a PhD in quantitative genetics from the University of Saskatchewan. He was a scientist at an international agricultural research center (ICARDA) in Syria and then an associate professor of agronomy with the University of Nebraska while working in Morocco. Upon returning to Canada, he founded a computer software company.

Responding to God's call, Dieter has become increasingly involved in the ministry of healing prayer for the whole person and has been ordained into the ministry of the gospel. He has authored three books on healing prayer. Dieter has taught courses at Christian colleges, spoken at conferences and churches and has conducted seminars on healing prayer and related topics. Since 1998, Dieter has been a director of Deeper Love Ministries, a Christian ministry for advancing spiritual wholeness, healing and growth in individuals, based on the model and ministry of Jesus Christ. He has a strong passion for equipping Christians in the local church for the ministry of healing prayer.

Dieter and his wife Ellen live in Winnipeg, Manitoba, Canada. They have one daughter, Karissa. The author may be contacted through his web site at www.dietermulitze.com.

This book helps individuals discover the roots to many of their adult problems by helping identify issues in their past that in many cases can have profound implications on their present emotional and spiritual well being. The book takes the reader through a deep journey into their past and highlights vulnerabilities at each stage of our natural development. It is wounds inflicted during these sensitive times of life that can be identified. The author explains how the reader can experience healing from these wounds and be free to live in their God given destiny!

Healing the Past, Releasing Your Future *by Frank & Catherine Fabiano*
£8.99 | 978-185240-4567 | 192pp | Sovereign World Ltd

THE TRUTH & FREEDOM SERIES

GOD'S COVERING

A PLACE OF HEALING

DAVID CROSS

God's covering is an expression which describes the spiritual protection and nurture which God provides for all those who are in a covenant relationship with Him. You cannot see His covering but you can certainly experience the effect which it has. Without Jesus, the world cannot truly understand God's covering but all of mankind desperately needs it! Outside this shelter, men and women are vulnerable to a hostile spiritual realm which governs this world and all those who remain in rebellion to the One who created them.

God's Covering: A Place of Healing *by David Cross*
£7.99 | 978-185240-4857 | 192pp | Sovereign World Ltd

We hope you enjoyed reading this Sovereign World book.
For more details of other Sovereign World books and
new releases please see our website:

www.sovereignworld.com

If you would like to help us send a copy of this book
and many other titles to needy pastors in developing
countries, please write for further information
or send your gift to:

Sovereign World Trust
PO Box 777
Tonbridge, Kent TN11 0ZS
United Kingdom

You can also visit www.sovereignworldtrust.com.
The Trust is a registered charity